The Project Physics Course

Reader

UNIT **5** Models of the Atom

A Component of the
Project Physics Course

Published by
HOLT, RINEHART and WINSTON, Inc.
New York, Toronto

This publication is one of the many instructional materials developed for the Project Physics Course. These materials include Texts, Handbooks, Teacher Resource Books, Readers, Programmed Instruction Booklets, Film Loops, Transparencies, 16mm films and laboratory equipment. Development of the course has profited from the help of many colleagues listed in the text units.

Directors of Harvard Project Physics

Gerald Holton, Department of Physics, Harvard University

F. James Rutherford, Capuchino High School, San Bruno, California, and Harvard University

Fletcher G. Watson, Harvard Graduate School of Education

Picture Credits

Cover drawing: "Relativity," 1953, lithograph by M. C. Escher. Courtesy of the Museum of Modern Art, New York City.

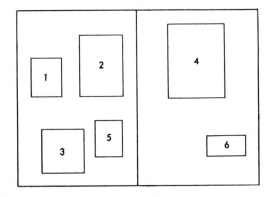

Picture Credits for frontispiece.

(1) Photograph by Glen J. Pearcy.

(2) *Jeune fille au corsage rouge lisant* by Jean Baptiste Camille Corot. Painting. Collection Bührle, Zurich.

(3) Harvard Project Physics staff photo.

(4) *Femme lisant* by Georges Seurat. Conté crayon drawing. Collection C. F. Stoop, London.

(5) *Portrait of Pierre Reverdy* by Pablo Picasso. Etching. Museum of Modern Art, N.Y.C.

(6) *Lecture au lit* by Paul Klee. Drawing. Paul Klee Foundation, Museum of Fine Arts, Berne.

Sources and Acknowledgments
Project Physics Reader 5

1. *Failure and Success—The Structure of Molecules* from *The Search*, pages 91–96, and 99–104, by Charles Percy Snow, reprinted with the permission of Charles Scribner's Sons. Copyright 1934 by Charles Scribner's Sons; renewal copyright © 1962.

2. *The Clock's Paradox in Relativity*, pages 976 and 977, *Nature*, published by Macmillan (Journals) Ltd. Reprinted with permission.

3. *The Island of Research* (map) by Ernest Harburg, *American Scientist*, Volume 54, No. 4, 1966. Reproduced with permission.

4. *Ideas and Theories* from *The Story of Quantum Mechanics*, pages 173–183, by Victor Guillemin, copyright © 1968 by Victor Guillemin. Reprinted with permission of Charles Scribner's Sons.

5. *Einstein* from *Quest*, pages 254–262 and 285–294, by Leopold Infeld, copyright 1941 by Leopold Infeld, published by Doubleday & Company, Inc. Reprinted with permission of Russell & Volkening, Inc.

6. *Mr. Tompkins and Simultaneity* from *Mr. Tompkins In Paperback*, pages 19–24, by George Gamow, copyright © 1965 by Cambridge University Press. Reprinted with permission.

7. *Mathematics: Accurate Language, Shorthand Machine and Brilliant Chancellor Relativity: New Science and New Philosophy* from *Physics for the Inquiring Mind: The Methods, Nature and Philosophy of Physical Science*, pages 468–500, by Eric M. Rogers, copyright © 1960 by Princeton University Press. Reprinted with permission.

8. *Parable of the Surveyors* by Edwin F. Taylor and John Archibald Wheeler, from *Spacetime Physics*, copyright © 1966 by W. H. Freeman and Company. Reprinted with permission.

9. *Outside and Inside the Elevator* from *The Evolution of Physics: The Growth of Ideas from Early Concepts to Relativity and Quanto*, pages 214–222, by Albert Einstein and Leopold Infeld, published by Simon and Schuster, copyright © 1961 by Estate of Albert Einstein. Reprinted with permission.

10. *Einstein and Some Civilized Discontents* by Martin Klein from *Physics Today*, 18, No. 1, 38–44 (January 1965). Reprinted with permission.

11. *The Teacher and the Bohr Theory of the Atom* from *The Search*, pages 10–12, by Charles Percy Snow, reprinted with the permission of Charles

Scribner's Sons. Copyright 1934 by Charles Scribner's Sons; renewal copyright © 1962.

12. *The New Landscape of Science* from *The Strange Story of the Quantum,* pages 174–199, by Banesh Hoffmann, copyright © 1959 by Banesh Hoffmann. Published by Dover Publications, Inc. Reprinted with permission.

13. *The Evolution of the Physicist's Picture of Nature* by Paul A. M. Dirac from *Scientific American,* May 1963. Copyright © 1963 by Scientific American, Inc. Reprinted with permission. All rights reserved. Available separately at 20¢ each as Offprint No. 292 from W. H. Freeman and Company, Inc., 660 Market Street, San Francisco, California 94104.

14. *Dirac and Born* from *Quest,* pages 202–212, by Leopold Infeld, copyright 1941 by Leopold Infeld, published by Doubleday & Company, Inc. Reprinted with permission of Russell & Volkening, Inc.

15. *I Am This Whole World: Erwin Schrödinger* from *A Comprehensible World,* pages 100–109, by Jeremy Bernstein, copyright © 1965 by Jeremy Bernstein. Published by Random House, Inc. Reprinted with permission. This article originally appeared in *The New Yorker.*

16. *The Fundamental Idea of Wave Mechanics* by Erwin Schrödinger from *Nobel Prize Lectures in Physics,* 1922–1941, Elsevier Publishing Company, Amsterdam, 1965. Reprinted with permission.

17. *The Sentinel* from *Expedition To Earth* by Arthur C. Clarke, copyright 1953 by Arthur C. Clarke. Published by Ballantine Books, Inc. Reprinted by permission of the author and his agents: Scott Meredith Literary Agency, Inc., New York, and David Higham Associates, Ltd., London.

18. *The Sea-Captain's Box* from *Science: Sense and Nonsense* by John L. Synge, copyright 1951. Reprinted with permission of W. W. Norton & Company, Inc., and Jonathan Cape Ltd.

19. *Space Travel: Problems of Physics and Engineering* by the Staff of Harvard Project Physics.

20. *Looking for a New Law* from *The Character of Physical Law,* pages 156–173, by Richard P. Feynman, copyright © 1965 by Richard P. Feynman. Published by the British Broadcasting Corporation and The M.I.T. Press. Reprinted with permission.

21. *A Portfolio of Computer-made Drawings* courtesy of California Computer Products, Inc., Lloyd Sumner, and Darel Esbach, Jr.

This is not a physics textbook. Rather, it is a physics reader, a collection of some of the best articles and book passages on physics. A few are on historic events in science, others contain some particularly memorable description of what physicists do; still others deal with philosophy of science, or with the impact of scientific thought on the imagination of the artist.

There are old and new classics, and also some little-known publications; many have been suggested for inclusion because some teacher or physicist remembered an article with particular fondness. The majority of articles is not drawn from scientific papers of historic importance themselves, because material from many of these is readily available, either as quotations in the Project Physics text or in special collections.

This collection is meant for your browsing. If you follow your own reading interests, chances are good that you will find here many pages that convey the joy these authors have in their work and the excitement of their ideas. If you want to follow up on interesting excerpts, the source list at the end of the reader will guide you for further reading.

Reader 5

Table of Contents

This author describes the frustrations and joy that can accompany a scientific discovery. The book is based on Snow's early experiences as a physical chemist.

---

1   Failure and Success

Charles Percy Snow

An excerpt from his novel *The Search,* published in 1934 and 1958.

Almost as soon as I took up the problem again, it struck me in a new light. All my other attempts have been absurd, I thought: if I turn them down and make another guess, then what? The guess didn't seem probable; but none of the others was any good at all. According to my guess, the structure was very different from anything one would have imagined; but that must be true, since the obvious structure didn't fit any of my facts. Soon I was designing structures with little knobs of plasticine for atoms and steel wires to hold them together; I made up the old ones, for comparison's sake, and then I built my new one, which looked very odd, very different from any structure I had ever seen. Yet I was excited—"I think it works," I said, "I think it works."

For I had brought back to mind some calculations of the scattering curves, assuming various models. None of the values had been anything like the truth. I saw at once that the new structure ought to give something much nearer. Hurriedly I calculated: it was a long and tiresome and complicated piece of arithmetic, but I rushed through it, making mistakes through impatience and having to go over it again. I was startled when I got the answer: the new model did not give perfect agreement, but it was far closer than any of the others. So far as I remember, the real value at one point was 1.32, my previous three models gave 1.1, 1.65 and 1.7, and the new one just under 1.4. 'I'm on it, at last,' I thought. 'It's a long shot, but I'm on it at last.'

For a fortnight I sifted all the evidence from the experiments since I first attacked the problem. There were a great many tables of figures, and a pile of X-ray photographs (for in my new instrument in Cambridge I was using a photographic detector); and I had been through most of them so often that I knew them almost by heart. But I went through them again, more carefully than ever, trying to interpret them in the light of the new structure. 'If it's right,' I was thinking, 'then these figures ought to run up to a maximum and then run down quickly.' And they did, though the maximum was less sharp than it should have been. And so on through experiments which represented the work of over a year; they all fitted the structure, with an allowance for a value a shade too big here, a trifle too small there. There were obviously approximations to make, I should have to modify the structure a little, but that it was on the right lines I was certain. I walked to my rooms to lunch one morning, overflowing with pleasure; I wanted to tell someone the news; I waved violently to a man whom I scarcely knew, riding by on a bicycle: I thought of sending a wire to Audrey, but decided to go and see her on the following day instead: King's Parade seemed a particularly admirable street, and young men shouting across it were all admirable young men. I had a quick lunch; I wanted to bask in satisfaction, but instead I hurried back to the laboratory so that I could have it all finished with no loose ends left, and then rest for a while. I was feeling the after-taste of effort.

There were four photographs left to inspect. They had been taken earlier in the week and I had looked over them once. Now they had to be definitely measured and entered, and the work was complete. I ran over the first, it was everything I expected. The structure was fitting even better than in the early experiments. And the second: I lit a cigarette. Then the third: I gazed over the black dots. All was well—and then, with a thud of the heart that shook me, I saw behind each distinct black dot another fainter speck. The bottom had fallen out of everything: I was wrong, utterly wrong. I hunted round for another explanation: the film might be a false one, it might be a fluke experiment; but the look of it mocked me: far from being false, it was the only experiment where I had arrived at precisely the right conditions.

Could it be explained any other way? I stared down at the figures, the sheets of results which I had forced into my scheme. My cheeks flushing dry, I tried to work this new photograph into my idea. An improbable assumption, another improbable assumption, a possibility of experimental error—I went on, fantastically, any sort of criticism forgotten. Still it would not fit. I was wrong, irrevocably wrong. I should have to begin again.

Then I began to think: If I had not taken this photograph, what would have happened? Very easily I might not have taken it. I should have been satisfied with my idea: everyone else would have been. The evidence is overwhelming, except for this. I should have pulled off a big thing. I should be made. Sooner or later, of course, someone would do this experiment, and I should be shown to be wrong: but it would be a long time ahead, and mine would have been an honourable sort of mistake. On my evidence I should have been right. That is the way everyone would have looked at it.

I suppose, for a moment, I wanted to destroy the photograph. It was all beyond my conscious mind. And I was swung back, also beyond my conscious mind, by all the forms of—shall I call it "conscience"—and perhaps more than that, by the desire which had thrown me into the search. For I had to get to what I myself thought was the truth. Honour, comfort and ambition were bound to move me, but I think my own desire went deepest. Without any posturing to myself, without any sort of conscious thought, I laughed at the temptation to destroy the photograph. Rather shakily I laughed. And I wrote in my note-book:

Mar. 30: *Photograph* 3 *alone has secondary dots, concentric with major dots. This removes all possibility of the hypothesis of structure B. The interpretation from Mar.* 4–30 *must accordingly be disregarded.*

From that day I understood, as I never had before, the frauds that creep into science every now and then. Sometimes they must be quite unconscious: the not-seeing of facts because they are inconvenient, the delusions of one's own senses. As though in my case I had not seen, because my unconscious self chose not to see, the secondary ring of dots. Sometimes, more rarely, the fraud must be nearer to consciousness; that is, the fraud must be realised, even though the man cannot control it. That was the point of my temptation. It could only be committed by a man in whom the scientific passion was weaker for the time than the ordinary desires for place or money. Sometimes it would be done, impulsively, by men in whom no faith was strong; and they could forget it cheerfully themselves and go on to do good and honest work. Sometimes it would be done by a man who reproached himself all his life. I think I could pick out most kinds of fraud from among the mistakes I have seen; after that afternoon I could not help being tolerant towards them.

For myself, there was nothing left to do but start again. I looked over the entry in my note-book; the ink was still shining, and yet it seemed to have stood, final, leaving me no hope, for a long time. Because I had nothing better to do, I made a list of the structures I had invented and, in the end, discarded. There were four of them now. Slowly, I devised another. I felt sterile. I distrusted it; and when I tried to test it, to think out its properties, I had to force my mind to work. I sat until six o'clock, working profitlessly; and when I walked out, and all through the night, the question was gnawing at me: 'What is this structure? Shall I ever get it? Where am I going wrong?'

I had never had two sleepless nights together before that week. Fulfilment deferred had hit me; I had to keep from reproaching myself that I had already wasted months over this problem, and now, just as I could consolidate my work, I was on the way to wasting another year. I went to bed late and heard the Cambridge clocks, one after another, chime out the small hours; I would have ideas with the uneasy clarity of night, switch on my light, scribble in my note-book, look at my watch, and try to sleep again; I would rest a little and wake up with a start, hoping that it was morning, to find that I had slept for twenty minutes: until I lay awake in a grey dawn, with all my doubts pressing in on me as I tried with tired eyes to look into the future. 'What is the structure? What line must I take?' And then, as an under-theme, 'Am I going to fail at my first big job? Am I always going to be a competent worker doing little problems?' And another, 'I shall be twenty-six in the winter: I ought to be established. But shall I be getting anywhere?' My ideas, that seemed hopeful when I got out of bed to write them, were ridiculous when I saw them in this cold light.

This went on for three nights, until my work in the day-time was only a pretence. Then there came a lull, when I forgot my worry for a night and slept until mid-day. But, though I woke refreshed, the questions began to whirl round again in my mind. For days it went on, and I could find no way out. I walked twenty miles one day, along the muddy fen-roads between the town and Ely, in order to clear my head; but it only made me very tired, and I drank myself to sleep. Another night I went to a play, but I was listening not to the actors' words, but to others that formed themselves inside me and were giving me no rest.

IV

I started. My thoughts had stopped going back upon themselves. As I had been watching Audrey's eyes, an idea had flashed through the mist, quite unreasonably, illogically. It had no bearing at all on any of the hopeless attempts I had been making; I had explored every way, I thought, but this was new; and, too agitated to say even to myself that I believed it, I took out some paper and tried to work it out. Audrey was staring with intent eyes. I could not get very far. I wanted my results and tables. But everything I could put down rang true.

"An idea's just come to me," I explained, pretending to be calm. "I don't think there's anything in it. But there might be a little. But anyway I ought to try it out. And I haven't my books. Do you mind if we go back pretty soon?" I fancy I was getting up from the table, for Audrey smiled.

"I'm glad you had some excuse for not listening," she said.

She drove back very fast, not speaking. I made my plans for the work. It couldn't take less than a week, I thought. I sat hunched up, telling myself that it might all be wrong again; but the structure was taking shape, and a part of me was beginning to laugh at my caution. Once I turned and saw Audrey's profile against the fields; but after a moment I was back in the idea.

When I got out at the Cavendish gateway, she stayed in the car. "You'd better be alone," she said.

"And you?"

"I'll sit in Green Street." She stayed there regularly on her week-end visits.

I hesitated. "It's——"

She smiled. "I'll expect you to-night. About ten o'clock," she said.

<h2 style="text-align:center">v</h2>

I saw very little of Audrey that week-end. When I went to her, my mind was active, my body tired, and despite myself it was more comfort than love I asked of her. I remember her smiling, a little wryly, and saying: "When this is over, we'll go away. Right away." I buried my head against her knees, and she stroked my hair. When she left me on the Monday morning, we clung to each other for a long time.

For three weeks I was thrusting the idea into the mass of facts. I could do nothing but calculate, read up new facts, satisfy myself that I had made no mistakes in measuring up the plates: I developed an uncontrollable trick of not being sure whether I had made a particular measurement correctly: repeating it: and then, after a day, the uncertainty returned, and to ease my mind I had to repeat it once more. I could scarcely read a newspaper or write a letter. Whatever I was doing, I was not at rest unless it was taking me towards the problem; and even then it was an unsettled rest, like lying in a fever half-way to sleep.

And yet, for all the obsessions, I was gradually being taken over by a calm which was new to me. I was beginning to feel an exultation, but it was peaceful, as different from wild triumph as it was from the ache in my throbbing nerves. For I was beginning to feel in my heart that I was near the truth. Beyond surmise, beyond doubt, I felt that I was nearly right; even as I lay awake in the dawn, or worked irritably with flushed cheeks, I was approaching a serenity which made the discomforts as trivial as those of someone else's body.

It was after Easter now and Cambridge was almost empty. I was glad; I felt free as I walked the deserted streets. One night, when I left the laboratory, after an evening when the new facts were falling into line and making the structure seem more than ever true, it was good to pass under the Cavendish! Good to be in the midst of the great days of science! Good to be adding to the record of those great days! And good to walk down King's Parade and see the Chapel standing against a dark sky without any stars!

The mingling of strain and certainty, of personal worry and deeper peace, was something I had never known before. Even at the time, I knew I was living in a strange happiness. Or, rather, I knew that when it was over I should covet its memory.

And so for weeks I was alone in the laboratory, taking photographs, gazing under the red lamp at films which still dripped water, carrying them into the light and studying them until I knew every grey speck on them, from the points which were testing my structures down to flaws and scratches on the surface. Then, when my eyes tired, I put down my lens and turned to the sheets of figures that contained the results, the details of the structure and the predictions I was able to make. Often I would say—if this structure is right, then this crystal here will have its oxygen atom 1.2 a.u. from the nearest carbon; and the crystal will break along this axis, and not along that; and it will be harder than the last crystal I measured, but not so hard as the one before, and so on. For days my predictions were not only vaguely right, but right as closely as I could measure.

I still possess those lists of figures, and I have stopped writing to look over them again. It is ten years and more since I first saw them and yet as I read:

Predicted	Observed
1.435	1.44
2.603	2.603

and so on for long columns, I am warmed with something of that first glow.

At last it was almost finished. I had done everything I could; and to make an end of it I thought out one prediction whose answer was irrefutable. There was one more substance in the organic group which I could not get in England, which had only been made in Munich; if my general structure was right, the atoms in its lattice could only have one pattern. For any other structure the pattern would be utterly different. An X-ray photograph of the crystal would give me all I wanted in a single day.

It was tantalising, not having the stuff to hand. I could write and get some from Munich, but it would take a week, and a week was very long. Yet there seemed nothing else to do. I was beginning to write in my clumsy scientist's German—and then I remembered Lüthy, who had returned to Germany a year ago.

I cabled to him, asking if he would get a crystal and photograph it on his instrument. It would only take him a morning at the most, I thought, and we had become friendly enough for me to make the demand on him. Later in the afternoon I had his answer: "I have obtained crystal will telegraph result to-morrow honoured to assist. Lüthy." I smiled at the "honoured to assist", which he could not possibly have left out, and sent off another cable: "Predict symmetry and distances. . . ."

Then I had twenty-four hours of waiting. Moved by some instinct to touch wood, I wanted to retract the last cable as soon as I had sent it. If—if I were wrong, no one else need know. But it had gone. And, nervous as I was, in a way I knew that I was right. Yet I slept very little that night; I could mock, with all the detached part of myself, at the tricks my body was playing, but it went on playing them. I had to leave my breakfast, and drank cup after cup of tea, and kept throwing away cigarettes I had just lighted. I watched myself do these things, but I could not stop them, in just the same way as one can watch one's own body being afraid.

The afternoon passed, and no telegram came. I persuaded myself there was scarcely time. I went out for an hour, in order to find it at my rooms when I returned. I went through all the antics and devices of waiting. I grew empty with anxiety as the evening drew on. I sat trying to read; the room was growing dark, but I did not wish to switch on the light, for fear of bringing home the passage of the hours.

At last the bell rang below. I met my landlady on the stairs, bringing in the telegram. I do not know whether she noticed that my hands were shaking as I opened it. It said: "Felicitations on completely accurate prediction which am proud to confirm apologise for delay due to instrumental adjustments. Lüthy." I was numbed for a moment; I could only see Lüthy bowing politely to the postal clerk as he sent off the telegram. I laughed, and I remember it had a queer sound.

Then I was carried beyond pleasure. I have tried to show something of the high moments that science gave to me; the night my father talked about the stars, Luard's lesson, Austin's opening lecture, the end of my first research. But this was different from any of them, different altogether, different in kind. It was further from myself. My own triumph and delight and success were there, but they seemed insignificant beside this tranquil ecstasy. It was as though I had looked for a truth outside myself, and finding it had become for a moment part of the truth I sought; as though all the world, the atoms and the stars, were wonderfully clear and close to me, and I to them, so that we were part of a lucidity more tremendous than any mystery.

I had never known that such a moment could exist. Some of its quality, perhaps, I had captured in the delight which came when I brought joy to Audrey, being myself content; or in the times among friends, when for some rare moment, maybe twice in my life, I had lost myself in a common purpose; but these moments had, as it were, the tone of the experience without the experience itself.

Since then I have never quite regained it. But one effect will stay with me as long as I live; once, when I was young, I used to sneer at the mystics who have described the experience of being at one with God and part of the unity of things. After that afternoon, I did not want to laugh again; for though I should have interpreted the experience differently, I thought I knew what they meant.

One of the most intriguing results of relativity theory, explained in a few paragraphs using only elementary arithmetic.

2 The Clock Paradox in Relativity

C. G. Darwin

An article in the scientific journal, *Nature,* 1957.

The Clock Paradox in Relativity

IN the course of reasoning on this subject with some of my more recalcitrant friends, I have come across a numerical example which I think makes the matter easier to follow than would any mathematical formulæ, and perhaps this might interest some readers of *Nature.*

There is no doubt whatever that the accepted theory of relativity is a complete and self-consistent theory (at any rate up to a range of knowledge far beyond the present matter), and it quite definitely implies that a space-traveller will return from his journey younger than his stay-at-home twin brother. We all of us have an instinctive resistance against this idea, but it has got to be accepted as an essential part of the theory. If Prof. H. Dingle should be correct in his disagreement, it would destroy the whole of relativity theory as it stands at present.

Some have found a further difficulty in understanding the matter. When two bodies are moving away from each other, each sees the occurrences on the other slowed down according to the Doppler effect, and relativity requires that they should both appear to be slowed down to exactly the same degree. Thus if there are clock-dials on each body visible from the other, both will appear to be losing time at the same rate. Conversely, the clocks will appear to be gaining equally as they approach one another again. At first sight this might seem to suggest that there is an exact symmetry between the two bodies, so that the clock of neither ought in the end to record a time behind that of the other. The present example will show how this argument fails.

In order to see how a time-difference will arise, it suffices to take the case of special relativity without complications from gravitation. Two space-ships, S_0 and S_1, are floating together in free space. By firing a rocket S_1 goes off to a distant star, and on arrival there he fires a stronger rocket so as to reverse his motion, and finally by means of a third rocket he checks his speed so as to come to rest alongside S_0, who has stayed quietly at home all the time. Then they compare their experiences. The reunion of the two ships is an essential of the proceedings, because it is only through it that the well-known difficulties about time-in-other-places are avoided.

The work is to be so arranged that it can be done by ordinary ships' navigators, and does not require the presence in the crews of anyone cognizant of the mysteries of time-in-other-places. To achieve this, I suppose that the two ships are equipped with identical cæsium clocks, which are geared so as to strike the hours. On the stroke of every hour each ship sends out a flash of light. These flashes are seen by the other ship and counted, and they are logged against the hour strokes of its own clock. Finally the two logs will be compared.

In the first place it must be noted that S_1's clock may behave irregularly during the short times of his three accelerations. This trouble can be avoided by instructing him to switch the clock off before firing his rockets, and only to start it again when he has got up to a uniform speed, which he can recognize from the fact that he will no longer be pressed against one wall of his ship. The total of his time will be affected by this error, but it will be to the same extent whether he is going to the Andromeda Nebula, or merely to Mars. Since the time that is the subject under dispute is proportional to the total time of his absence, this direct effect of acceleration can be disregarded.

I choose as the velocity of S_1's travel $v = \frac{4}{5}c$, because in this special case there are no tiresome irrationalities to consider. I take the star to be 4 light-years away from S_0. The journey there and back will therefore take 10 years according to S_0.

Immediately after the start each will observe the other's flashes slowed down by the Doppler effect. The formula for this in relativity theory is $\sqrt{(c+v)/(c-v)}$, which in the present case gives exactly 3. That is to say, each navigator will log the other's flashes at a rate of one every three hours of his own clock's time. Conversely, when they are nearing one another again, each will log the other's flashes at a rate of three an hour.

So far everything is perfectly symmetrical between the ships, but the question arises, for each ship respectively, how soon the slow flashes will change over into fast ones. First take the case of S_1. During his outward journey he will get slow flashes, but when he reverses direction at the star, they will suddenly change to fast ones. Whatever his clock shows at this time it is certainly just half what it will show when he gets home. Thus for half the journey he will get flashes at the rate of $\frac{1}{3}$ per hour, and for the other half at a rate of 3 per hour. The average for the whole journey will thus be at a rate $\frac{1}{2}(\frac{1}{3}+3)=\frac{5}{3}$ per hour. During this time S_0 will have sent out 10 years' worth of flashes, and so in the end S_1's clock will record $\frac{3}{5}\times 10=6$ years, which, of course, he can verify directly from his detailed log.

S_0's log will be quite different. He will start with slow flashes and end with fast ones, but the changeover is determined by S_1's reversal, which is occurring 4 light years away from him. Consequently, he will get slow flashes for $5+4=9$ years, and therefore fast flashes for only 1 year. The total number he will count is $\frac{1}{3}\times 9+3\times 1=6$ years' worth. His nine years of slow flashes and one of fast are in marked contrast with S_1's experience of three years of each. Thus when the navigators compare their logs together they will be completely different, but both will agree that S_0's clock went for ten years and S_1's for only six.

It may be that S_0 will suggest that for some reason S_1's clock was going slow during the motion, but S_1 will point out that there was no sign of anything wrong with it, and that anyhow his heart-beat and other bodily functions matched the rate of his clock and he may even direct attention to the fact that his forehead is perceptibly less wrinkled than that of his twin brother. In fact—as the relativist knows—he is now actually four years younger than his brother.

In giving this example, I have assumed S_0 at rest for the sake of simplicity, but it is not hard to verify that the two logs will be exactly the same if a uniform motion of any amount is superposed on the system. However, to show this would go beyond the scope of this communication.

C. G. Darwin

Newnham Grange,
    Cambridge.
        Sept. 30.

One rule: Do not block the path of inquiry.

---

3 The Island of Research

Ernest Harburg

1966.

Discussion of ways in which fields and quanta are related to one another in cases ranging from electrostatics to gravitation.

---

4   Ideas and Theories

V. Guillemin

A chapter from his textbook, *The Story of Quantum Mechanics*, 1968.

QUANTUM FIELD THEORY

THE size of particles compares to that of atoms as atoms compare to the scale of things in the world of familiar objects; both involve roughly a hundred-thousand-fold ratio in magnitude. A tiny grain of sand, perhaps a thousandth (10^{-3}) centimeter across, behaves in every way like an object of the large-scale world. But a downward plunge to a hundred millionth (10^{-8}) centimeter leads to a realm in which everything existing in space and happening in time is a manifestation of changing patterns of matter waves. Things arrange themselves in sequences of discrete configurations, changes occur in abrupt quantum jumps and the pertinent laws of motion determine only the probabilities of events, not the individual events themselves. These profound changes in behavior are due primarily to differences in the relative size of objects and their de Broglie waves. Large objects are enormous compared to their associated waves; atoms and their waves are similar in size.

In the second downward plunge of minuteness, from a scale of 10^{-8} to one of 10^{-13} centimeter, a contrast of this sort does not exist. Here the matter waves are again comparable in size to the tiny regions in which particle events occur. Their radically new characteristics must be laid to other causes, in part to the change of scale itself. By quantum-mechanical principles the wave packets associated with events restricted to tiny regions of space must be constituted of very short matter waves; and because of the de Broglie relation between wavelength and momentum, this implies large values of velocity and energy and brief interaction times. Therefore, particle phenomena are necessarily rapid and violent, so violent that mass and energy interchange freely, and matter loses the stability it displays under less drastic conditions.

Atoms are a "half-way stopover" between the things of everyday experience and the weird realm of particles. They could still be treated to some extent in terms of familiar concepts. Thus, the Bohr atom model is frankly a mechanism operating in a familiar, albeit altered, manner. Particles are, however, conceptually more remote from atoms than are atoms from sticks and stones.

It is hardly surprising that attempts to extend the methods of quantum mechanics, so sucessful in dealing with atomic phenomena, to the realm of particles have met with difficulties. To make progress, it has been necessary to devise different methods of attack for various kinds of problems, for the properties of particles, for their groupings, their interactions, and so forth. There exists, however, one generally recognized theoretical method of dealing with particle phenomena, the *quantum field theory*, which is adequate, in principle, to cope with all aspects of particle physics. As the name implies, it is concerned with the relations of quanta and fields.

Electric and magnetic fields have already been discussed briefly as regions in which charges experience electric and magnetic forces. To physicists in the mid-nineteenth century, fields had a more tangible meaning. They were assumed to be conditions of *strain* in an ether, a tenuous elastic "jelly" filling all space. Where there is a field, the ether jelly is under a strain of tension or compression, different from its normal relaxed state; and these strains were thought to produce the forces acting upon electric charges. There was also the luminiferous ether, possibly different from the electric and magnetic ethers which, when set into oscillation at one point, could transmit the oscillatory strains as a light wave.

Maxwell began the development of his monumental synthesis of electromagnetism and optics (page 48) by constructing an elaborate model of a mechanical ether, presumably capable of transmitting the various field effects. But after having built the electromagnetic theory of light, in which light appears as a combination of oscillating electric and magnetic fields propagated together through space, he saw that his mathematical equations contained everything of importance. In the publication of his studies *On a Dynamical Theory of the Electro-magnetic Field* (1864), he presented only the mathematical theory with no mention of the ether model. Although he had thus made the ether unnecessary, neither he nor his contemporaries thought of casting it aside. Even up to the beginning of the twentieth century almost all physicists continued to believe in the reality of the ether or at least in the need of retaining it as an intuitive conception. But in 1905, in his famous publication on the theory of relativity, Einstein showed that the idea of an entity filling all space and acting as a stationary reference, relative to which all motions could be described in an absolute manner, is untenable, that only the *relative* motions of objects have meaning. After the ether had thus been abolished, the fields remained, like the grin of the vanished Cheshire cat.

Yet fields, in particular the traveling electromagnetic fields of the light waves, still retained a measure of reality. These carried energy and momentum and could cause electric charges to oscillate. Again, it was Einstein who robbed them of these trappings of reality when, by postulating the photons, he relegated the light waves to a mere ghostly existence as nothing more than mathematical abstractions determining the gross average propagation of flocks of photons.

Quantum field theory has wrought a curious revival in the status of fields. Although they are still largely mathematical conceptions, they have acquired strong overtones of reality. In fact, this theory asserts that fields alone are real, that *they* are the substance of the universe, and that particles are merely the momentary manifestations of interacting fields.

The way in which particles are derived from fields is analogous to the construction of atoms out of patterns of matter waves in Schrödinger's original conception of wave mechanics. Here the properties of atoms, and their interactions with each other and with photons, are described in terms of the configurations and changes of these wave patterns. Similarly, the solution of the quantum field equations leads to quantized energy values which manifest themselves with all the properties of particles. The activities of the fields seem particlelike because fields interact very abruptly and in very minute regions of space. Nevertheless, even avowed quantum field theorists are not above talking about "particles" as if there really were such things, a practice which will be adopted in continuing this discussion.

The ambitious program of explaining all properties of particles and all of their interactions in terms of fields has actually been successful only for three of them: the photons, electrons and positrons. This limited quantum field theory has the special name of *quantum electrodynamics*. It results from a union of classical electrodynamics and quantum theory, modified to be compatible with the principles of relativity. The three particles with which it deals are well suited to theoretical treatment because they are stable, their properties are well understood and they interact through the familiar electromagnetic force.

Quantum electrodynamics was developed around 1930, largely through the work of Paul Dirac. It yielded two important results: it showed that the electron has an *alter ego*, the positron, and it gave the electron its spin, a property which previously had to be added arbitrarily. When it was applied to the old problem of the fine structure of the hydrogen spectrum (the small differences between the observed wavelengths and those given by the Bohr theory), it produced improved values in good agreement with existing measures. However, in 1947 two experimenters, Willis Lamb and Robert Retherford, made highly precise measurements of the small differences in energy levels, using instead of photons the quanta of radio waves, which are more delicate probes of far lower energy. Their results, which showed distinct discrepancies from Dirac's theory, stimulated renewed theoretical efforts. Three men, Sin-Itiro Tomonaga of Tokyo University, Richard Feynman of the University of California and Julian Schwinger of Harvard, working independently, produced an improved theory which at long last gave precise agreement with experiment. For this work the three shared the 1965 Nobel Prize in physics.

The study of particles by the methods of quantum field theory was begun at a time when only a few were known. Since the field associated with a particle represents all of its properties, there had to be a distinct kind of field for each kind of particle; and as their number increased, so did the number of different fields, a complication which pleased no one. Actually, little further progress was made in the two decades following the success of quantum electrodynamics. Attempts to deal with the strongly interacting particles, the mesons and baryons, were frustrated by seemingly insurmountable mathematical difficulties. Still, the idea of developing a basic and comprehensive theory of particles continued to have strong appeal. In the mid-1960's the introduction of powerful new mathematical techniques has yielded results which indicate that this may yet be accomplished.

THE ELECTROSTATIC FIELD

THE interaction of the electromagnetic fields, whose energy is carried by photons, and the electron fields, which manifest themselves as electrons, is already familiar in the production of photons by the activity of atomic electrons. It is, however, not apparent how photons, which travel through space with the highest possible velocity, might be involved in *static* electric fields such as those which hold electrons close to the atomic nucleus.

Here a new concept is needed, that of *virtual photons*. Their existence is due in a remarkable, yet logical manner to the Heisenberg uncertainty principle. One form of this principle (page 99) asserts that the uncertainty ΔE in the energy possessed by a system and the uncertainty Δt in the time at which it has this energy are related by the formula:

$$\Delta E \times \Delta t \geqslant h/2\pi$$

Because of the relativistic correspondence between energy and mass, this relation applies as well to the uncertainty Δm in mass, which is $\Delta E/c^2$. Applied to an electron, this means physically that its mass does not maintain one precise value; rather, it *fluctuates*, the magnitude of the fluctuations being in inverse proportion to the time interval during which they persist. Electrons effect their mass or equivalent energy fluctuations by emitting photons, but these exist only on the sufferance of the uncertainty principle. When their time Δt is up, they must vanish. They cannot leave the electron permanently, carrying off energy, nor can they deliver energy to any detection device, including the human eye. It is impossible for them to be seen or detected; therefore they are called *virtual*, not real. Yet there is a warrant for their existence; theories in which they are postulated yield results in agreement with experimental observation. In the language of quantum field theory the interaction of electron and photon fields brings about a condition in which by permission of the uncertainty principle virtual photons are continually created and destroyed.

Virtual photons of greater energy exist for shorter times and travel shorter distances away from the electron before they are annihilated; those of lesser energy reach out farther. In fact, they travel a distance equal to the length of their associated waves (radio waves, light waves and others), which may vary over the whole range of values from zero to infinity. This swarm of virtual photons darting outward from the central electron in all directions constitutes the electric field surrounding the electron. Calculations based on this concept show that the field is strongest close by and drops off in inverse proportion to the square of the distance, in agreement with Coulomb's law of electric force (page 27). Virtual photons are the *quanta* of all electrostatic fields. For large charged objects they are so numerous that they produce a sensibly smooth and continuous effect, identical with the classical field.

Two electrically charged objects exchange virtual photons. This produes an *exchange force* between them, a result which follows directly from the principles of quantum electrodynamics, but which has unfortunately no analogy in classical physics and cannot be visualized in terms of familiar experience. The theory shows that the force between charges of like sign is one of repulsion, that for opposite signs it is an attraction, again in agreement with experiment.

There are, however, further complications. The virtual photons, produced by the electron, interact with the electron field to produce additional virtual electrons, which in turn yield virtual photons, and so on. Thus the theory, starting with one electron, ends up with an infinite number of them. Fortunately, the magnitudes of the successive steps in this sequence drop off rapidly so that after much effort the results of all this complex activity could be calculated very precisely.

This production of secondary virtual electrons manifests itself in the hydrogen atom as a slight alteration of energy levels. It was this effect which Tomonaga, Feynman and Schwinger succeeded in determining correctly.

For situations in which sufficient energy is made available, one of the virtual photons surrounding an electron may be "promoted" to a real one. This explains real photon emission when atoms release energy by making transitions to lower energy states.

This discussion implies that electrostatic fields are created by the activity of virtual photons. The point of view of field theory is rather the other way about, the photons being thought of merely as the way in which electric fields interact with electron fields. It is quite in order, however, to use either concept, depending on which is more appropriate to the problem at hand.

THE STRONG-FORCE FIELD

A FEW years after it had been found that atomic nuclei are built of protons and neutrons, Hideki Yukawa, working toward his Ph.D. at Osaka University, undertook a theoretical study of the force which binds nucleons together. The successful description of the electromagnetic force in terms of virtual photons suggested to him that the strong nuclear force might be accounted for in a similar manner.

It was known that this force does not decrease gradually toward zero with increasing distance; rather, its range ends abruptly at about 10^{-13} centimeter. Yukawa concluded that the virtual particles associated with the strong-force field should be all of one mass. Assuming that they dart out at velocities close to that of light, he could estimate that they exist for about 10^{-23} second; and from this value of Δt he calculated that their mass Δm, as given by the uncrtainty principle, is somewhat greater than two hundred electron masses. Since particles having a mass intermediate between the electron and proton were unheard of at the time this prediction was made, it was received with considerable skepticism.

The way in which Yukawa's prediction was verified has already been discussed (page 144). The pions discovered in cosmic-ray studies are the real particles, not the predicted virtual ones. As is true of photons, virtual pions may be promoted to the real state if sufficient energy is provided. In this manner pions are produced in considerable numbers in the violent collisions of protons or neutrons.

Further studies of the strong-force field have shown that its quanta include not only the three kinds of pions, but the other mesons, the kaons and eta particles, as well. Just as electrons are centers surrounded by virtual photons, so protons and neutrons, and all the other baryons, are to be pictured as centers of darting virtual mesons. A proton is constantly fluctuating between being just a proton and being a proton plus a neutral pion or a neutron plus a positive pion. Similarly, a neutron may be just a neutron or a neutron plus a neutral pion or a proton plus a negative pion. These fluctuations may be indicated thus:

$$p^+ \longleftrightarrow p^+ + \pi^0 \qquad n \longleftrightarrow n + \pi^0$$
$$p^+ \longleftrightarrow n + \pi^+ \qquad n \longleftrightarrow p^+ + \pi^-$$

The double-headed arrows imply that the interactions proceed in both directions. Similarly, an antineutron may be at times a negative antiproton plus a positive pion.

The neutron, in fact, must be in the form of a proton plus a negative pion a good part of the time, for it acts as if it were a tiny magnet. Since magnetic effects are produced only by moving electric charge, the neutron cannot be devoid of charge; rather, it must have equal amounts of both kinds spinning together about a common axis. The idea that both the proton and the neutron consist part of the time of central particles surrounded by charged pions is supported by experimental measurements of their magnetic effects, which are due mainly to the whirling pions. In the protons, where this whirling charge is *positive*, the magnet and the mechanical spin point in the *same* direction; in the neutron with its *negative* pions the two are *opposed*.

Direct evidence for the complex structure of protons and neutrons has been obtained through bombardment experiments with high-energy electrons (page 135). The proton experiments are carried out by bombarding ordinary hydrogen while the observations on neutrons are made with heavy hydrogen, whose atoms have nuclei which are proton-neutron pairs (since free neutrons in quantity are not available). From observations on the scattering of the bombarding electrons, it is possible to determine the distribution of electric charge within the bombarded particles. It is found that the pions have a range of about 10^{-13} centimeter, in agreement with Yukawa's theory. This theory gives only the *range* of the strong force and yields no information about its strength or details of its nature.

Attempts have been made to formulate a theory of the *weak-force* field, involving yet another kind of unknown virtual particle. All attempts to track down this *W-particle* experimentally have been unsuccessful. Finally, the gravitational field is thought to be mediated by virtual *gravitons* which, like photons, must be massless since the gravitational field, like the electrical field, has a long range. There is at present no expectation of observing real gravitons, for their creation in sensible amounts would require the violent agitation of huge masses. The particles related to the four kinds of fields are the only ones not constrained by number conservation laws; all four may be created and destroyed freely in any numbers.

Force fields consisting of darting virtual photons and mesons are again a radically new conception regarding the nature of matter. Material particles do not simply exist statically; they are centers of intense activity, of continual creation and annihilation. Every atom is a seat of such activity. In the nucleus there is a constant interplay of mesons, and the space around it is filled with swarms of virtual photons darting between the nucleus and the electrons.

ACTION AT A DISTANCE

QUANTUM field theory is, from one viewpoint, an attack on a problem of ancient origin, the problem of *action at a distance*. The natural philosophers of Aristotle's Lyceum may well have been puzzled to observe that a piece of rubbed amber exerts an attraction on bits of straw over a short intervening space, a phenomenon which eighteenth-century physicists would ascribe to the electric field in the vicinity of the charge on the amber. But they were no doubt more concerned with the analogous but more conspicuous observation of the downward pull experienced by all objects on the surface of the earth. Classical physics attributed this pull to the gravitational field which surrounds all pieces of matter but is of appreciable magnitude only near very large pieces such as the earth. To say that a stone held in the hand is pulled downward because it is in the earth's gravitational field, however, is merely puting a name to ignorance. It does not detract a whit from the mystery that the stone "feels" a pull with no visible or tangible agent acting upon it.

Isaac Newton, who formulated the law of action of the gravitational force, was well aware of this mystery. In one of his letters to the classical scholar and divine Richard Bentley he expressed himself thus:

> . . . that one body may act upon another at a distance through a vacuum without the mediation of anything else, by and through which their action and force may be conveyed from one to another, is to me so great an absurdity that, I believe, no man who has in philosophic matters a competent faculty of thinking could ever fall into it.

Newton saw clearly that his universal law of gravitation is a *description* not an *explanation*. The German philosopher and mathematician Baron Gottfried von Leibnitz (1646-1716), among others of Newton's contemporaries, criticized his work on this account, holding that his famous formula for the gravitational force ($F = Gm_1m_2/r^2$) is merely a rule of computation not worthy of being called a law of nature. It was compared adversely with existing "laws," with Aristotle's animistic explanation of the stone's fall as due to its "desire" to return to its "natural place" on the ground, and with Descartes's conception of the planets caught up in huge ether whirlpools carrying them on their orbits around the sun.

This unjust valuation of his work was repudiated in many of Newton's writings, as in the following passage from his *Optics*:

> To tell us that every species of thing is endow'd with an occult specific quality, by which it acts and produces manifest effects, is to tell us nothing. But to derive two or three general principles of motion from phenomena, and afterwards to tell us how the properties and actions of all corporeal things follow from these principles would be a very great step in philosophy, though the causes of those principles were not yet discovered.

Concerning his law of gravitation, which he discussed in the *Principia*, Newton made his position clear:

> I have not yet been able to discover the cause of these properties of gravity from phenomena, and I frame no hypotheses. . . . It is enough that gravity does really exist and acts according to the laws I have explained, and that it abundantly serves to account for all the motions of celestial bodies.

This quotation shows how thoroughly Newton espoused the experimental philosophy. He clearly expected that, if ever the "cause" of gravity is found, it will be deduced "from phenomena," that is, from experimental observations, and that in the meantime it is advisable to "frame no hypotheses."

The conception of fields of force as streams of virtual particles supplies the means "through which their action and force may be conveyed," which Newton so urgently demanded. It mitigates the problem of action at a distance, for with virtual photons producing the electric field, what happens *to* the electron happens *at* the electron.

Here is a lesson about the need for caution as to what "makes sense" in science. Nothing would seem more sensible than the observation that a stone tossed into the air falls back to earth; it would be surprising if the stone failed to do so. Yet upon closer study this simple event is seen to involve the metaphysical difficulties of action at a distance, difficulties which achieve a measure of intuitive resolution only in terms of the strange conception of virtual gravitons. This may serve as a warning that what passes for an understanding of simple things may well be no more than a tacit consensus to stop asking questions.

A noted Polish theoretical physicist and co-worker of
Albert Einstein takes us into the study of the great
twentieth-century physicist.

---

5   Einstein

Leopold Infeld

Excerpts from his book, *Quest, The Evolution of a Scientist*,

published in 1941.

I CAME TO PRINCETON on a Saturday, lived through a dead
Sunday and entered the office of Fine Hall on Monday, to make
my first acquaintances. I asked the secretary when I could see
Einstein. She telephoned him, and the answer was:

"Professor Einstein wants to see you right away."

I knocked at the door of 209 and heard a loud "*herein.*" When I opened the door I saw a hand stretched out energetically. It was Einstein, looking older than when I had met him in Berlin, older than the elapsed sixteen years should have made him. His long hair was gray, his face tired and yellow, but he had the same radiant deep eyes. He wore the brown leather jacket in which he has appeared in so many pictures. (Someone had given it to him to wear when sailing, and he had liked it so well that he dressed in it every day.) His shirt was without a collar, his brown trousers creased, and he wore shoes without socks. I expected a brief private conversation, questions about my crossing, Europe, Born, etc. Nothing of the kind:

"Do you speak German?"

"Yes," I answered.

"Perhaps I can tell you on what I am working."

Quietly he took a piece of chalk, went to the blackboard and started to deliver a perfect lecture. The calmness with which Einstein spoke was striking. There was nothing of the restlessness of a scientist who, explaining the problems with which he has lived for years, assumes that they are equally familiar to the listener and proceeds quickly with his exposition. Before going into details Einstein sketched the philosophical background for the problems on which he was working. Walking slowly and with dignity around the room, going to the blackboard from time to time to write down mathematical equations, keeping a dead pipe in his mouth, he formed his sentences perfectly. Everything that he said could have been printed as he said it and every sentence would make perfect sense. The exposition was simple, profound and clear.

I listened carefully and understood everything. The ideas behind Einstein's papers are aways so straightforward and fundamental that I believe I shall be able to express some of them in simple language.

There are two fundamental concepts in the development of physics: *field* and *matter.* The old physics which developed from Galileo and Newton, up to the middle of the nineteenth century, is a physics of matter. The old mechanical point of view is based upon the belief that we can explain all phenomena in nature by assuming particles and simple forces acting among them. In mechanics, while investigating the motion of the planets around the sun, we have the most triumphant model of the old view. Sun and planets are treated as particles, with the forces among them depending only upon their relative distances. The forces decrease if the distances increase. This is a typical model which the mechanist would like to apply, with some unessential changes, to the description of all physical phenomena.

A container with gas is, for the physicist, a conglomeration of small particles in haphazard motion. Here—from the planetary system to a gas—we pass in one great step from "macrophysics" to "microphysics," from phenomena accessible to our immediate observation to phenomena described by pictures of particles with masses so small that they lie beyond any possibility of direct measurement. It is our "spiritual" picture of gas, to which there is no immediate access for our senses, a microphysical picture which we are forced to form in order to understand experience.

Again this picture is of a mechanical nature. The forces among the particles of a gas depend only upon distances. In the motions of the stars, planets, gas particles, the human mind of the nineteenth century saw the manifestation of the same mechanical view. It understood the world of sensual impressions by forming pictures of particles and assuming simple forces acting among them. The philosophy of nature from the beginning of physics to the nineteenth century is based upon the belief that to understand phenomena means to use in their explanation the concepts of particles and forces which depend only upon distances.

To understand means always to reduce the complicated to the simple and familiar. For the physicists of the nineteenth century, to explain meant to form a mechanical picture from which the phenomena could be deduced. The physicists of the past century believed that it is possible to form a mechanical picture of the universe, that the whole universe is in this sense a great and complicated mechanical system.

Through slow, painful struggle and progress the mechanical view broke down. It became apparent that the simple concepts of particles and forces are not sufficient to explain all phenomena of nature. As so often happens in physics, in the time of need and doubt, a great new idea was born: that of the *field*. The old theory states: particles and the forces between them are the basic concepts. The new theory states: changes in space, spreading in time through all of space, are the basic concepts of our descriptions. These basic changes characterize the *field*.

Electrical phenomena were the birthplace of the field concept. The very words used in talking about radio waves—*sent, spread, received*—imply changes in space and therefore *field*. Not particles in certain points of space, but the whole continuous space forms the scenery of events which change with time.

The transition from particle physics to field physics is undoubtedly one of the greatest, and, as Einstein believes, *the* greatest step accomplished in the history of human thought. Great courage and imagination were needed to shift the responsibility for physical phenomena from particles into the previously empty space and to formulate mathematical equations describing the changes in space and time. This great change in the history of physics proved extremely fruitful in the theory of electricity and magnetism. In fact this change is mostly responsible for the great technical development in modern times.

We now know for sure that the old mechanical concepts are insufficient for the description of physical phenomena. But are the field concepts sufficient? Perhaps there is a still more primitive question: I see an object; how can I understand its existence? From the point of view of a mechanical theory the answer would be obvious: the object consists of small particles held together by forces. But we can look upon an object as upon a portion of space where the field is very intense or, as we say, where the energy is especially dense. The mechanist says: here is the object localized at this point of space. The field physicist says: field is everywhere, but it diminishes outside this portion so rapidly that my senses are aware of it only in this particular portion of space.

Basically, three views are possible:

1. The mechanistic: to reduce everything to particles and forces acting among them, depending only on distances.

2. The field view: to reduce everything to field concepts concerning continuous changes in time and space.

3. The dualistic view: to assume the existence of both matter and field.

For the present these three cases exhaust the possibilities of a philosophical approach to basic physical problems. The past generation believed in the first possibility. None of the present generation of physicists believes in it any more. Nearly all physicists accept, for the present, the third view, assuming the existence of both matter and field.

But the feeling of beauty and simplicity is essential to all scientific creation and forms the vista of future theories; where does the development of science lead? Is not the mixture of field and matter something temporary, accepted only out of necessity because we have not yet succeeded in forming a consistent picture based on the field concepts alone? Is it possible to form a pure field theory and to create what appears as matter out of the field?

These are the basic problems, and Einstein is and always has been interested in basic problems. He said to me once:

"I am really more of a philosopher than a physicist."

There is nothing strange in this remark. Every physicist is a philosopher as well, although it is possible to be a good experimentalist and a bad philosopher. But if one takes physics seriously, one can hardly avoid coming in contact with the fundamental philosophic questions.

General relativity theory (so called in contrast to special relativity theory, developed earlier by Einstein) attacks the problem of gravitation for the first time since Newton. Newton's theory of gravitation fits the old mechanical view perfectly. We could say more. It was the success of Newton's theory that caused the mechanical view to spread over all of physics. But with the triumphs of the field theory of physics a new task appeared: to fit the gravitational problem into the new field frame.

This is the work which was done by Einstein. Formulating the equations for the gravitational field, he did for gravitational theory what Faraday and Maxwell did for the theory of electricity. This is of course only one aspect of the theory of relativity and perhaps not the most important one, but it is a part of the principal problems on which Einstein has worked for the last few years and on which he is still working.

Einstein finished his introductory remarks and told me why he did not like the way the problem of a unitary field theory had been attacked by Born and me. Then he told me of his unsuccessful attempts to understand matter as a concentration of the field, then about his theory of "bridges" and the difficulties which he and his collaborator had encountered while developing that theory during a whole year of tedious work.

At this moment a knock at the door interrupted our conversation. A very small, thin man of about sixty entered, smiling and gesticulating, apologizing vividly with his hands, undecided in what language to speak. It was Levi-Civita, the famous Italian mathematician, at that time a professor in Rome and invited to Princeton for half a year. This small, frail man had refused some years before to swear the fascist oath designed for university professors in Italy.

Einstein had known Levi-Civita for a long time. But the form in which he greeted his old friend for the first time in Princeton was very similar to the way he had greeted me. By gestures rather than words Levi-Civita indicated that he did not want to disturb us, showing with both his hands at the door that he could go away. To emphasize the idea he bent his small body in this direction.

It was my turn to protest:

"I can easily go away and come some other time."

Then Einstein protested:

"No. We can all talk together. I shall repeat briefly what I said to Infeld just now. We did not go very far. And then we can discuss the later part."

We all agreed readily, and Einstein began to repeat his introductory remarks more briefly. This time "English" was chosen as the language of our conversation. Since I had heard the first part before, I did not need to be very attentive and could enjoy the show. I could not help laughing. Einstein's English was very simple, containing about three hundred words pronounced in a peculiar way. He had picked it up without having learned the language formally. But every word was understandable because of his quietness, slow tempo and the distinct, attractive sound of his voice. Levi-Civita's English was much worse, and the sense of his words melted in the Italian pronunciation and vivid gestures. Understanding was possible between us only because mathematicians hardly need words to understand each other. They have their symbols and a few technical terms which are recognizable even when deformed.

I watched the calm, impressive Einstein and the small, thin, broadly gesticulating Levi-Civita as they pointed out formulae on the blackboard and talked in a language which they thought to be English. The picture they made, and the sight of Einstein pulling up his baggy trousers every few seconds, was a scene, impressive and at the same time comic, which I shall never forget. I tried to restrain myself from laughing by saying to myself:

"Here you are talking and discussing physics with the most famous scientist in the world and you want to laugh because he does not wear suspenders!" The persuasion worked and I managed to control myself just as Einstein began to talk about his latest, still unpublished paper concerning the work done during the preceding year with his assistant Rosen.

It was on the problem of gravitational waves. Again I believe that, in spite of the highly technical, mathematical character of this work, it is possible to explain the basic ideas in simple words.

The existence of electromagnetic waves, for example, light waves, X rays or wireless waves, can be explained by one theory embracing all these and many other phenomena: by Maxwell's equations governing the electromagnetic field. The prediction that electromagnetic waves *must* exist was prior to Hertz's experiment showing that the waves *do* exist.

General relativity is a field theory and, roughly speaking, it does for the problem of gravitation what Maxwell's theory did for the problem of electromagnetic phenomena. It is therefore apparent that the existence of gravitational waves can be deduced from general relativity just as the existence of electromagnetic waves can be deduced from Maxwell's theory. Every physicist who has ever studied the theory of relativity is convinced on this point. In their motion the stars send out gravitational waves, spreading in time through space, just as oscillating electrons send out electromagnetic waves. It is a common feature of all field theories that the influence of one object on another, of one electron or star on another electron or star, spreads through space with a great but finite velocity in the form of waves. A superficial mathematical investigation of the structure of gravitational equations showed the existence of gravitational waves, and it was always believed that a more thorough examination could only confirm this result, giving some finer features of the gravitational waves. No one cared about a deeper investigation of this subject because in nature gravitational waves, or gravitational radiation, seem to play a very small role. It is different in Maxwell's theory, where the electromagnetic radiation is essential to the description of natural phenomena.

So everyone believed in gravitational waves. In the previous two years Einstein had begun to doubt their existence. If we investigate the problem superficially, they seem to exist. But Einstein claimed that a deeper analysis flatly contradicts the previous statement. This result, if true, would be of a fundamental nature. It would reveal something which would astound every physicist: that field theory and the existence of waves are not as closely connected as previously thought. It would show us once more that the first intuition may be wrong, that deeper mathematical analysis may give us new and unexpected results quite different from those foreseen when only scratching the surface of gravitational equations.

I was very much interested in this result, though somewhat skeptical. During my scientific career I had learned that you may admire someone and regard him as the greatest scientist in the world but you must trust your own brain still more. Scientific creation would become sterile if results were authoritatively or dogmatically accepted. Everyone has his own intuition. Everyone has his fairly rigidly determined level of achievement and is capable only of small up-and-down oscillations around it. To know this level, to know one's place in the scientific world, is essential. It is good to be master in the restricted world of your own possibilities and to outgrow the habit of accepting results before they have been thoroughly tested by your mind.

Both Levi-Civita and I were impressed by the conclusion regarding the nonexistence of gravitational waves, although there was no time to develop the technical methods which led to this conclusion. Levi-Civita indicated that he had a luncheon appointment by gestures so vivid that they made me feel hungry. Einstein asked me to accompany him home, where he would give me the manuscript of his paper. On the way we talked physics. This overdose of science began to weary me and I had difficulty in following him. Einstein talked on a subject to which we returned in our conversations many times later. He explained why he did not find the modern quantum mechanics aesthetically satisfactory and why he believed in its provisional character which would be changed fundamentally by future development.

He took me to his study with its great window overlooking the bright autumn colors of his lovely garden, and his first and only remark which did not concern physics was:

"There is a beautiful view from this window."

Excited and happy, I went home with the manuscript of Einstein's paper. I felt the anticipation of intense emotions which always accompany scientific work: the sleepless nights in which imagination is most vivid and the controlling criticism weakest, the ecstasy of seeing the light, the despair when a long and tedious road leads nowhere; the attractive mixture of happiness and unhappiness. All this was before me, raised to the highest level because I was working in the best place in the world.

THE PROGRESS OF MY WORK with Einstein brought an increasing intimacy between us. More and more often we talked of social problems, politics, human relations, science, philosophy, life and death, fame and happiness and, above all, about the future of science and its ultimate aims. Slowly I came to know Einstein better and better. I could foresee his reactions; I understood his attitude which, although strange and unusual, was always fully consistent with the essential features of his personality.

Seldom has anyone met as many people in his life as Einstein has. Kings and presidents have entertained him; everyone is eager to meet him and to secure his friendship. It is comparatively easy to meet Einstein but difficult to know him. His mail brings him letters from all over the world which he tries to answer as long as there is any sense in answering. But through all the stream of events, the impact of people and social life forced upon him, Einstein remains lonely, loving solitude, isolation and conditions which secure undisturbed work.

A few years ago, in London, Einstein made a speech in Albert Hall on behalf of the refugee scientists, the first of whom had begun to pour out from Germany all over the world. Einstein said then that there are many positions, besides those in universities, which would be suitable for scientists. As an example he mentioned a lighthouse keeper. This would be comparatively easy work which would allow one to contemplate and to do scientific research. His remark seemed funny to every scientist. But it is quite understandable from Einstein's point of view. One of the consequences of loneliness is to judge everything by one's own standards, to be unable to change one's co-ordinate system by putting oneself into someone else's being. I always noticed this difficulty in Einstein's reactions. For him loneliness, life in a lighthouse, would be most stimulating, would free him from so many of the duties which he hates. In fact it would be for him the ideal life. But nearly every scientist thinks just the opposite. It was the curse of my life that for a long time I was not in a scientific atmosphere, that I had no one with whom to talk physics. It is commonly known that stimulating environment strongly influences the scientist, that he may do good work in a scientific atmosphere and that he may become sterile, his ideas dry up and all his research activity die if his environment is scientifically dead. I knew that put back in a gymnasium, in a provincial Polish town, I should not publish anything, and the same would have happened to many another scientist better than I. But genius is an exception. Einstein could work anywhere, and it is difficult to convince him that he is an exception.

He regards himself as extremely lucky in life because he never had to fight for his daily bread. He enjoyed the years spent in the patent office in Switzerland. He found the atmosphere more friendly, more human, less marred by intrigue than at the universities, and he had plenty of time for scientific work.

In connection with the refugee problem he told me that he would not have minded working with his hands for his daily bread, doing something useful like making shoes and treating physics only as a hobby; that this might be more attractive than earning money from physics by teaching at the university. Again something deeper is hidden behind this attitude. It is the "religious" feeling, bound up with scientific work, recalling that of the early Christian ascetics. Physics is great and important. It is not quite right to earn money by physics. Better to do something different for a living, such as tending a lighthouse or making shoes, and keep physics aloof and clean. Naïve as it may seem, this attitude is consistent with Einstein's character.

I learned much from Einstein in the realm of physics. But what I value most is what I was taught by my contact with him in the human rather than the scientific domain. Einstein is the kindest, most understanding and helpful man in the world. But again this somewhat commonplace statement must not be taken literally.

The feeling of pity is one of the sources of human kindness. Pity for the fate of our fellow men, for the misery around us, for the suffering of human beings, stirs our emotions by the resonance of sympathy. Our own attachments to life and people, the ties which bind us to the outside world, awaken our emotional response to the struggle and suffering outside ourselves. But there is also another entirely different source of human kindness. It is the detached feeling of duty based on aloof, clear reasoning. Good, clear thinking leads to kindness and loyalty because this is what makes life simpler, fuller, richer, diminishes friction and unhappiness in our environment and therefore also in our lives. A sound social attitude, helpfulness, friendliness, kindness, may come from both these different sources; to express it anatomically, from heart and brain. As the years passed I learned to value more and more the second kind of decency that arises from clear thinking. Too often I have seen how emotions unsupported by clear thought are useless if not destructive.

Here again, as I see it, Einstein represents a limiting case. I had never encountered so much kindness that was so completely detached. Though only scientific ideas and physics really matter to Einstein, he has never refused to help when he felt that his help was needed and could be effective. He wrote thousands of letters of recommendation, gave advice to hundreds. For hours he talked with a crank because the family had written that Einstein was the only one who could cure him. Einstein is kind, smiling, understanding, talkative with people whom he meets, waiting patiently for the moment when he will be left alone to return to his work.

Einstein wrote about himself:

My passionate interest in social justice and social responsibility has always stood in curious contrast to a marked lack of desire for direct association with men and women. I am a horse for single harness, not cut out for tandem or teamwork. I have never belonged wholeheartedly to country or state, to my circle of friends or even to my own family. These ties have always been accompanied by a vague aloofness, and the wish to withdraw into myself increases with the years.

Such isolation is sometimes bitter, but I do not regret being cut off from the understanding and sympathy of other men. I lose something by it, to be sure, but I am compensated for it in being rendered independent of the customs, opinions and prejudices of others and am not tempted to rest my peace of mind upon such shifting foundations.

For scarcely anyone is fame so undesired and meaningless as for Einstein. It is not that he has learned the bitter taste of fame, as frequently happens, after having desired it. Einstein told me that in his youth he had always wished to be isolated from the struggle of life. He was certainly the last man to have sought fame. But fame came to him, perhaps the greatest a scientist has ever known. I often wondered why it came to Einstein. His ideas have not influenced our practical life. No electric light, no telephone, no wireless is connected with his name. Perhaps the only important technical discovery which takes its origin in Einstein's theoretical work is that of the photoelectric cell. But Einstein is certainly not famous because of this discovery. It is his work on relativity theory which has made his name known to all the civilized world. Does the reason lie in the great influence of Einstein's theory upon philosophical thought? This again cannot be the whole explanation. The latest developments in quantum mechanics, its connection with determinism and indeterminism, influenced philosophical thought fully as much. But the names of Bohr and Heisenberg have not the glory that is Einstein's. The reasons for the great fame which diffused deeply among the masses of people, most of them removed from creative scientific work, incapable of estimating his work, must be manifold and, I believe, sociological in character. The explanation was suggested to me by discussions with one of my friends in England.

It was in 1919 that Einstein's fame began. At this time his great achievement, the structure of the special and general relativity theories, was essentially finished. As a matter of fact it had been completed five years before. One of the consequences of the general relativity theory may be described as follows: if we photograph a fragment of the heavens during a solar eclipse and the same fragment in normal conditions, we obtain slightly different pictures. The gravitational field of the sun slightly disturbs and deforms the path of light, therefore the photographic picture of a fragment of the heavens will vary somewhat during the solar eclipse from that under normal conditions. Not only qualitatively but quantitatively the theory of relativity predicted the difference in these two pictures. English scientific expeditions sent in 1919 to different parts of the world, to Africa and South America, confirmed this prediction made by Einstein.

Thus began Einstein's great fame. Unlike that of film stars, politicians and boxers, the fame persists. There are no signs of its diminishing; there is no hope of relief for Einstein. The fact that the theory predicted an event which is as far from our everyday life as the stars to which it refers, an event which follows from a theory through a long chain of abstract arguments, seems hardly sufficient to raise the enthusiasm of the masses. But it did. And the reason must be looked for in the postwar psychology.

It was just after the end of the war. People were weary of hatred, of killing and international intrigues. The trenches, bombs and murder had left a bitter taste. Books about war did not sell. Everyone looked for a new era of peace and wanted to forget the war. Here was something which captured the imagination: human eyes looking from an earth covered with graves and blood to the heavens covered with stars. Abstract thought carrying the human mind far away from the sad and disappointing reality. The mystery of the sun's eclipse and the penetrating power of the human mind. Romantic scenery, a strange glimpse of the eclipsed sun, an imaginary picture of bending light rays, all removed from the oppressive reality of life. One further reason, perhaps even more important: a new event was predicted by a *German* scientist Einstein and confirmed by *English* astronomers. Scientists belonging to two warring nations had collaborated again! It seemed the beginning of a new era.

It is difficult to resist fame and not to be influenced by it. But fame has had no effect on Einstein. And again the reason lies in his internal isolation, in his aloofness. Fame bothers him when and as long as it impinges on his life, but he ceases to be conscious of it the moment he is left alone. Einstein is unaware of his fame and forgets it when he is allowed to forget it.

Even in Princeton everyone looks with hungry, astonished eyes at Einstein. During our walks we avoided the more crowded streets to walk through fields and along forgotten byways. Once a car stopped us and a middle-aged woman got out with a camera and said, blushing and excited:

"Professor Einstein, will you allow me to take a picture of you?"

"Yes, sure."

He stood quiet for a second, then continued his argument. The scene did not exist for him, and I am sure after a few minutes he forgot that it had ever happened.

Once we went to a movie in Princeton to see the *Life of Émile Zola*. After we had bought our tickets we went to a crowded waiting room and found that we should have to wait fifteen minutes longer. Einstein suggested that we go for a walk. When we went out I said to the doorman:

"We shall return in a few minutes."

But Einstein became seriously concerned and added in all innocence:

"We haven't our tickets any more. Will you recognize us?"

The doorman thought we were joking and said, laughing:

"Yes, Professor Einstein, I will."

Einstein is, if he is allowed to be, completely unaware of his fame, and he furnishes a unique example of a character untouched by the impact of the greatest fame and publicity. But there are moments when the aggressiveness of the outside world disturbs his peace. He once told me:

"I envy the simplest working man. He has his privacy."

Another time he remarked:

"I appear to myself as a swindler because of the great publicity about me without any real reason."

Einstein understands everyone beautifully when logic and thinking are needed. It is much less easy, however, where emotions are concerned; it is difficult for him to imagine motives and emotions other than those which are a part of his life. Once he told me:

"I speak to everyone in the same way, whether he is the garbage man or the president of the university."

I remarked that this is difficult for other people. That, for example, when they meet him they feel shy and embarrassed, that it takes time for this feeling to disappear and that it was so in my case. He said:

"I cannot understand this. Why should anyone be shy with me?"

If my explanation concerning the beginning of Einstein's fame is correct, then there still remains another question to be answered: why does this fame cling so persistently to Einstein in a changing world which scorns today its idols of yesterday? I do not think the answer is difficult.

Everything that Einstein did, everything for which he stood, was always consistent with the primary picture of him in the minds of the people. His voice was always raised in defense of the suppressed; his signature always appeared in defense of liberal causes. He was like a saint with two halos around his head. One was formed of ideas of justice and progress, the other of abstract ideas about physical theories which, the more abstruse they were, the more impressive they seemed to the ordinary man. His name became a symbol of progress, humanity and creative thought, hated and despised by those who spread hate and who attack the ideas for which Einstein's name stands.

From the same source, from the desire to defend the oppressed, arose his interest in the Jewish problem. Einstein himself was not reared in the Jewish tradition. It is again his detached attitude of sympathy, the rational idea that help must be given where help is needed, that brought him near to the Jewish problem. Jews have made splendid use of Einstein's gentle attitude. He once said:

"I am something of a Jewish saint. When I die the Jews will take my bones to a banquet and collect money."

In spite of Einstein's detachment I had often the impression that the Jewish problem is nearer his heart than any other social problem. The reason may be that I met him just at the time when the Jewish tragedy was greatest and perhaps, also, because he believes that there he can be most helpful.

Einstein also fully realized the importance of the war in Spain and foresaw that on its outcome not only Spain's fate but the future of the world depended. I remember the gleam that came into his eyes when I told him that the afternoon papers carried news of a Loyalist victory.

"That sounds like an angel's song," he said with an excitement which I had hardly ever noticed before. But two minutes later we were writing down formulae and the external world had again ceased to exist.

It took me a long time to realize that in his aloofness and isolation lie the simple keys leading to an understanding of many of his actions. I am quite sure that the day Einstein received the Nobel prize he was not in the slightest degree excited and that if he did not sleep well that it was because of a problem which was bothering him and not because of the scientific distinction. His Nobel prize medal, together with many others, is laid aside among papers, honorary degrees and diplomas in the room where his secretary works, and I am sure that Einstein has no clear idea of what the medal looks like.

Einstein tries consciously to keep his aloofness intact by small idiosyncrasies which may seem strange but which increase his freedom and further loosen his ties with the external world. He never reads articles about himself. He said that this helps him to be free. Once I tried to break his habit. In a French newspaper there was an article about Einstein which was reproduced in many European papers, even in Poland and Lithuania. I have never seen an article which was further from the truth than this one. For example, the author said that Einstein wears glasses, lives in Princeton in one room on the fifth floor, comes to the institute at 7 A.M., always wears black, keeps many of his technical discoveries secret, etc. The article could be characterized as the peak of stupidity if stupidity could be said to have a peak. Fine Hall rejoiced in the article and hung it up as a curiosity on the bulletin board at the entrance. I thought it so funny that I read it to Einstein, who at my request listened carefully but was little interested and refused to be amused. I could see from his expression that he failed to understand why I found it so funny.

One of my colleagues in Princeton asked me:

"If Einstein dislikes his fame and would like to increase his privacy, why does he not do what ordinary people do? Why does he wear long hair, a funny leather jacket, no socks, no suspenders, no collars, no ties?"

The answer is simple and can easily be deduced from his aloofness and desire to loosen his ties with the outside world. The idea is to restrict his needs and, by this restriction, increase his freedom. We are slaves of millions of things, and our slavery progresses steadily. For a week I tried an electric razor—and one more slavery entered my life. I dreaded spending the summer where there was no electric current. We are slaves of bathrooms, Frigidaires, cars, radios and millions of other things. Einstein tried to reduce them to the absolute minimum. Long hair minimizes the need for the barber. Socks can be done without. One leather jacket solves the coat problem for many years. Suspenders are superfluous, as are nightshirts and pajamas. It is a minimum problem which Einstein has solved, and shoes, trousers, shirt, jacket, are the very necessary things; it would be difficult to reduce them further.

I like to imagine Einstein's behavior in an unusual situation. For example: Princeton is bombed from the air; explosives fall over the city, people flee to shelter, panic spreads over the town and everyone loses his head, increasing the chaos and fear by his behavior. If this situation should find Einstein walking through the street, he would be the only man to remain as quiet as before. He would think out what to do in this situation; he would do it without accelerating the normal speed of his motions and he would still keep in mind the problem on which he was thinking.

There is no fear of death in Einstein. He said to me once:

"Life is an exciting show. I enjoy it. It is wonderful. But if I knew that I should have to die in three hours it would impress me very little. I should think how best to use the last three hours, then quietly order my papers and lie peacefully down."

Mr. Tompkins takes a holiday trip in a physically possible science-fiction land. In solving a murder case there he learns the meaning of the concept of simultaneity in the theory of relativity.

6   Mr. Tompkins and Simultaneity

George Gamow

Excerpt from his book, *Mr. Tompkins In Paperback*, published in 1965

Mr Tompkins was very amused about his adventures in the relativistic city, but was sorry that the professor had not been with him to give any explanation of the strange things he had observed: the mystery of how the railway brakeman had been able to prevent the passengers from getting old worried him especially. Many a night he went to bed with the hope that he would see this interesting city again, but the dreams were rare and mostly unpleasant; last time it was the manager of the bank who was firing him for the uncertainty he introduced into the bank accounts... so now he decided that he had better take a holiday, and go for a week somewhere to the sea. Thus he found himself sitting in a compartment of a train and watching through the window the grey roofs of the city suburb gradually giving place to the green meadows of the countryside. He picked up a newspaper and tried to interest himself in the Vietnam conflict. But it all seemed to be so dull, and the railway carriage rocked him pleasantly....

When he lowered the paper and looked out of the window again the landscape had changed considerably. The telegraph poles were so close to each other that they looked like a hedge, and the trees had extremely narrow crowns and were like Italian cypresses. Opposite to him sat his old friend the professor, looking through the window with great interest. He had probably got in while Mr Tompkins was busy with his newspaper.

'We are in the land of relativity,' said Mr Tompkins, 'aren't we?'

'Oh!' exclaimed the professor, 'you know so much already! Where did you learn it from?'

'I have already been here once, but did not have the pleasure of your company then.'

'So you are probably going to be my guide this time,' the old man said.

'I should say not,' retorted Mr Tompkins. 'I saw a lot of unusual things, but the local people to whom I spoke could not understand what my trouble was at all.'

'Naturally enough,' said the professor. 'They are born in this world and consider all the phenomena happening around them as self-evident. But I imagine they would be quite surprised if they happened to get into the world in which you used to live. It would look so remarkable to them.'

'May I ask you a question?' said Mr Tompkins. 'Last time I was here, I met a brakeman from the railway who insisted that owing to the fact that the train stops and starts again the passengers grow old less quickly than the people in the city. Is this magic, or is it also consistent with modern science?'

'There is never any excuse for putting forward magic as an explanation,' said the professor. 'This follows directly from the laws of physics. It was shown by Einstein, on the basis of his analysis of new (or should I say as-old-as-the-world but newly discovered) notions of space and time, that all physical processes slow down when the system in which they are taking place is changing its velocity. In our world the effects are almost unobservably small, but here, owing to the small velocity of light, they are usually very obvious. If, for example, you tried to boil an egg here, and instead of letting the saucepan stand quietly on the stove moved it to and fro, constantly changing its velocity, it would take you not five but perhaps six minutes to boil it properly. Also in the human body all processes slow down, if the person is sitting (for example) in a rocking chair or in a train which changes its speed; we live more slowly under such conditions. As, however, all processes slow down to the same extent, physicists prefer to say that *in a non-uniformly moving system time flows more slowly*.'

'But do scientists actually observe such phenomena in our world at home?'

'They do, but it requires considerable skill. It is technically very difficult to get the necessary accelerations, but the conditions existing in a non-uniformly moving system are analogous, or should I say identical, to the result of the action of a very large force of gravity. You may have noticed that when you are in an elevator which is rapidly accelerated upwards it seems to you that you have grown heavier; on the contrary, if the elevator starts downward (you realize it best when the rope breaks) you feel as though you were losing weight. The explanation is that the gravitational field created by acceleration is added to or subtracted from the gravity of the earth. Well, the potential of gravity on the sun is much larger than on the surface of the earth and all processes there should be therefore slightly slowed down. Astronomers do observe this.'

'But they cannot go to the sun to observe it?'

'They do not need to go there. They observe the light coming to us from the sun. This light is emitted by the vibration of different atoms in the solar atmosphere. If all processes go slower there, the speed of atomic vibrations also decreases, and by comparing the light emitted by solar and terrestrial sources one can see the difference. Do you know, by the way'—the professor interrupted himself—'what the name of this little station is that we are now passing?'

The train was rolling along the platform of a little countryside station which was quite empty except for the station master and a young porter sitting on a luggage trolley and reading a newspaper. Suddenly the station master threw his hands into the air and fell down on his face. Mr Tompkins did not hear the sound of shooting, which was probably lost in the noise of the train, but the pool of blood forming round the body of the station master left no doubt. The professor immediately pulled the emergency cord and the train stopped with a jerk. When they got out of the carriage the young porter was running towards the body, and a country policeman was approaching.

'Shot through the heart,' said the policeman after inspecting the body, and, putting a heavy hand on the porter's shoulder, he went on: 'I am arresting you for the murder of the station master.'

'I didn't kill him,' exclaimed the unfortunate porter. 'I was reading a newspaper when I heard the shot. These gentlemen from the train have probably seen all and can testify that I am innocent.'

'Yes,' said Mr Tompkins, 'I saw with my own eyes that this man was reading his paper when the station master was shot. I can swear it on the Bible.'

'But you were in the moving train,' said the policeman, taking an authoritative tone, 'and what you saw is therefore no evidence at all. As seen from the platform the man could have been shooting at the very same moment. Don't you know that simultaneousness depends on the system from which you observe it? Come along quietly,' he said, turning to the porter.

'Excuse me, constable,' interrupted the professor, 'but you are absolutely wrong, and I do not think that at headquarters they will like your ignorance. It is true, of course, that the notion of simultaneousness is highly relative in your country. It is also true that two events in different places could be simultaneous or not, depending on the motion of the observer. But, even in your country, no observer could see the consequence before the cause. You have never received a telegram before it was sent, have you? or got drunk before opening the bottle? As I understand you, you suppose that owing to the motion of the train the shooting would have been seen by us much *later* than its effect and, as we got out of the train immediately we saw the station master fall, we still had not seen the shooting itself. I know that in the police force you are taught to believe only what is written in your instructions, but look into them and probably you will find something about it.'

The professor's tone made quite an impression on the policeman and, pulling out his pocket book of instructions, he started to read it slowly through. Soon a smile of embarrassment spread out across his big, red face.

'Here it is,' said he, 'section 37, subsection 12, paragraph e: "As a perfect alibi should be recognized any authoritative proof, from any moving system whatsoever, that at the moment of the crime or within a time interval $\pm cd$ (c being natural speed limit and d the distance from the place of the crime) the suspect was seen in another place."'

'You are free, my good man,' he said to the porter, and then, turning to the professor: 'Thank you very much, Sir, for saving me from trouble with headquarters. I am new to the force and not yet accustomed to all these rules. But I must report the murder anyway,' and he went to the telephone box. A minute later he was shouting across the platform. 'All is in order now! They caught the real murderer when he was running away from the station. Thank you once more!'

'I may be very stupid,' said Mr Tompkins, when the train started again, 'but what is all this business about simultaneousness? Has it really no meaning in this country?'

'It has,' was the answer, 'but only to a certain extent; otherwise I should not have been able to help the porter at all. You see, the existence of a natural speed limit for the motion of any body or the propagation of any signal, makes simultaneousness in our ordinary sense of the word lose its meaning. You probably will see it more easily this way. Suppose you have a friend living in a far-away town, with whom you correspond by letter, mail train being the fastest means of communication. Suppose now that something happens to you on Sunday and you learn that the same thing is going to happen to your friend. It is clear that you cannot let him know about it before Wednesday. On the other hand, if he knew in advance about the thing that was going to happen to you, the last date to let you know about it would have been the previous Thursday. Thus for six days, from Thursday to next Wednesday, your friend was not able either to influence your fate on Sunday or to learn about it. From the point of view of causality he was, so to speak, excommunicated from you for six days.'

'What about a telegram?' suggested Mr Tompkins.

'Well, I accepted that the velocity of the mail train was the maximum possible velocity, which is about correct in this country. At home the velocity of light is the maximum velocity and you cannot send a signal faster than by radio.'

'But still,' said Mr Tompkins, 'even if the velocity of the mail train could not be surpassed, what has it to do with simultaneousness? My friend and myself would still have our Sunday dinners simultaneously, wouldn't we?'

'No, that statement would not have any sense then; one observer would agree to it, but there would be others, making their observations from different trains, who would insist that you eat your Sunday dinner at the same time as your friend has his Friday breakfast or Tuesday lunch. But in no way could anybody observe you and your friend simultaneously having meals more than three days apart.'

'But how can all this happen?' exclaimed Mr Tompkins unbelievingly.

'In a very simple way, as you might have noticed from my lectures. The upper limit of velocity must remain the same as observed from different moving systems. If we accept this we should conclude that. . . .'

But their conversation was interrupted by the train arriving at the station at which Mr Tompkins had to get out.

Rogers, a noted physics teacher, introduces the fundamental concepts of the theory of relativity and illustrates the relation of mathematics to physics.

7 Mathematics and Relativity

Eric M. Rogers

Chapter from his textbook, *Physics for the Inquiring Mind*, 1960.

Mathematics as Language

The scientist, collecting information, formulating schemes, building knowledge, needs to express himself in clear language; but ordinary languages are much more vague and unreliable than most people think. "I love vegetables" is so vague that it is almost a disgrace to a civilized language—a few savage cries could make as full a statement. "A thermometer told me the temperature of the bath water." Thermometers don't "tell." All you do is try to decide on its reading by staring at it—and you are almost certainly a little wrong. A thermometer does not show the temperature of the water; it shows its own temperature. Some of these quarrels relate to the physics of the matter, but they are certainly not helped by the wording. We can make our statements safer by being more careful; but our science still emerges with wording that needs a series of explanatory footnotes. In contrast, the language of mathematics says what it means with amazing brevity and honesty. When we write $2x^2 - 3x + 1 = 0$ we make a very definite, though very dull, statement about x. One advantage of using mathematics in science is that we can make it write what we want to say with accuracy, avoiding vagueness and unwanted extra meanings. The remark "$\Delta v/\Delta t = 32$" makes a clear statement without dragging in a long, wordy description of acceleration. $y = 16t^2$ tells us how a rock falls without adding any comments on mass or gravity.

Mathematics is of great use as a shorthand, both in stating relationships and in carrying out complicated arguments, as when we amalgamate several relationships. We can say, for uniformly accelerated motion, "the distance travelled is the sum of the product of initial velocity and time, and half the product of the acceleration and the square of the time," but it is shorter to say, "$s = v_0 t + \frac{1}{2} at^2$." If we tried to operate with wordy statements instead of algebra, we should still be able to start with two accelerated-motion relations and extract a third one, as when we obtained $v^2 = v_0^2 + 2as$ in Chapter 1, Appendix A; but, without the compact shorthand of algebra, it would be a brain-twister argument. Going still further, into discussions where we use the razor-sharp algebra called calculus, arguing in words would be impossibly complex and cumbersome. In such cases mathematics is like a sausage-machine that operates with the rules of logical argument instead of wheels and pistons. It takes in the scientific information we provide—facts and relationships from experiment, and schemes from our minds, dreamed up as guesses to be tried—and rehashes them into new form. Like the real sausage-machine, it does not always deliver to the new sausage all the material fed in; but it never delivers anything that was not supplied to it originally. It cannot manufacture science of the real world from its own machinations.

Mathematics: the Good Servant

Yet in addition to routine services mathematics can indeed perform marvels for science. As a lesser marvel, it can present the new sausage in a form that suggests further uses. For example, suppose you had discovered that falling bodies have a constant acceleration of 32 ft/sec/sec, and that any downward motion they are given to start with is just added to the motion gained by acceleration. Then the mathematical machine could take your experimental discovery and measurement of "g" and predict the relationship $s = v_0 t + \frac{1}{2}(32)t^2$. Now suppose you had never thought of including upward-thrown things in your study, had never seen a ball rise and fall in a parabola. The mathematical machine, not having been warned of any such restriction, would calmly offer its prediction as if unrestricted. Thus you might try putting in an upward start, giving v_0 a negative value in the formula. At once the formula tells a different-looking story. In that case, it says,

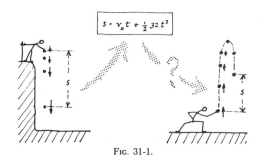

$$s = v_0 t + \frac{1}{2} 32 t^2$$

FIG. 31-1.

the stone would fly up slower and slower, reach a highest point, and then fall faster and faster. This is not a rash guess on the algebra's part. It is an unemotional routine statement. The algebra-machine's defense would be, "You never told me v_0 had to be downward. I do not know whether the new prediction is right. All I can say is that IF an upward throw follows the rules I was told to use for downward throws, THEN an upward thrown ball will rise, stop, fall." It is we who make the rash guess that the basic rules may be general. It is we who welcome the machine's new hint; but we then go out and try it.[1] To take another example from projectile mathematics, the following problem, which you met earlier, has two answers.

PROBLEM:

"A stone is thrown upward, with initial speed 64 ft/sec, at a bird in a tree. How long after its start will the stone hit the bird, which is 48 feet above the thrower?"

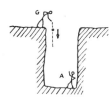

48 ft

ANSWER:

1 second or 3 seconds.

FIG. 31-2.

This shows algebra as a very honest, if rather dumb, servant. There are two answers and there should be, for the problem as presented to the machine. The stone may hit the bird as it goes up (1 sec from start), or as it falls down again (after 3 secs). The machine, if blamed for the second answer would complain, "But you never told me the stone had to *hit* the bird, still less that it must hit it on the way *up*. I only calculated *when the stone would be 48 feet above the thrower*. There are two such times." Looking back, we see we neither wrote anything in the mathematics to express contact between stone and bird nor said which way the stone was to be moving. It is *our* fault for giving incomplete instructions, and it is to the credit of the machine that it politely tells us all the answers which are possible within those instructions.

If the answer to some algebra problem on farming emerges as 3 cows *or* 2¼ cows, we rightly reject the second answer, but we blame ourselves for not telling the mathematical machine an important fact about cows. In physics problems where several answers emerge we are usually unwise to throw some of them away. They may all be quite true; or, if some are very queer, accepting them provisionally may lead to new knowledge. If you look back at the projectile problem, No. 7 in Chapter 1, Appendix B, you may now see what its second answer meant.

Here is one like it:

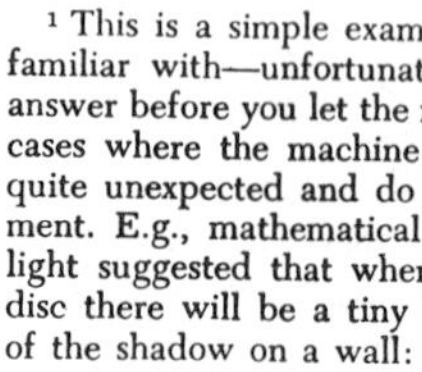

PROBLEM:

A man throws a stone down a well which is 96 feet deep. It starts with *downward* velocity 16 ft/sec. When will it reach the bottom?

FIG. 31-4.

[1] This is a simple example, chosen to use physics you are familiar with—unfortunately so simple that you know the answer before you let the machine suggest it. There are many cases where the machine can produce suggestions that are quite unexpected and do indeed send us rushing to experiment. E.g., mathematical treatment of the wave theory of light suggested that when light casts a sharp shadow of a disc there will be a tiny bright spot of light in the middle of the shadow on a wall: "There is a hole in every coin."

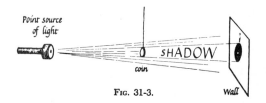

Point source of light

SHADOW

coin

Wall

FIG. 31-3.

Assign suitable + and − signs to the data, substitute them in a suitable relation for free fall, and solve the equation. You will obtain two answers: One a sensible time with + sign (the "right" answer), the other a negative time. Is the negative answer necessarily meaningless and silly? A time such as "−3 seconds" simply means, "3 seconds before the clock was started." The algebra-machine is not told that *the stone was flung down by the man.* It is only told that when the clock started at zero *the stone was moving DOWN with speed 16 ft/sec,* and thereafter fell freely. For all the algebra knows, the stone may have just skimmed through the man's hand at time zero. It may have been started much earlier by an assistant at the bottom of the well who hurled it upward fast enough to have just the right velocity at time zero. So, while our story runs, "George, standing at the top of the well, hurled the stone down . . . ," an answer −3 seconds suggests an alternative story: "Alfred, at the bottom of the well, hurled the stone up with great speed. The stone rose up through the well and into the air above, with diminishing speed, reached a highest point, fell with increasing speed, moving down past George 3 seconds after Alfred threw it. George missed it (at $t = 0$), so it passed him at 16 ft/sec and fell on down the well again." According to the algebra, the stone will reach the bottom of the well one second after it leaves George, and it *might* have started from the bottom 3 seconds before it passes George.

Return to Problem 7 of Chapter 1, Appendix B and try to interpret its two answers.

PROBLEM 7:

A man standing on the top of a tower throws a stone up into the air with initial velocity 32 feet/sec upward. The man's hand is 48 feet above the ground. How long will the stone take to reach the ground?

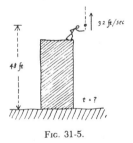

FIG. 31-5.

In these problems mathematics shows itself to be the completely honest servant—rather like the honest boy in one of G. K. Chesterton's "Father Brown" stories. (There, a slow-witted village lad delivered a telegram to a miser. The miser meant to tip the boy with the smallest English coin, a bright bronze farthing (¼¢), but gave him a golden pound ($3) by mistake. What was the boy to do when he discovered the obvious mistake? Keep the pound, trading on the mistake dishonestly? Or bring it back with unctuous virtue and embarrass the miser into

saying "Keep it, my boy"? He did neither. He simply brought the exact change, 19 shillings and 11¾ pence. The miser was delighted, saying, "At last I have found an honest man"; and he bequeathed to the boy all the gold he possessed. The boy, in wooden-headed honesty, interpreted the miser's will literally, even to the extent of taking gold fillings from his teeth.)

Mathematics: the Clever Servant

As a greater marvel, mathematics can present the new sausage in a form that suggests entirely new viewpoints. With vision of genius the scientist may see, in something new, a faint resemblance to something seen before—enough to suggest the next step in imaginative thinking and trial. If we tried to do without mathematics we should lose more than a clear language, a shorthand script for argument and a powerful tool for reshaping information. We should also lose an aid to scientific vision on a higher plane.

With mathematics, we can codify present science so clearly that it is easier to discover the essential simplicity many of us seek in science. That is no crude simplicity such as finding all planetary orbits circles, but a sophisticated simplicity to be read only in the language of mathematics itself. For example, imagine we make a hump in a taut rope by slapping it (Fig. 31-6). Using Newton's Law II, we

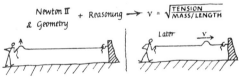

FIG. 31-6. WAVE TRAVELS ALONG A ROPE

can codify the behavior of the hump in compact mathematical form. There emerges, quite uninvited, the clear mathematical trademark of *wave* motion.[*] The mathematical form predicts that the hump will travel along as a wave, and tells us how to compute the wave's speed from the tension and mass of the

---

[*] The wave-equation reduces to the essential form:
$$\nabla^2 V = (1/c^2) \; d^2V/dt^2$$
For *any* wave of constant pattern that travels with speed c. (If you are familiar with calculus, ask a physicist to show you this remarkable piece of general mathematical physics.) This equation connects a spreading-in-space with a rate-of-change in time. $\nabla^2 V$ would be zero for an inverse-square field at rest in space: but here it has a value that looks like some acceleration. In the electromagnetic case, we may trace the d^2V/dt^2 back to an accelerating electron emitting the wave.

rope. Another example: A century ago, Maxwell reduced the experimental laws of electromagnetism to especially simple forms by boiling them down mathematically. He removed the details of shape and size of apparatus, etc., much as we remove the shape and size of the sample when we calculate the density of a metal from some weighing and measuring. Having thus removed the "boundary conditions," he had electrical laws that are common to all apparatus and all circumstances, just as density is common to all samples of the same metal. His rules were boiled down by the calculus-process of differentiation to a final form called differential equations. You can inspect their form without understanding their terminology. Suppose that at time t there are fields due to electric charges and magnets, whether moving or not; an electric field of strength E, a vector with components E_x, E_y, E_z, and a magnetic field H with components H_x, H_y, H_z. Then, *in open space* (air or vacuum), the experimental laws known a century ago reduce to the relations shown in Fig. 31-7.

I	II
$\dfrac{dE_x}{dx} + \dfrac{dE_y}{dy} + \dfrac{dE_z}{dz} = 0$	$\dfrac{dH_x}{dx} + \dfrac{dH_y}{dy} + \dfrac{dH_z}{dz} = 0$

III	IV
$\left(\dfrac{dE_z}{dy} - \dfrac{dE_y}{dz}\right) = K_H \dfrac{dH_x}{dt}$	$-\left(\dfrac{dH_z}{dy} - \dfrac{dH_y}{dz}\right) = 0$
$\left(\dfrac{dE_x}{dz} - \dfrac{dE_z}{dx}\right) = K_H \dfrac{dH_y}{dt}$	$-\left(\dfrac{dH_x}{dz} - \dfrac{dH_z}{dx}\right) = 0$
$\left(\dfrac{dE_y}{dx} - \dfrac{dE_x}{dy}\right) = K_H \dfrac{dH_z}{dt}$	$-\left(\dfrac{dH_y}{dx} - \dfrac{dH_x}{dy}\right) = 0$

FIG. 31-7. MAXWELL'S EQUATIONS (INCOMPLETE)
The constant K_H relates to magnetic fields. It appears in the expression for the force exerted by a magnetic field on an electric current. (See the discussion in this chapter and in Ch. 37.) There is a corresponding electric constant, K_E, which appears in Coulomb's Law (See Ch. 33).

Look at IV and compare it with III. The equations of IV look incomplete, spoiling the general symmetry.[2] Maxwell saw the defect and filled it by inventing an extra electric current, a spooky one in space, quite unthought-of till then, but later observed experimentally. How would *you* change IV to match III if told that part of the algebra had been left out because it was then unknown? Try this.

The addition was neither a lucky guess nor a mysterious inspiration. To Maxwell, fully aware of the state of developing knowledge, it seemed *compulsory*, a necessary extension of symmetry—that is the difference between the scientific advance of the disciplined, educated expert and the free invention of the enthusiastic amateur.

Having made his addition, fantastic at the time, Maxwell could pour the whole bunch of equations into the mathematical sausage-machine and grind out a surprising equation which had a familiar look, the same trademark of wave-motion that appears for a hump on a rope. That new equation suggested strongly that changes of electric and magnetic fields would travel out as waves with speed $v = 1/\sqrt{K_H K_E}$. Here K_H is a constant involved in the magnetic effects of moving charges; and K_E is the corresponding electrostatic constant inserted by Maxwell in his improvement.[3] (K_E is involved in the inverse-square force between electric charges.)

An informal fanciful derivation is sketched near the end of Chapter 37.

To Maxwell's delight and the wonder of his contemporaries, the calculated v agreed with the speed of light, which was already known to consist of waves of some sort. This suggested that light might be one form of Maxwell's predicted electromagnetic waves.

It was many years before Maxwell's prediction was verified directly by generating electromagnetic waves with electric currents. As a brilliant intuitive guess, a piece of synthetic theory, Maxwell's work was one of the great developments of physics—its progeny, new guesses along equally fearless lines, are making the physics of today.

One of the great contributions of mathematics to physics is Relativity, which is both mathematics and physics: you need good knowledge of both mathematics and physics to understand it. We shall give an account of Einstein's "Special Relativity" and then return to comments on mathematics as a language.

[2] In completing IV, you will need to insert a constant K_E corresponding to K_H in III. The minus sign is obviously unnecessary in the present form of IV, and when IV is completed it will spoil the symmetry somewhat; but the experimental facts produce it, conservation of energy requires it, and without it there would be no radio waves.

[3] In this course we use different symbols. See Ch. 33 and Ch. 37. We write the force between electric charges $F = B(Q_1 Q_2)/d^2$. Comparison with Maxwell's form shows our B is the same as $1/K_E$. Again, we write the force between two short pieces of current-carrying wire, due to magnetic-field effects, $F = B'(C_1 L_1)(C_2 L_2)/d^2$, and our B' is the same as K_H. Then Maxwell's prediction, $v = 1/\sqrt{K_E K_H}$, becomes, in our terminology, $v = 1/\sqrt{(1/B)(B')} = \sqrt{B/B'}$. So, if you measure B and B' you can predict the speed of electromagnetic waves. The arithmetic is easy. Try it and compare the result with the measured speed of light, 3.0×10^8 meters/sec. ($B = 9.00 \times 10^9$ and $B' = 10^{-7}$, in our units).

RELATIVITY

The theory of Relativity, which has modified our mechanics and clarified scientific thinking, arose from a simple question: *"How fast are we moving through space?"* Attempts to answer that by experiment led to a conflict that forced scientists to think out their system of knowledge afresh. Out of that reappraisal came Relativity, a brilliant application of mathematics and philosophy to our treatment of space, time, and motion. Since Relativity *is* a piece of mathematics, popular accounts that try to explain it without mathematics are almost certain to fail. To understand Relativity you should either follow its algebra through in standard texts, or, as here, examine the origins and final results, taking the mathematical machine-work on trust.

What can we find out about space? Where is its fixed framework and how fast are we moving through it? Nowadays we find the Copernican view comfortable, and picture the spinning Earth moving around the Sun with an orbital speed of about 70,000 miles/hour. The whole Solar system is moving towards the constellation Hercules at some 100,000 miles/hour, while our whole galaxy. . . .

We must be careering along a huge epicycloid through space without knowing it. Without knowing it, because, as Galileo pointed out, the mechanics of motion—projectiles, collisions, . . . , etc.—is the same in a steadily moving laboratory as in a stationary one.[4] Galileo quoted thought-experiments of men walking across the cabin of a sailing ship or dropping stones from the top of its mast. We illustrated this "Galilean relativity" in Chapter 2 by thought-experiments in moving trains. Suppose one train is passing another *at constant velocity* without bumps, and in a fog that conceals the countryside. Can the passengers really say which is moving? Can mechanical experiments in either train tell them? They can only observe their *relative* motion. In fact, we developed the rules of vectors and laws of motion in earthly labs that *are* moving; yet those statements show no effect of that motion.

We give the name *inertial frame* to any frame of reference or laboratory in which Newton's Laws

seem to describe nature truly: objects left alone without force pursue straight lines with constant speed, or stay at rest; forces produce proportional accelerations. We find that any frame moving at constant velocity relative to an inertial frame is also an inertial frame—Newton's Laws hold there too. In all the following discussion that concerns Galilean relativity and Einstein's special Relativity, *we assume that every laboratory we discuss is an inertial frame*—as a laboratory at rest on Earth is, to a close approximation.[4] In our later discussion of General Relativity, we consider other laboratory frames, such as those which accelerate.

We are not supplied by nature with an obvious inertial frame. The spinning Earth is not a perfect inertial frame (because its spin imposes central accelerations), but if we could ever find one perfect one then our relativity view of nature assures us we could find any number of other inertial frames. Every frame moving with constant velocity relative to our first inertial frame proves to be an equally good inertial frame—Newton's laws of motion, which apply *by definition* in the original frame, apply in all the others. When we do experiments on force and motion and find that Newton's Laws seem to hold, we are, from the point of view of Relativity, simply showing that our earthly lab does provide a practically perfect inertial frame. Any experiments that demonstrate the Earth's rotation could be taken instead as showing the imperfection of our choice of frame. However, by saying "the Earth *is* rotating" and blaming that, we are able to imagine a perfect frame, in which Newton's Laws would hold exactly.

We incorporate Galilean Relativity in our formulas. When we write, $s = v_0 t + \frac{1}{2}at^2$ for a rocket accelerating horizontally, we are saying, "Start the rocket with v_0 and its effect will persist as a plain addition, $v_0 t$, to the distance travelled."

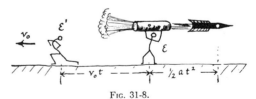

Fig. 31-8.

This can be reworded: "An experimenter ε, starts a rocket from rest and observes the motion: $s = \frac{1}{2}at^2$. Then another experimenter, ε', running away with speed v_0 will measure distances-travelled given by $s' = v_0 t + \frac{1}{2}at^2$. He will include $v_0 t$ due to his own motion."

We are saying that the effects of steady motion

---

[4] Though the Earth's velocity changes around its orbit, we think of it as steady enough during any short experiment. In fact, the steadiness is perfect, because any changes in the Earth's velocity exactly compensate the effect of the Sun's gravitation field that "causes" those changes. We see no effect on the Earth as a whole, at its center; but we do see *differential* effects on outlying parts—solar tides. The Earth's *rotation* does produce effects that can be seen and measured—Foucault's pendulum changes its line of swing, g shows differences between equator and poles, &c.—but we can make allowances for these where they matter.

and accelerated motion do not disturb each other; they just add.

ε and ε' have the following statements for the distance the rocket travels in time t.

EXPERIMENTER ε   EXPERIMENTER ε'
$$s = \tfrac{1}{2}at^2 \qquad\qquad s' = v_0 t + \tfrac{1}{2}at^2$$

Both statements say that the rocket travels with constant acceleration.[5]

Both statements say the rocket is at distance zero (the origin) at $t = 0$.

The *first statement* says ε sees the rocket start from rest. When the the clock starts at $t = 0$ the rocket has no velocity relative to him. At that instant, the rocket is moving with his motion, if any—so *he* sees it at rest—and he releases it to accelerate.

The difference between the two statements says the relative velocity between ε and ε' is v_0. There is no information about absolute motion. ε may be at rest, in which case ε' is running *backward* with speed v_0. Or ε' may be at rest, and ε running *forward* v_0 (releasing the rocket as he runs, at $t = 0$). Or both ε and ε' may be carried along in a moving train with terrific speed V, still with ε moving ahead with speed v_0 relative to ε'. In every case, v_0 is the relative velocity between the observers; and nothing in the analysis of their measurements can tell us (or them) who is "really" moving.

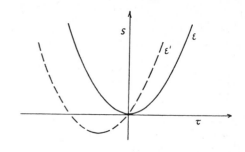
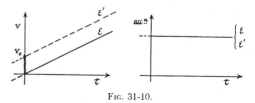

Fig. 31-10.

Adding $v_0 t$ only *shifts* the graph of s vs. t. It does not affect estimates of *acceleration, force*, etc. Then, to the question, "How fast are we moving through *space*?" simple mechanics replies, "No experiments with weights, springs, forces, . . . , can reveal our *velocity*. Accelerations could make themselves known, but uniform velocity would be unfelt." We could only measure our *relative velocity*—relative to some other object or material framework.

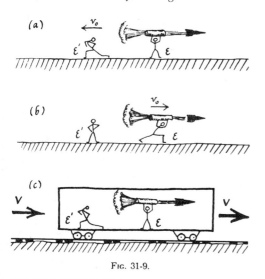

(a)

(b)

(c)

Fig. 31-9.

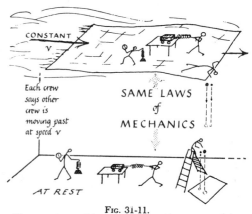

Fig. 31-11.
Observers in two laboratories, one moving with constant velocity v relative to the other, will find the same *mechanical* laws.

Yet we are still talking as if there *is* an absolute motion, past absolute landmarks in space, however hard to find. Before exploring that hope into greater disappointments, we shall codify rules of relative motion in simple algebraic form.

---

[5] The first statement is simpler because it belongs to the observer who releases the rocket from rest relative to him, at the instant the clock starts, $t = 0$.

Galilean Transformation for Coordinates

We can put the comparison between two such observers in a simple, general way. Suppose an observer ε records an event in his laboratory. Another

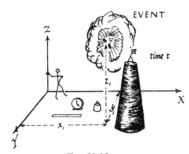

FIG. 31-12a
Observer ready to observe an event at time t and place x, y, z.

observer, ε', flies through the laboratory with constant velocity and records the same event as he goes. As sensible scientists, ε and ε' manufacture identical clocks and meter-sticks to measure with. Each carries a set of x-y-z-axes with him. For convenience, they start their clocks ($t = 0$ and $t' = 0$) at the instant they are together. At that instant their coordinate origins and axes coincide. Suppose ε records the event as happening at time t and place (x, y, z) referred to his axes-at-rest-with-him.[6] The same event is recorded by observer ε' using *his* instruments as occurring at t' and (x', y', z') referred to the axes-he-carries-with-him. How will the two records compare? Common sense tells us that time

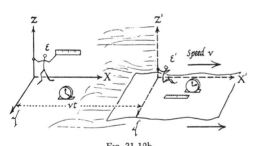

FIG. 31-12b.
Another observer, moving at constant velocity v relative to the first, also makes observations.

is the same for both, so $t' = t$. Suppose the relative velocity between the two observers is v meters/sec

---

[6] For example: he fires a bullet along OX from the origin at $t = 0$ with speed 1000 m./sec. Then the event of the bullet reaching a target 3 meters away might be recorded as $x = 3$ meters, $y = 0$, $z = 0$, $t = 0.003$ sec.

along OX. Measurements of y and z are the same for both: $y' = y$ and $z' = z$. But since ε' and his coordinate framework travel ahead of ε by vt meters in t seconds, all his x'-measurements will be vt shorter. So every x' must $= x - vt$. Therefore:

$$x' = x - vt \qquad y' = y \qquad z' = z \qquad t' = t$$

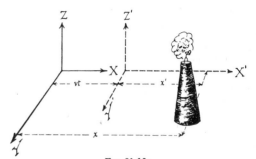

FIG. 31-12c.
For measurements along direction of relative motion v, the second observer measures x'; the first measures x. Then it seems obvious that $x' = x - vt$.

These relations, which connect the records made by ε' and ε, are called the *Galilean Transformation*.

The reverse transformation, connecting the records of ε and ε', is:

$$x = x' + vt \qquad y = y' \qquad z = z' \qquad t = t'$$

These two transformations treat the two observers impartially, merely indicating their *relative* velocity, $+ v$ for ε' $-$ ε and $- v$ for ε $-$ ε'. They contain our common-sense knowledge of space and time, written *in algebra*.

Velocity of Moving Object

If ε sees an object moving forward along the x direction, he measures its velocity, u, by $\Delta x/\Delta t$. Then ε' sees that object moving with velocity u' given by his $\Delta x'/\Delta t'$. Simple algebra, using the Galilean Transformation, shows that $u' = u - v$. (To obtain this relation for motion with constant velocity, just divide $x' = x - vt$ by t.) For example: suppose ε stands beside a railroad and sees an express train moving with $u = 70$ miles/hour. Another observer, ε', rides a freight train moving 30 miles/hour in the same direction. Then ε' sees the express moving with

$$u' = u - v = 70 - 30 = 40 \text{ miles/hour.}$$

(If ε' is moving the opposite way, as in a head-on collision, $v = -30$ miles/hour, and ε' sees the express approaching with speed

$$u' = 70 - (-30) = 100 \text{ miles/hour.})$$

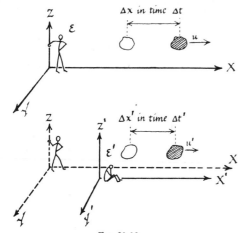

FIG. 31-13.
Each experimenter calculates the velocity of a moving object from his observations of time taken and distance travelled.

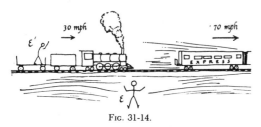

FIG. 31-14.

Stationary experimenter ε observes the velocities shown and calculates the relative velocity that moving experimenter ε′ should observe.

This is the "common sense" way of adding and subtracting velocities. It seems necessarily true, and we have taken it for granted in earlier chapters. Yet we shall find we must modify it for very high speeds.

?Absolute Motion?

If we discover our laboratory is in a moving train, we can add the train's velocity and refer our experiments to the solid ground. Finding the Earth moving, we can shift our "fixed" axes of space to the Sun, then to a star, then to the center of gravity of all the stars. If these changes do not affect our knowledge of mechanics, do they really matter? Is it honest to worry about finding an absolutely fixed framework? Curiosity makes us reply, "Yes. If we *are* moving through space it would be interesting to know how fast." Though mechanical experiments cannot tell us, could we not find out by electrical experiments? Electromagnetism is summed up in Maxwell's equations, for a stationary observer. Ask what a *moving* observer should find, by changing x to x′, etc., with the Galilean Transformation: then Maxwell's equations take on a different, more complicated, form. An experimenter who trusted that transformation could decide which is really moving, himself or his apparatus: absolute motion would be revealed by the changed form of electrical laws. An easy way to look for such changes would be to use the travelling electric and magnetic fields of light waves—the electromagnetic waves predicted by Maxwell's equations. We might find our velocity through space by timing flashes of light. Seventy-five years ago such experiments were being tried. When the experiments yielded an unexpected result—failure to show any effect of motion—there were many attempts to produce an explanation. Fitzgerald in England suggested that whenever any piece of matter is set in motion through space it must contract, along the direction of motion, by a fraction that depended only on its speed. With the fraction properly chosen, the contraction of the apparatus used for timing light signals would prevent their revealing motion through space. This strange contraction, which would make even measuring rods such as meter-sticks shrink like everything else when in motion, was too surprising to be welcome; and it came with no suggestion of mechanism to produce it. Then the Dutch physicist Lorentz (also Larmor in England) worked out a successful electrical "explanation."

The Lorentz Transformation

Lorentz had been constructing an electrical theory of matter, with atoms containing small electric charges that could move and emit light waves. The experimental discovery of electron streams, soon after, had supported his speculations; so it was natural for Lorentz to try to explain the unexpected result with his electrical theory. He found that if Maxwell's equations are *not* to be changed in form by the motion of electrons and atoms of moving apparatus, then lengths along the motion must shrink, in changing from x to x′, by the modifying factor:

$$\frac{1}{\sqrt{1 - \left(\dfrac{\text{SPEED OF OBSERVER}}{\text{SPEED OF LIGHT}}\right)^2}}$$

He showed that this shrinkage (the same as Fitzgerald's) of the apparatus would just conceal any motion through absolute space and thus explain the experimental result. But he also gave a reason for the change: he showed how electrical forces—in the new form he took for Maxwell's equations—would compel the shrinkage to take place.

It was uncomfortable to have to picture matter in motion as invisibly shrunk—invisibly, because we should shrink too—but that was no worse than the previous discomfort that physicists with a sense of mathematical form got from the uncouth effect of the Galilean Transformation on Maxwell's equations. Lorentz's modifying factor has to be applied to t' as well as x', and a strange extra term must be added to t'. And then Maxwell's equations maintain their same simple symmetrical form for all observers moving with any constant velocity. You will see this "Lorentz Transformation" put to use in Relativity; but first see how the great experiments were made with light signals.

Measuring Our Speed through "Space"?

A century ago, it was clear that light consists of waves, which travel with very high speed through glass, water, air, even "empty space" between the stars and us. Scientists imagined space filled with "ether"[7] to carry light waves, much as air carries sound waves. Nowadays we think of light (and all other radio waves) as a travelling pattern of electric and magnetic fields and we need no "ether"; but before we reached that simple view a tremendous contradiction was discovered.

Experiments with light to find how fast *we* are moving through the "ether" gave a surprising result: "no comment." These attempts contrast with successful measurements with sound waves and air.

Sound travels as a wave in air. A trumpet-toot is handed on by air molecules at a definite speed *through the air*, the same speed whether the trumpet is moving or not. But a moving observer finds *his* motion added to the motion of sound waves. When he is running towards the trumpet, the toot passes by him faster. He can find how fast he is moving *through air* by timing sound signals passing him.

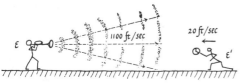

FIG. 31-15.
Experimenter running towards source of sound finds the speed of sound 1120 ft/sec, in excess of normal by his own speed.

---

[7] This ether or æther was named after the universal substance that Greek philosophers had pictured filling all space beyond the atmosphere.

A moving observer will notice another effect if he is out to one side, listening with a direction-finder. He will meet the sound slanting from a new

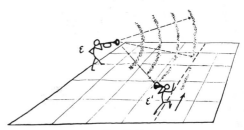

FIG. 31-16.
Observer running across the line-of-travel of sound notices a change of apparent direction of source.

direction if he runs. Again he can estimate his running speed if he knows the speed of sound.

In either case, his measurements would tell him his speed *relative to the air*. A steady wind blowing would produce the same effects and save him the trouble of running. Similar experiments with light should reveal our speed relative to the "ether," which is our only remaining symbol of absolute space. Such experiments were tried, with far-reaching results.

Aberration of Starlight

Soon after Newton's death, the astronomer Bradley discovered a tiny yearly to-and-fro motion of all stars that is clearly due to the Earth's motion around its orbit. Think of starlight as rain showering down (at great speed) from a star overhead. If you stand in vertical rain holding an umbrella upright, the rain will hit the umbrella top at right angles. Drops falling through a central gash will hit your head. Now run quite fast. To you the rain will seem slanting. To catch it squarely you must tilt the umbrella at the angle shown by the vectors in the sketch. Then drops falling through the gash will still hit your head. If you run around in a circular orbit, or to-and-fro along a line, you must wag the umbrella this way and that to fit your motion. This is what Bradley found when observing stars precisely with a telescope.[*] Stars near the ecliptic seemed to slide to-and-fro, their directions swinging through a small angle. Stars up near the pole of the ecliptic

---

[*] This *aberration* is quite distinct from *parallax*, the apparent motion of near stars against the background of remoter stars. Aberration makes a star seem to move in the same kind of pattern, but it applies to *all* stars; and it is dozens of times bigger than the parallax of even the nearest stars. (Also, a star's aberration, which goes with the Earth's *velocity*, is three months out of phase with its parallax.)

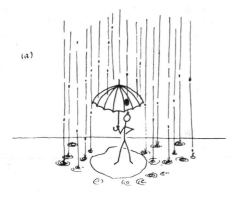

(a)

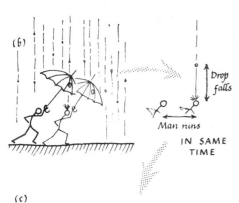

(b)

Drop falls

Man runs

IN SAME TIME

(c)

Tilt of umbrella

Velocity of raindrops

Velocity of runner

(d)

Fig. 31-17. "Aberration" of Rain

move in small circles in the course of a year. The telescope following the star is like the tilting umbrella. In six months, the Earth's velocity around the Sun changes from one direction to the reverse, so the telescope tilt must be reversed in that time. From the tiny measured change in 6 months, Bradley estimated the speed of light. It agreed with the only other estimate then available—based on the varying delays of seeing eclipses of Jupiter's moons, at varying distances across the Earth's orbit.[8]

WIND

Man stands still in rain falling in wind

Umbrella tilt

Velocity of raindrops relative to air

Velocity of wind

Fig. 31-18. "Aberration" of Rain Falling in Wind
If you stand still but a steady wind carries the air past you, you should still tilt the umbrella.

To catch rain drops fair and square, you must tilt your umbrella if you are running *or* if there is a steady wind, but not if you are running *and* there is also a wind carrying the air and raindrops along *with you*—if you just stand in a shower inside a closed railroad coach speeding along, you do not tilt the umbrella. Therefore, Bradley's successful measurement of aberration showed that *as the Earth runs around its orbit it is moving through the "ether" in changing directions*, moving through space if you like, nearly 20 miles/sec.

An overall motion of the solar system towards some group of stars would remain concealed, since that would give a permanent slant to star directions,

---

[8] It was another century before terrestrial experiments succeeded.

($\sim$ 1600): Galileo recorded an attempt with experimenters signalling by lantern flashes between two mountain tops. ε_1 sent a flash to ε_2 who immediately returned a flash to ε_1. At first ε_2 was clumsy and they obtained a medium speed for light. As they improved with practice, the estimated speed grew greater and greater, towards "infinity"—light travels too fast to clock by hand.

($\sim$ 1700): Newton knew only Roemer's estimate from Jupiter's moons.

(1849): Fizeau succeeded, by using a distant mirror to return the light and a spinning toothed wheel as a chopper to make the flashes and catch them one tooth later on their return. His result confirmed the astronomical estimate. His and all later terrestrial methods use some form of chopper—as in some methods for the speeds of bullets, and electrons.

The result: speed of light is 300,000,000 meters/sec or 186,000 miles/sec.

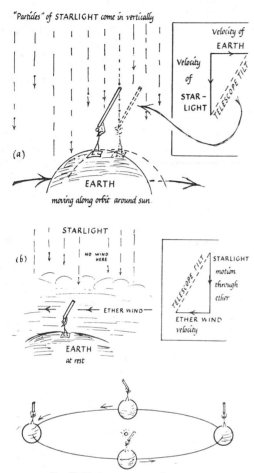

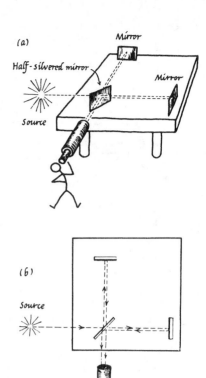

FIG. 31-20. THE MICHELSON-MORLEY EXPERIMENT

FIG. 31-19. ABERRATION OF STARLIGHT

whereas Bradley measured *changes* of slant from one season to another.

The Michelson-Morley Experiment

Then, seventy-five years ago, new experiments were devised to look for our absolute motion in space. One of the most famous and decisive was devised and carried out by A. A. Michelson and E. W. Morley in Cleveland; this was one of the first great scientific achievements in modern physics in the New World. In their experiment, two flashes of light travelling in different directions were made to pace each other. There was no longer a moving observer and fixed source, as with Bradley and a star. Both source and observer were carried in a laboratory, but the experimenters looked for motion of the intervening ether that carried the light waves.

A semi-transparent mirror split the light into two beams, one travelling, say, North-South and the other East-West. The two beams were returned along their paths by mirrors and rejoined to form an interference pattern. The slightest change in trip-time for one beam compared with the other would shift the pattern. Now suppose at some season the whole apparatus is moving upward in space: an outside observer would see the light beams tilted up or down by the "ether-wind" the same tilt for both routes. At another season, suppose the whole Earth is moving due North horizontally in space, then the N-S light beam would take longer for its round trip than the E-W one. You will find the experiments described in standard texts, with the algebra to show that if the whole laboratory is sweeping through the ether, light must take longer on the trip along the stream and back than on the trip across and back.

You can see that this is so in the following example. Instead of light, consider a bird flying across a cage and back, when the cage is moving relative

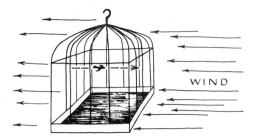

FIG. 31-21. GIANT BIRDCAGE IN WIND

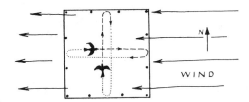

FIG. 31-22.
Bird flies either against the wind and back;
or across the wind and back across the wind.

to the air. Either (a) drag the cage steadily along through still air, or (b) keep the cage still and have an equal wind blow through it the opposite way. We shall give the wind version; but you can re-tell the story for a moving cage, with the same results. Suppose the bird has air-speed 5 ft/sec, the cage is 40 ft square, and the wind blows through at 3 ft/sec. To fly across-stream from side to side and back takes

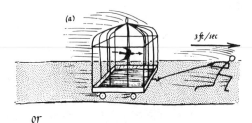

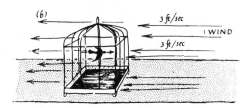

FIG. 31-23.
Cage moving 3 ft/sec through still air has same effect on bird's flight as wind blowing 3 ft/sec through stationary cage.

the bird 10 sec + 10 sec,[9] or 20 sec for the round trip. To fly from end to end, upstream and back, takes

$$\frac{40 \text{ ft}}{(5-3)\text{ft/sec}} + \frac{40 \text{ ft}}{(5+3)\text{ft/sec}}$$

or 20 sec + 5 sec, a much longer time.[10] Put a bird in a cage like this and compare his round-trip times E-W and N-S, and you will be able to tell how fast the cage is moving through the air; or use twin birds and compare their returns. Twist the cage to different orientations, and returns of the twins will tell you which way the cage is travelling through air and how fast. A similar experiment with sound waves in an open laboratory moving through air would tell us the laboratory's velocity. Let a trumpeter stand in one corner and give a toot. The arrivals of returning echoes will reveal general motion, of lab or wind. (Of course, if the moving laboratory

---

[9] This requires some geometrical thinking. The bird must fly a 50-ft hypotenuse to cross the 40-ft cage while the wind carries him 30 ft downstream. The simple answer 8 + 8 sec, which is incorrect, is even shorter.

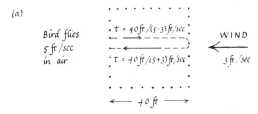

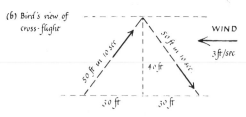

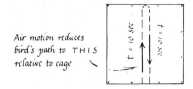

FIG. 31-24. DETAILS OF FLIGHTS
Bird flies 5 ft/sec.   Steady wind 3 ft/sec.

---

[10] If you are still not convinced and feel sure the trips up and downstream should average out, try a thought-experiment with the wind blowing faster, say 6 ft/sec. Then the bird could never make the trip upstream—that time would be infinite!

is closed and carries its air with it, the echoes will show no motion.)

The corresponding test with light-signals is difficult, but the interference pattern affords a very delicate test of trip-timing. When it was tried by Michelson and Morley, and repeated by Miller, it gave a surprising answer: NO MOTION through the "ether." It was repeated in different orientations, at different seasons: always the same answer, NO MOTION. If you are a good scientist you will at once ask, "How big were the error-boxes? How sensitive was the experiment?" The answer: "It would have shown reliably ¼ of the Earth's orbital speed around the Sun, and in later[11] work, ⅒. Yet aberration shows us moving through the "ether" with ¹⁰⁄₁₀ of that speed. Still more experiments added their testimony, some optical, some electrical. Again and again, the same "null result." Here then was a confusing contradiction:

"ABERRATION" OF STARLIGHT	MICHELSON, MORLEY, MILLER EXPERIMENTS
Light from star to telescope showed change of tilt in 6 months.	Light signals compared for perpendicular round trips: pattern showed no change when apparatus was rotated or as seasons changed.
EARTH, MOVING IN ORBIT AROUND SUN, IS MOVING FREELY THROUGH "ETHER"	EARTH IS NOT MOVING THROUGH "ETHER"; or EARTH IS CARRYING ETHER WITH IT

CONTRADICTION

Growing electrical theory added confusion, because Maxwell's equations seemed to refer to currents and fields in an absolute, fixed, space (= ether). Unlike Newton's Laws of Motion, they are changed by the Galilean Transformation to a different form in a moving laboratory. However, the modified transformation devised by Lorentz kept the form of Maxwell's equations the same for moving observers. This seemed to fit the facts—in "magnets and coils experiments" (Experiment C in Ch. 41), we get the same effects whether the magnet moves or the coil does. With the Lorentz Trans-

[11] The latest test (Townes, 1958) made by timing microwaves in a resonant cavity, gave a null result when it would have shown a velocity as small as 1/1000 of the Earth's orbital speed.

formation, electrical experiments would show *relative* velocity (as they do), but would never reveal uniform *absolute* motion. But then the Lorentz Transformation made mechanics suffer; it twisted $F = Ma$ and $s = v_0 + \frac{1}{2}at^2$ into unfamiliar forms that contradicted Galileo's common-sense relativity and Newton's simple law of motion.

Some modifications of the Michelson-Morley experiment rule out the Fitzgerald contraction as a sufficient "explanation." For example, Kennedy and Thorndike repeated it with *unequal* lengths for the two perpendicular trips. Their null result requires the Lorentz change of time-scale as well as the shrinkage of length.

Pour these pieces of information into a good logic machine. The machine puts out a clear, strong conclusion: "Inconsistent." Here is a very disturbing result. Before studying Einstein's solution of the problem it posed, consider a useful fable.

A Fable

[This is an annoying, untrue, fable to warn you of the difficulty of accepting Relativity. Counting items is an absolute process that no change of viewpoint can alter, so this fable is very distressing to good mathematical physicists with a strong sense of nature—take it with a grain of tranquilizer. You will find, however, that what it alleges so impossibly for adding up balls does occur in relativistic adding of velocities.]

I ask you to watch a magic trick. I take a black cloth bag and convince you it is empty. I then put into it 2 white balls. You count them as they go in—one, two—and then two more—three, four. Now I take out 5 white balls, and the bag is empty.

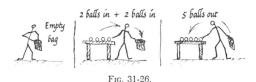

FIG. 31-26.

Pour this record into the logic machine and it will say, "Inconsistent." What is your solution here? First, "It's an illusion." It is not. You are allowed to repeat the game yourself. (Miller repeated the Michelson-Morley experiment with great precision.) Next, "Let me re-examine the bag for concealed pockets." There are none. Now let us re-state the record. The bag is simple, the balls are solid, the

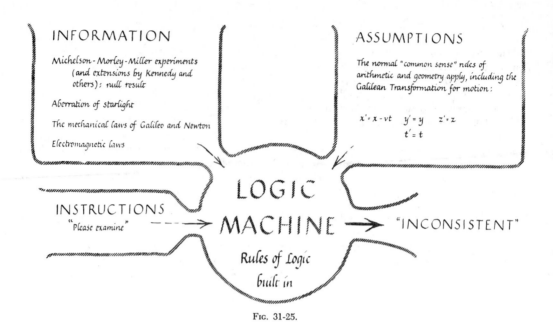

INFORMATION

Michelson-Morley-Miller experiments
(and extensions by Kennedy and
others); null result

Aberration of starlight

The mechanical laws of Galileo and Newton

Electromagnetic laws

ASSUMPTIONS

The normal "common sense" rules of
arithmetic and geometry apply, including the
Galilean Transformation for motion:

$$x' = x - vt \quad y' = y \quad z' = z$$
$$t' = t$$

INSTRUCTIONS
"Please examine" ---→ LOGIC MACHINE ---→ "INCONSISTENT"

Rules of Logic
built in

Fig. 31-25.

tally is true: $2 + 2$ go in and 5 come out. What can you say now? If you cannot refute tried and true observations, you must either give up science—and go crazy—or attack the rules of logic, including the basic rules of arithmetic. Short of neurotic lunacy, you would have to say, "*In some cases*, $2 + 2$ do not make 4." Rather than take neurotic refuge in a catch-phrase such as "It all adds up to anything," you might set yourself to cataloguing events in which 2 and 2 make 4—e.g. adding beans on a table, coins in a purse; and cataloguing events for which $2 + 2$ make something else.[12]

[12] There *are* cases where $2 + 2$ do not make 4. Vectors $2 + 2$ may make anything between 0 and 4. Two quarts of alcohol $+$ two quarts of water mix to make less than 4 quarts. In the circuit sketched, all the resistors, R, are identical but the heating effects do not add up. Two currents each delivering 2 joules/sec add to one delivering 8 joules/sec.

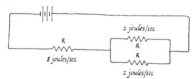

Fig. 31-27.

In studying Nature, scientists have been seeking and *selecting* quantities that do add simply, such as masses of liquids rather than volumes, copper-plating by currents rather than heating. The essence of the "exceptions" is that they are cases where the items to be added *interact*; they do not just act independently so that their effects can be superposed.

In this fable, you have three explanations to choose from:

(a) "It is witchcraft." That way madness lies.
(b) "There is a special invisible mechanism": hardly any better—it turns science into a horde of demons.
(c) "The rules of arithmetic must be modified."

However unpleasant (c) looks, you had better try it—desperate measures for desperate cases. Think carefully what you would do, in this plight.

You are not faced with that arithmetical paradox in real life, but now turn again to motion through space. Ruling out mistaken experimenting, there were similar choices: blame witchcraft, invent special mechanisms, or modify the physical rules of motion. At first, scientists invented mechanisms, such as electrons that squash into ellipsoids when moving; but even these led to more troubles. Poincaré and others prepared to change the rules for measuring time and space. Then Einstein made two brilliant suggestions: an *honest viewpoint*, and a *single hypothesis*, in his Theory of Relativity.

The Relativity *viewpoint* is this: scientific thinking should be built of things that can be observed in real experiments; details and pictures that cannot be observed must not be treated as real; questions about such details are not only unanswerable, they are improper and unscientific. On this view, fixed space (and the "ether" thought to fill it) must be thrown out of our scientific thinking if we become convinced that all experiments to detect it or to measure motion through it are doomed to failure. This viewpoint merely says, "let's be realistic," on a ruthless scale.

All attempts like the Michelson-Morley-Miller experiment failed to show any change of light's speed. Aberration measurements did not show light moving with a new speed, but only gave a new direction to its apparent velocity. So, the Relativity *hypothesis* is this: *The measured speed of light (electromagnetic waves) will be the same, whatever the motion of observer or source.* This is quite contrary to common sense; we should expect to meet light faster or slower by running against it or with it. Yet this is a clear application of the realistic viewpoint to the experimental fact that all experiments with light fail to show the observer's motion or the motion of any "ether wind." Pour this hypothesis into the logic machine that previously answered, "Inconsistent"; but remove the built-in "geometry rules" of space-&-time and motion, with their Galilean Transformation. Ask instead for the (*simplest*) *new rules that will make a consistent scheme.* However, since Newtonian mechanics has stood the test of time, in moving ships and trains, in the Solar System, etc.,

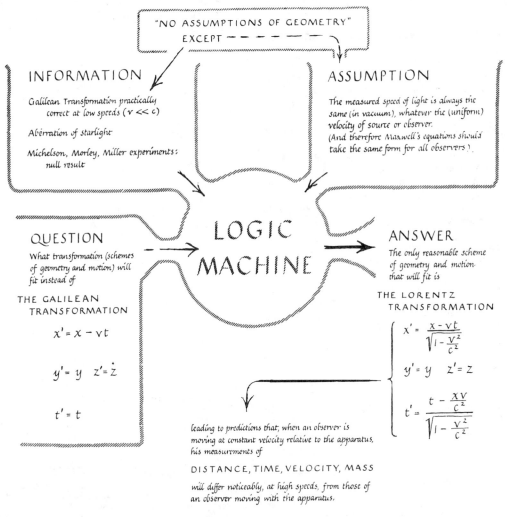

"NO ASSUMPTIONS OF GEOMETRY" EXCEPT ─ ─ ─ ─ ─ ─

INFORMATION

Galilean Transformation practically correct at low speeds ($v \ll c$)

Aberration of starlight

Michelson, Morley, Miller experiments: null result

ASSUMPTION

The measured speed of light is always the same (in vacuum), whatever the (uniform) velocity of source or observer.
(And therefore Maxwell's equations should take the same form for all observers.)

LOGIC MACHINE

QUESTION

What transformation (schemes of geometry and motion) will fit instead of

THE GALILEAN TRANSFORMATION

$$x' = x - vt$$

$$y' = y \quad z' = z$$

$$t' = t$$

leading to predictions that, when an observer is moving at constant velocity relative to the apparatus, his measurements of

DISTANCE, TIME, VELOCITY, MASS

will differ noticeably, at high speeds, from those of an observer moving with the apparatus.

ANSWER

The only reasonable scheme of geometry and motion that will fit is

THE LORENTZ TRANSFORMATION

$$x' = \frac{x - vt}{\sqrt{1 - \frac{v^2}{c^2}}}$$

$$y' = y \quad z' = z$$

$$t' = \frac{t - \frac{xv}{c^2}}{\sqrt{1 - \frac{v^2}{c^2}}}$$

Fig. 31-28.

the new rules must reduce to the Galilean Transformation at low speeds.[13] The logic machine replies: "There is only one reasonable scheme: the transformation suggested by Lorentz and adopted by Einstein."

Instead of the GALILEAN TRANSFORMATION

$$x' = x - vt \qquad y' = y \qquad z' = z \qquad t' = t$$

the LORENTZ-EINSTEIN TRANSFORMATION runs

$$x' = \frac{x - vt}{\sqrt{1 - v^2/c^2}} \quad y' = y \quad z' = z \quad t' = \frac{t - xv/c^2}{\sqrt{1 - v^2/c^2}}$$

and these turn into the reverse transformation, with relative velocity v changing to $-v$

$$x = \frac{x' + vt'}{\sqrt{1 - v^2/c^2}} \quad y = y' \quad z = z' \quad t = \frac{t' + x'v/c^2}{\sqrt{1 - v^2/c^2}}$$

where c is the *speed of light in vacuum*. That speed is involved essentially in the new rules of measurement, because the new transformation was chosen to make all attempts to measure that speed yield the same answer. And the symmetrical form shows that absolute motion is never revealed by experiment. We can measure relative motion of one experimenter past another, but we can never say which is really moving.

Of course the new transformation accounts for the Michelson-Morley-Miller null result—it was chosen to do so. It also accounts for aberration, predicting the same aberration whether the star moves or we do. *But* it modifies Newtonian mechanics. In other words, we have a choice of troubles: the old transformation upsets the form of electromagnetic laws; the new transformation upsets the form of mechanical laws. Over the full range of experiment, high speeds as well as low, the old electromagnetic laws seem to remain good simple descriptions of nature; but the mechanical laws do fail, in their classical form, at high speeds. So we choose the new transformation, and let it modify mechanical laws, and are glad to find that the modified laws describe nature excellently when mechanical experiments are made with improved accuracy.

The new transformation looks unpleasant° because it is more complicated, and its implications are less pleasant. To maintain his Galilean relativity, Newton could assume that length, mass, and time are independent of the observer and of each other. He could assert that mechanical experiments will fail to reveal uniform motion through "space."[14] When Einstein extended the assertion of failure to experiments with light, he found it necessary to have measurements of length and time, and therefore mass, different for observers with different motions. We shall not show the steps of the logic machine grinding out the transformation and its implications, but you may trust them as routine algebra.[15] We shall follow custom and call it the Lorentz Transformation.

Implications of the Lorentz Transformation

Take the new modified geometry that will fit the experimental information, and argue from it how measurements by different observers will compare.

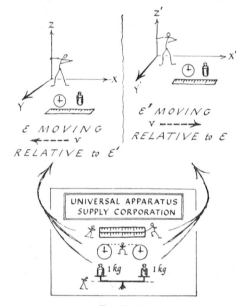

FIG. 31-29
One experimenter is moving with constant velocity relative to the other. They arrange to use standard measuring instruments of identical construction.

Return to our two observers ε and ε′, who operate with identical meter sticks, clocks, and standard kilograms. ε′ and his coordinate framework are moving with speed v relative to ε; and ε is moving backward with speed v relative to ε′. The trans-

---

[13] This is an application of Bohr's great "Principle of Correspondence": in any extreme case where the new requirement is trivial—here, at low speeds—the new theory must reduce to the old.

°This transformation may seem more reasonable if you see that it represents a rotation of axes in space-&-time. For that, see later in this chapter, page 495.

[14] When an experiment leads us to believe Newton's Laws I and II are valid, it is really just telling us that we are lucky enough to be in a laboratory that is (practically) an inertial frame. If we had always experimented in a tossing ship, we should not have formulated those simple laws.
[15] For details, see standard texts. There is a simple version in *Relativity . . . A Popular Exposition* by A. Einstein (published by Methuen, London, 15th edn., 1955).

formations $\varepsilon \to \varepsilon'$ and $\varepsilon' \to \varepsilon$ are completely symmetrical, and show only the relative velocity v—the same in both cases—with no indication of absolute motion, no hint as to which is "really moving."

The results of arguing from the transformation differ strangely from earlier common sense, but only at exceedingly high speeds. An observer flying past a laboratory in a plane, or rocket, would apply Galilean Transformations safely. He would agree to the ordinary rules of vectors and motion, the Newtonian laws of mechanics.

The speed of light, c, is huge:

$$c = 300{,}000{,}000 \text{ meters/sec} = 186{,}000 \text{ miles/sec}$$
$$\approx \text{a billion ft/sec} \approx 700 \text{ million miles/hour}$$
$$\approx 1 \text{ ft/nonasecond, in the latest terminology.}$$

For relative motion with any ordinary velocity v, the fraction v/c is tiny, v^2/c^2 still smaller. The factor $\sqrt{1 - v^2/c^2}$ is 1 for all practical purposes, and the time-lag xv/c^2 is negligible—so we have the Galilean Transformation.

Now suppose ε' moves at tremendous speed relative to ε. Each in his own local lab will observe the same mechanical laws; and any beam of light passing through both labs will show the same speed, universal c, to each observer. But at speeds like 20,000 miles/sec, 40,000, 60,000 and up towards the speed of light, experimenter ε would see surprising things as ε' and his lab whizz past. ε would say, "The silly fellow ε' is using inaccurate apparatus.

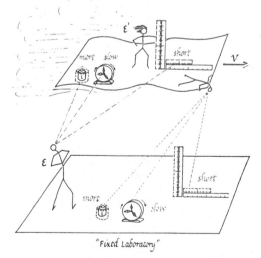

"Fixed Laboratory"

Fig. 31-30.
Each experimenter finds, by using his own standard instruments, that the other experimenter is using incorrect instruments: a shrunken meter stick, a clock that runs too slowly, and a standard mass that is too big.

His meter stick is shrunken—less than my true meter. His clock is running slow—taking more than one of my true seconds for each tick." Meanwhile ε' finds nothing wrong in his own laboratory, but sees ε and his lab moving away backwards, and says, "The silly fellow ε . . . his meter stick is shrunken . . . clock running slow."

Suppose ε measures and checks the apparatus used by ε' just as they are passing. ε finds the meter stick that ε' holds as standard shrunk to $\sqrt{1 - v^2/c^2}$ meter. ε finds the standard clock that ε' holds to tick seconds is ticking longer periods, of $1/\sqrt{1 - v^2/c^2}$ second. And ε finds the 1 kg standard mass that ε' holds is greater, $1/\sqrt{1 - v^2/c^2}$ kg. These are changes that a "*stationary*" observer sees in a *moving* laboratory; but, equally, a moving observer watching a "stationary" laboratory sees the *same* peculiarities: the stationary meter stick shorter, clock running slower, and masses increased. The Lorentz Transformations $\varepsilon' - \varepsilon$ and $\varepsilon - \varepsilon'$ are symmetrical. If ε' and ε compare notes they will quarrel hopelessly, since each imputes the *same* errors to the other! Along the direction of relative motion, each sees all the other's apparatus shrunk, even electrons. Each sees all the other's clocks running slowly, even the vibrations of atoms. (Across the motion, in y- and z-directions, ε and ε' agree.) In this symmetrical "relativity" we see the same thing in the other fellow's laboratory, *whether he is moving or we are*. Only the *relative* motion between us and apparatus matters—we are left without any hint of being able to distinguish *absolute* motion through space.

The shrinkage-factor and the slowing-factor are the same, $1/\sqrt{1 - v^2/c^2}$. This factor is practically 1 for all ordinary values of v, the relative speed between the two observers. Then the transformation reduces to Galilean form where geometry follows our old "common sense." Watch a supersonic 'plane flying away from you 1800 miles/hour ($= \frac{1}{2}$ mile/sec). For that speed, the factor is

$$\frac{1}{\sqrt{1 - \left(\dfrac{\frac{1}{2}\text{ mile/sec}}{186{,}000 \text{ miles/sec}}\right)^2}} \quad \text{or } 1.000000000004$$

The plane's length would seem shrunk, and its clock ticking slower, by less than half a billionth of 1%. At 7,000,000 miles/hour (nearly 1/100 of c) the factor rises to 1.00005. At 70,000,000 miles/hour it is 1.005, making a $\frac{1}{2}$% change in length.

Until this century, scientists never experimented with speeds approaching the speed of light—except for light itself, where the difference is paramount.

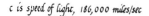

c is speed of light, 186,000 miles/sec

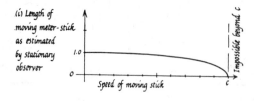

(i) Length of moving meter-stick as estimated by stationary observer

1.0
o
Speed of moving stick
Impossible beyond c

(ii) Length of stationary meter-stick, as estimated by moving observer

1.0
o o
Speed of observer
Impossible beyond c

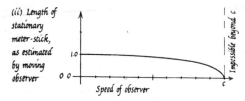

(iii) Time between ticks of moving standard clock, as estimated by stationary observer.

1.0 sec
o
Speed of moving clock
Impossible beyond c

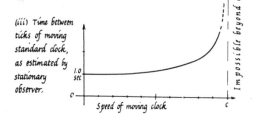

(iv) Mass of moving standard kilogram, estimated by stationary observer

1.0
o
Speed of moving mass
Up to infinity at c
Impossible beyond c

FIG. 31-31.
CHANGES OF MEASUREMENT PREDICTED BY RELATIVITY

Nowadays we have protons hurled out from small cyclotrons at 2/10 of *c*, making the factor 1.02; electrons hitting an X-ray target at 6/10 of *c*, making the factor 1.2; beta-rays flung from radioactive atoms with 98/100 of *c*, making the factor 5; and billion-volt electrons from giant accelerators, with .99999988 *c*, factor 2000.

Among cosmic rays we find some very energetic particles, mu-mesons; some with energy about 1000 million electron · volts moving with 199/200 of the speed of light. For them

$$1/\sqrt{1 - v^2/c^2} = 1/\sqrt{1 - 199^2/200^2} = 1/\sqrt{\tfrac{1}{100}} = 10.$$

Now these mesons are known to be unstable, with lifetime about 2×10^{-6} sec (2 microseconds). Yet they are manufactured by collisions high up in the atmosphere and take about 20×10^{-6} seconds on the trip down to us. It seemed puzzling that they could last so long and reach us. Relativity removes the puzzle: we are looking at the flying meson's internal life-time-clock. To us that is slowed by a factor of 10. So the flying meson's lifetime *should seem to us* 20×10^6 seconds. Or, from the meson's own point of view, its lifetime is a normal 2 microseconds, but the thickness of our atmosphere, which rushes past it, is foreshortened to 1/10 of *our* estimate—so it can make the shrunk trip in its short lifetime.

Measuring Rods and Clocks

We used to think of a measuring rod such as a meter stick as an unchanging standard, that could be moved about to step off lengths, or pointed in different directions, without any change of length. True, this was an idealized meter stick that would not warp with moisture or expand with some temperature change, but we felt no less confident of its properties. Its length was *invariant*. So was the time between the ticks of a good clock. (If we distrusted pendulum-regulated clocks, we could look forward to completely constant atomic clocks.) Now, Relativity warns us that measuring rods are *not* completely rigid with invariant length. The whole idea of a rigid body—a harmless and useful idealization to 19th-century physicists—now seems misleading. And so does the idea of an absolutely constant stream of time flowing independently of space. Instead, our measurements are affected by our motion, and only *the speed of light, c, is invariant.* A broader view treats *c* as merely a constant scale-factor for *our* choice of units in a compound space-&-time, which different observers slice differently.

Changes of Mass

If length- and time-measurements change, mass must change too. We shall now find out *how* mass must change, when a moving observer estimates it, by following a thought-experiment along lines suggested by Tolman. We shall assume that *the conservation of momentum holds true* in any (inertial frame) laboratory whatever its speed relative to the observer—we must cling to some of our working rules or we shall land in a confusion of unnecessary changes.

Consider ε and ε' in their labs, moving with relative velocity *v* in the *x*-direction. Suppose they make two platinum blocks, each a standard kilogram, that they know are *identical*—they can count the

66

atoms if necessary. Each places a 1-kg block at rest in his lab on a frictionless table. Just as they are passing each other ε and ε' stretch a long light spiral spring between their blocks, along the y-direction. They let the spring tug for a short while and then remove it, leaving each block with some y-momentum. Then each experimenter measures the y-velocity of his block and calculates its momentum.

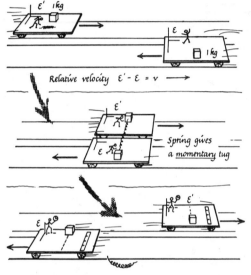

Fig. 31-32. Two Observers Measuring Masses
(A thought-experiment to find how mass depends on speed of object relative to observer.) ε says: I have 1 kg, moving across my lab with velocity 3 meters/sec. I know ε' has 1 kg, and I see that *he* records its velocity as 3 meters/sec; but I know his clock is ticking slowly, so that the velocity of his lump is *less* than 3 meters/sec. Therefore his lump has mass *more* than 1 kg.

They compare notes: each records 3 meters/sec for his block in his own framework. They conclude: equal and opposite velocities; equal and opposite momenta. They are pleased to adopt Newton's Law III as a workable rule. Then ε, watching ε' at work, sees that ε' uses a clock that runs slowly (but they agree on normal meter sticks in the y-directions). So ε sees that when ε' said he measured 3 meters travel in 1 sec, it was "really" 3 meters in *more-than-1-second* as ε would measure it by *his* clock. Therefore ε computes that velocity as *smaller than 3 meters/second* by $\sqrt{1 - v^2/c^2}$. Still believing in Newton III and momentum-conservation, ε concludes that, since his own block acquired momentum 1 kg · 3 meters/sec, the other, which he calculates is moving slower must have greater mass[16]—in-

creased by the factor $1/\sqrt{1 - v^2/c^2}$. While that block is drifting across the table after the spring's tug, ε also sees it whizzing along in the x-direction, table and all, with great speed v. Its owner, ε', at rest with the table, calls his block 1 kg. But ε, who sees it whizzing past, estimates its mass as greater, by $1/\sqrt{1 - v^2/c^2}$.

This result applies to all moving masses: mass, as we commonly know it, has different values for different observers. Post an observer on a moving body and he will find a standard value, the "rest-mass," identical for every electron, the same for every proton, standard for every pint of water, etc. But an observer moving past the body, or seeing it move past him, will find it has greater mass $m = \dfrac{m_0}{\sqrt{1 - v^2/c^2}}$. Again, the factor $1/\sqrt{1 - v^2/c^2}$ makes practically no difference at ordinary speeds. However, in a cyclotron, accelerated ions increase their mass significantly. They take too long on their wider trips, and arrive late unless special measures are taken. Electrons from billion-volt accelerators are so massive that they practically masquerade as protons.

For example, an electron from a 2-million-volt gun emerges with speed about 294,000,000 meters/sec or 0.98 c. The factor $1/\sqrt{1 - (.98c)^2/c^2}$ is $1/\sqrt{1 - (98/100)^2} \approx 1/\sqrt{4/100} = 5$. To a stationary observer the electron has 5 times its rest-mass.[*] (Another way of putting this is: that electron's kinetic energy is 2 million electron · volts; the energy associated with an electron's rest-mass is half a million ev, and therefore this electron has K.E. that has mass 4 rest-masses; and that with the original rest-mass makes 5 rest-masses.)

This dependence on speed has been tested by deflecting very fast electrons (beta-rays) with electric and magnetic fields, and the results agree excellently with the prediction. Another test: in a cloud chamber a *very fast electron* hitting a *stationary electron* ("at rest" in some atom of the wet air) does not make the expected 90° fork. In the photograph of Fig. 31-34c, the measured angles

[16] Suppose ε and ε' are passing each other with relative velocity 112,000 miles/sec. Then ε sees the clock used by ε' running slow, ticking once every 1.2 seconds. So he knows the block belonging to ε' has velocity 3 meters/1.2 secs or 2.5 meters/sec. His own block has momentum 1 kg · 3 m./sec. To preserve momentum conservation, he must say that the other block has momentum 1.2 kg. · 2.5 m./sec. So he estimates the mass of the other block as 1.2 kg, a 20% increase.

[*] To the moving electron, or to a neighbor flying along beside it, its mass is the normal rest-mass; and it is the experimenter rushing towards it who has 5 times *his* normal rest-mass and is squashed to ⅕ his normal thickness.

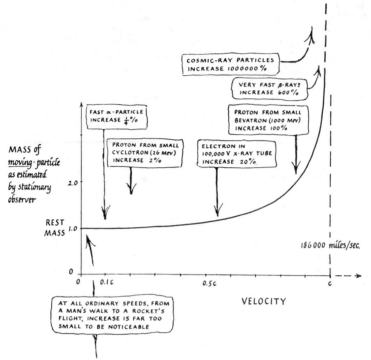

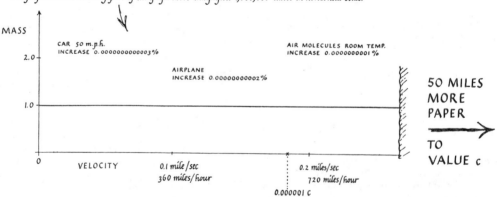

FIG. 31-33. CHANGES OF MASS OF OBJECTS MOVING RELATIVE TO OBSERVER
(The graphs of Fig. 31-31 cover the whole range of speeds from zero to the speed of light; and they may give a mistaken impression of noticeable increase of mass at ordinary speeds. This graph is a copy of the mass-graph there, with comments.)

agree well with those predicted by Relativity for a moving mass 12.7m hitting a stationary mass m, in an elastic collision. The tracks are curved because there was a strong magnetic field perpendicular to the picture. Measurements of the curvatures give the momentum of each electron after collision, and the momentum of the bombarding electron before collision. Measurements of the angles shown in the sketch confirm the proportions of these momenta. If non-relativistic mechanics [K.E. = ½mv^2, etc.] is used to calculate the masses, assuming an elastic collision, the projectile's mass appears to be about four times the target particle's mass. Yet the tracks look like those of an electron-

FIG. 31-34. RELATIVISTIC MASS IN ELASTIC COLLISIONS

ELASTIC COLLISIONS

(a) Nuclei

(b) Electrons

(a) Collision of alpha-particle with stationary atom. Even with its high energy, an alpha-particle from a radioactive atom has a speed that is less than 0.1 c, so its mass is not noticeably increased. It makes the expected 90° fork when it hits a stationary particle (He) of its own mass. With a hydrogen atom as target, it shows its greater mass.

(b) When a slow electron hits a stationary one, the fork shows the expected 90°. When a fast electron hits a stationary one, the angles show that the fast one has much greater mass.

ELECTRONS COLLIDE

(c) Cloud chamber photo

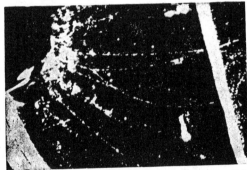

(c) Cloud-chamber photograph of very fast electron colliding with a stationary one. (Photograph by H. R. Crane, University of Michigan.)

(d) Measurements

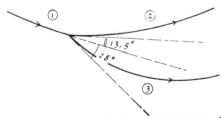

(d) Measurements of original photograph, (c), gave the following radii: (1) 0.15 ± 0.01 meter, (2) 0.105 m., (3) 0.050 m. Magnetic field strength was 1,425,000 (in our units for H in $F = 10^{-7}(Qv)(H)$, discussed in Ch. 37.)

electron collision; and we do not expect $4m$ and m *classically* for two electrons. So we try assuming *relativistic* mechanics [K.E. = $(m - m_0)c^2$,

MOMENTUM = mv, with $m = m_0/\sqrt{1 - v^2/c^2}$].

Then we find a consistent story: from the magnetic field and our measurements of curvature we find:

BEFORE COLLISION:

projectile had mass $12.7m_0$, speed $0.9969\ c$;

Since the track is short and only slightly curved, its radius cannot be measured very precisely; so the projectile's momentum, and thence mass, is uncertain within about 6%. We should say

mass = $12.7\ m_0 \pm 6\%$ or mass = $12.7\ m_0 \pm 0.8\ m_0$

AFTER COLLISION:

projectile had mass $8.9\ m_0$, speed $0.9936\ c$;
target particle had mass $4.3\ m_0$, speed $0.9728\ c$,

where m_0 is the standard rest-mass of an electron and c is the speed of light. Before collision the total mass was $13.7\ m_0$ (including the target); after collision it was $13.2\ m_0$. Mass is conserved in this collision—within the 6% experimental uncertainty—and so is energy, now measured by mc^2.

A Meaning for Mass Change

There is an easy physical interpretation of the change of mass: the extra mass is the mass of the body's kinetic energy. Try some algebra, using the binomial theorem to express the $\sqrt{}$ as a series, for fairly low speeds:

$$m = \frac{m_0}{\sqrt{1 - v^2/c^2}}$$

$$= m_0 \left[1 - \frac{v^2}{c^2} \right]^{-\frac{1}{2}}$$

$$= m_0 \left[1 - (-\tfrac{1}{2})\frac{v^2}{c^2} + (-\tfrac{1}{2})(-\tfrac{3}{2})\frac{v^4}{c^4} + \cdots \right]$$

$$= m_0 \left[1 + \tfrac{1}{2}\frac{v^2}{c^2} + \text{higher powers of } \frac{v^2}{c^2} \text{ which are very small at low speeds} \right]$$

$$= m_0 + \tfrac{1}{2}m_0 v^2/c^2 + \text{negligible terms at low speeds}$$

$$= \text{REST-MASS} + \text{K.E.}/c^2$$

$$= \text{REST-MASS} + \text{MASS OF K.E.}$$

Maximum Speed: c

As a body's speed grows nearer to the speed of light, it becomes *increasingly* harder to accelerate—the mass sweeps up towards infinite mass at the speed of light. Experimenters using "linear accelerators" (which drive electrons straight ahead) find that at high energies their victims approach the speed of light but never exceed it. The electrons gain more energy at each successive push (and therefore more mass) but hardly move any faster (and therefore the accelerating "pushers" can be spaced evenly along the stream—a welcome simplification in design).

Mass growing towards infinity at the speed of light means unaccelerability growing to infinity. Our efforts at making an object move faster seem to run along the level of constant mass, till it reaches very high speeds; then they climb a steeper and steeper mountain towards an insurmountable wall at the speed of light itself. No wonder Relativity predicts that *no piece of matter can move faster than light*; since in attempting to accelerate it to that speed we should encounter more and more mass and thereby obtain less and less response to our accelerating force.

Adding Velocities, Relativistically

Faster than light? Surely that is possible: mount a gun on a rocket that travels with speed $\frac{3}{4}c$ and have the gun fire a bullet forward with muzzle velocity $\frac{1}{2}c$. The bullet's speed should be $\frac{1}{2}c + \frac{3}{4}c$ or $1\frac{1}{4}c$. No: that is a Galilean addition of velocities. We must find the relativistic rule.

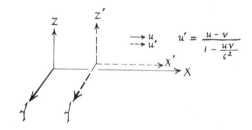

FIG. 31-35a. OBSERVERS MEASURE A VELOCITY
Two experimenters observe the same moving object. How do their estimates of its velocity compare? The Lorentz transformation leads to the relation shown, between u as measured by ε and u' as measured by ε'.

Suppose ε sees an object moving in his laboratory with velocity u, along the x-direction. What speed will ε' measure for the object? As measured by ε, $u = \Delta x/\Delta t$. As measured by ε', $u' = \Delta x'/\Delta t'$ and simple algebra leads from the Lorentz Transformation to

$$u' = \frac{(u - v)}{\left[1 - \dfrac{uv}{c^2} \right]}$$

instead of the Galilean $u' = (u - v)$. And the inverse relation runs:

$$u = \frac{(u' + v)}{\left[1 + \dfrac{u'v}{c^2} \right]}$$

The factor in [ ] is practically 1 for all ordinary speeds, and then the relations reduce to Galilean form. Try that on a bullet fired by an ordinary rifle inside an ordinary express train. ε', riding in the train, sees the rifle fire the bullet with speed u'. ε, sitting at the side of the track, sees the bullet move with speed u. He sees the train passing him with speed v. Then $u = (u' + v)/[1]$. The Galilean version fits closely:

SPEED OF BULLET RELATIVE TO GROUND

= SPEED OF BULLET RELATIVE TO TRAIN + SPEED OF TRAIN RELATIVE TO GROUND

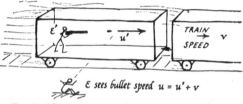

FIG. 31-35b. ADDING VELOCITIES AT ORDINARY SPEEDS
Two experimenters observe the same bullet, shot from a gun in a moving train. With such speeds, the Lorentz transformation leads to the simple Galilean relations: $u' = u - v$ and $u = u' + v$.

Now return to the gun on a $\frac{3}{4}c$ rocket firing a $\frac{1}{2}c$ bullet forward. ε' rides on the rocket and sees the bullet emerge with $u' = \frac{1}{2}c$. ε on the ground sees ε' and his rocket moving with speed $\frac{3}{4}c$; and ε learns from ε' how fast the gun fired the bullet. Then, using the relativity-formula above, ε predicts the bullet-speed that *he* will observe, thus:

FIG. 31-36. ADDING VELOCITIES AT VERY HIGH SPEEDS

(a)

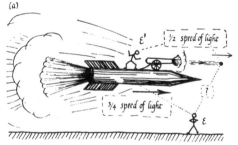

(a) Experimenter ε on ground observes a rocket moving at $\frac{3}{4}c$. Experimenter ε' riding on the rocket fires a bullet at $\frac{1}{2}c$ relative to the rocket. What will be the speed of the bullet, as measured by ε on the ground?

$$u = \frac{u' + v}{1 + u'v/c^2} = \frac{\frac{1}{2}c + \frac{3}{4}c}{1 + \frac{1}{2}c \cdot \frac{3}{4}c/c^2} = \frac{1\frac{1}{4}c}{1 + \frac{3}{8}}$$

$$= \frac{(\frac{5}{4})c}{(1\frac{1}{8})} = \frac{10}{11}c, \text{ still just less than } c.$$

SPEED OF BULLET RELATIVE TO GROUND

$$= \frac{\dfrac{\text{SPEED OF GUN}}{\text{RELATIVE TO GROUND}} + \dfrac{\text{SPEED OF BULLET}}{\text{RELATIVE TO GUN}}}{1 - \dfrac{\text{SPEED OF BULLET}}{\text{SPEED OF LIGHT}} \cdot \dfrac{\text{SPEED OF GUN}}{\text{SPEED OF LIGHT}}}$$

Have another try at defeating the limit of velocity, c. Run two rockets head on at each other, with speeds $\frac{3}{4}c$ and $\frac{1}{2}c$. ε on the ground sees ε' riding on

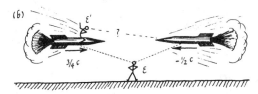

(b) Experimenter ε on ground sees two rockets approaching each other, one with speed $\frac{3}{4}c$, the other with speed $\frac{1}{2}c$. What speed of approach will experimenter ε' riding on the first rocket see?

one rocket with velocity $v = \frac{3}{4}c$ and the other rocket travelling with $u = -\frac{1}{2}c$; and he thinks they must be approaching each other with relative velocity $1\frac{1}{4}c$. ε', riding on the first rocket, sees the second rocket moving with predicted speed

$$u' = \frac{u - v}{1 - uv/c^2} = \frac{(-\frac{1}{2}c) - (\frac{3}{4}c)}{1 - (-\frac{1}{2}c)(\frac{3}{4}c)/c^2}$$

$$= \frac{-1\frac{1}{4}c}{1 + \frac{3}{8}} = -\frac{10}{11}c$$

Their rate of approach is less than c. Whatever we do, we cannot make a material object move faster than light—as seen by any observer.

Speed of Light

Finally, as a check on our velocity-addition formula, make sure it does yield the same speed of light for observers with different speeds. Take a flash of light travelling with speed $u = c$, as observed by ε. Observer ε' is travelling with speed v relative to ε, in the same direction. ε' observes the flash moving with speed

$$u' = \frac{u - v}{1 - uv/c^2} = \frac{c - v}{1 - cv/c^2} = \frac{c(1 - v/c)}{(1 - v/c)} = c$$

Every observer measures the same speed c for light.

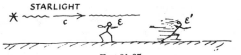

STARLIGHT

FIG. 31-37.
Two experimenters measure the speed of the same sample of light. Experimenter ε sees that ε' is running with velocity v in the direction the light is travelling.

(No wonder, since the Lorentz Transformation was chosen to produce this.) This certainly accounts for the Michelson-Morley-Miller null results.

Energy

We rebuild the Newtonian view of energy to fit Relativity as follows. Define MOMENTUM as mv, where m is the observed mass of the body in motion: $m = m_0/\sqrt{1 - v^2/c^2}$. Define force, F, as $\Delta(mv)/\Delta t$. Define change from potential energy to K.E. as WORK, $F \cdot \Delta s$. Combine these to calculate the K.E. of a mass m moving with speed v. We shall give the result, omitting the calculus derivation.

$$m = \frac{m_0}{\sqrt{1 - v^2/c^2}} \quad \begin{bmatrix} \text{part of Lorentz} \\ \text{Transformation} \end{bmatrix}$$

$$F = \frac{\Delta(mv)}{\Delta t} \quad \begin{bmatrix} \text{Newton Law II} \\ \text{Relativity form} \end{bmatrix}$$

$$\left.\begin{aligned} \Delta(\text{K.E.}) &= F \cdot \Delta s \\ &= F \cdot v \cdot \Delta t \\ \text{K.E.} &= 0 \text{ if } v = 0 \end{aligned}\right\} \begin{bmatrix} \text{Definition} \\ \text{of K.E.} \end{bmatrix}$$

↓

CALCULUS

↓

$$\text{K.E.} = mc^2 - m_0c^2$$
$$= (m - m_0)c^2$$

We assign the body a permanent store of "rest-energy" m_0c^2—locked up in its atomic force-fields, perhaps. We add that to the K.E.; then the *total* energy, E, of the body is $m_0c^2 + (mc^2 - m_0c^2) = mc^2$. Therefore total $E = mc^2$. This applies whatever its speed—but remember that m itself changes with speed. At low speeds, mc^2 reduces[17] to

(rest-energy m_0c^2) + (K.E. $\frac{1}{2}mv^2$).

For a short, direct derivation of $E = mc^2$, see the note at the bottom of the next page.

This view that energy and mass go together according to $E = mc^2$ has been given many successful tests in nuclear physics. Again and again we find some mass of material particles disappears in a

[17] See the discussion above, with the binomial theorem.

nuclear break-up; but then we find a release of energy—radiation in some cases, K.E. of flying fragments in others—and that energy carries the missing mass.

The expression for mass, $m = m_0/\sqrt{1 - v^2/c^2}$ follows from the Lorentz Transformation and conservation of momentum. So $E = mc^2$ follows from Newton's Laws II and III combined with the Lorentz Transformation.

Then if an observer assigns to a moving body a mass m, momentum mv, and total energy mc^2 he finds that, in any closed system, *mass is conserved*, *momentum is conserved* (as a vector sum), and *energy is conserved*. In all this he must use the observed mass m, which is $m_0/\sqrt{1 - v^2/c^2}$ for any body moving with speed v relative to him. Then he is doubling up his claim of conservation because, if the sum of all the masses $(m_1 + m_2 + \ldots)$, is constant, the total energy $(m_1c^2 + m_2c^2 + \ldots)$ must also be constant. If energy is conserved, mass must also be conserved. One rule will cover both. That is why some scientists say rather carelessly, "mass and energy are the same, but for a factor c^2." In fact, since c^2 is universally constant, there is little harm in saying that mass and energy are the same thing, though commonly measured in different units. But there is also little harm if you prefer to think of them still with quite different flavors as physical concepts. And a very important distinction remains between *matter* and *radiation* (and other forms of energy). Matter comes in particles, *whose total number remains constant* if we count the production or destruction of a [particle + anti-particle]

pair as no change. Radiation comes in photons; and the total number of photons *does* change when one is emitted or absorbed by matter.

Covariance

Finally, Einstein treated momentum as a vector with three components in space-&-time, and kinetic energy with them as a fourth, time-like, component of a "supervector." Thus, conservation rules for mass, momentum, and energy can be rolled into one great formula in relativistic mechanics. The Lorentz Transformation gives this formula *the same form* with respect to any (steadily moving) set of axes whatever their velocity. We say such a formula or relation is "covariant." We put great store by covariance: covariant laws have the most general form possible and we feel they are the most perfect mathematical statement of natural laws. "We lose a frame of reference, but we gain a universally valid symbolic form."[18]

"A Wrong Question"

The physical laws of mechanics and electromagnetism are covariant: they give no hope of telling how fast we move through absolute space. This brings us back to Einstein's basic principle of being realistic. Where the answer is "impossible," the question is a foolish one. We are unscientific to imply there *is* an absolute space, as we do when we ask "How fast . . . *through space?*" We are begging the question, inside our own question, by mentioning space. We are asking a wrong question,

[18] Frederic Keffer.

NOTE: Derivation of $E = mc^2$

This short derivation, due to Einstein, uses the experimental knowledge that when radiation with energy E joules is absorbed by matter, it delivers momentum E/c kg·m./sec. (Experiment shows that PRESSURE of radiation on an *absorbing* wall is ENERGY-PER-UNIT-VOLUME of radiation-beam. Suppose a beam of area A falls on an absorbing surface head-on. In time Δt, a length of beam $c \cdot \Delta t$ arrives. Then MOMENTUM delivered in Δt

$= $ FORCE $\cdot \Delta t$ $\qquad = $ PRESSURE $\cdot$ AREA $\cdot \Delta t$
$= $ (ENERGY/VOLUME) $\cdot$ AREA $\cdot \Delta t$
$= $ (ENERGY/$A \cdot c \cdot \Delta t$) $\cdot A \cdot \Delta t$
$= $ ENERGY/ c

This also follows from Maxwell's equations).

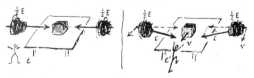

We take two views of the same thought-experiment:

(A) Place a block of matter at rest on a frictionless table. Give it some energy E by firing two chunks of radiation at it, ½E from due East, ½E from due West. The block absorbs the radiation and gains energy E; but its net gain of momentum is zero: it stays at rest. (B) Now let a running observer watch the same event. He runs with speed v due North; but according to Relativity he can equally well think he is at rest and see the table, etc. moving towards him with speed v due South. Then he sees the block moving South with momentum Mv. He sees the two chunks of radiation moving towards the block, each with speed c but in directions, slanted southward with slope v/c. (This is like the *aberration of starlight*.) In his view, each chunk has momentum $(\frac{1}{2}E/c)$ with a southward component $(\frac{1}{2}E/c)(v/c)$. Thinking himself at rest, he sees total southward momentum $Mv + 2(\frac{1}{2}E/c)(v/c)$. After the block has absorbed the radiation, he still sees it moving South with the same speed v—since in version (A) we saw that the block gained no net momentum. However, the block may gain some mass, say m. Find out how big m is by trusting *conservation of momentum*:

$$Mv + 2(\tfrac{1}{2}E/c)(v/c) = (M + m)v$$
$$\therefore \quad m = E/c^2 \quad \text{or} \quad E = mc^2,$$

where m is the MASS gained when ENERGY E is gained.

like the lawyer who says, "Answer me 'yes' or 'no.' Have you stopped beating your wife?" The answer to *that* is, "A reasonable man does not answer unreasonable questions." And Einstein might suggest that a reasonable scientist does not *ask* unreasonable questions.

Simultaneity

The observers ε and ε' do not merely see each other's clocks running slowly; worse still, clocks at different *distances* seem to disagree. Suppose each observer posts a series of clocks along the x-direction in his laboratory and sets them all going together. And when ε and ε' pass each other at the origin, they set their central clocks in agreement. Then each will blame the other, saying: "*His* clocks are not even synchronized. He has set his distant clocks wrong by his own central clock—the greater the distance, the worse his mistake. The farther I look down his corridor, along the direction he is moving, the more he has set his clocks there back— they read early, behind my proper time. And looking back along his corridor, opposite to the direction of his motion, I see his clocks set more and more forward, to read later than my correct time." (That judgment, which each makes of the other's clocks, is not the result of forgetting the time-delay of seeing a clock that is far away. Each observer allows for such delays—or reads one of his own clocks that is close beside the other's—and then finds the disagreement. This disagreement about setting of remote clocks belongs with the view that each observer takes of clock *rates*. Each claims that all the other's clocks are running too slowly; so they should not be surprised to find that their central clocks, originally synchronized at the origin, disagree after a while. Each says: "*His* central clock, that was opposite me, has moved ahead and was running too slowly all the while; so no wonder its hands have not moved around as fast as my clock.")

ε observes his own row of clocks ticking simultaneously all in agreement. But ε' does not find those ticks simultaneous. *Events that are simultaneous for ε are not simultaneous for ε'.* This is a serious change from our common-sense view of universal time; but it is a part of the Lorentz Transformation. In fact, the question of simultaneity played an essential role in the development of relativity by Poincaré and Einstein. Arguing with thought-experiments that keep "c" constant, you can show this change is necessary. The following example illustrates this.

Suppose ε and ε' have their laboratories in two transparent railroad coaches on parallel tracks, one moving with speed v relative to the other. Just

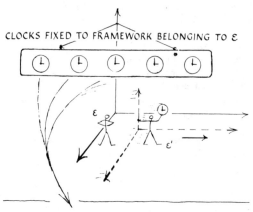

CLOCKS FIXED TO FRAMEWORK BELONGING TO ε

SAME CLOCKS AS REPORTED BY ε'

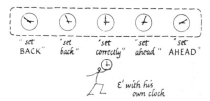

"set BACK" "set back" "set correctly" "set ahead" "set AHEAD"

ε' with his own clock

FIG. 31-38. "SIMULTANEOUS" CLOCK SETTINGS
Each experimenter sets his own clocks *all in agreement* (allowing carefully for the time taken by any light signals he uses in looking at them). Each experimenter finds that the other man's clocks *disagree among themselves*, progressively with distance. (That is, after he has allowed carefully for the time taken by the light signals he uses in checking the other man's clocks against his own.) The sketch shows a series of clocks all fixed in the framework belonging to ε. As adjusted and observed by ε, they all agree: they are synchronized. As investigated by ε' those clocks disagree with each other. The lower sketch shows what ε' finds by comparing those clocks simultaneously (as he, ε', thinks) with his own clock. The two sketches of clocks disagree because each experimenter thinks *he* compares them all simultaneously but disagrees with the other man's idea of simultaneity.

as the coaches are passing, ε and ε' lean out of their center windows and shake hands. They happen to be electrically charged, + and −, so there is a flash of light as they touch. Now consider the light from this flash. Some of it travels in each coach starting from the mid-point where the experimenter is standing. ε finds it reaches the front and hind ends of his coach simultaneously. And ε' finds it reaches the ends of *his* coach simultaneously. Each considers he is in a stationary coach with light travelling out from the center with constant speed c. But ε can also observe the light flash reaching the ends of the other coach that carries ε'. He observes the events that ε' observes; but he certainly does not find them simultaneous, as ε' claims. By the time the flash has travelled a half-length of the ε′ coach, that coach has moved forward past ε. As ε sees it, the light travels farther to reach the front end of that moving coach, and less to the hind end. So ε sees the flash hit the hind end first, while ε′ claims the hits are simultaneous.[19] (Reciprocally, ε′ sees the light reach the ends of the coach carrying ε at different instants, while ε claims they are simultaneous.) You will meet no such confusion in ordinary life, because such disagreements over priority arise only when the events are very close in time, or very far apart in distance. Where events P and Q are closer in time than the travel-time for light between them, observers with different motions may take different views: one may find P and Q simultaneous, while another finds P occurs before Q, and

still another finds P later than Q. To maintain Einstein's Relativity, we must regard time as interlocked with space in a compound space-time, whose slicing into separate time and space depends somewhat on the observer's motion. If we accept this compound space-time system, we must modify our philosophy of cause and effect.

Cause and Effect

Earlier science was much concerned with causality. Greeks looked for "first causes"; later scientists looked for immediate causes—"the heating caused the rock to melt"; "the pressure caused the liquid to flow"; "the alpha-particle caused the ions to be formed." It is difficult to define cause and effect. "P causes Q": what does that mean? The best we can say is that cause is something that *precedes* the effect so consistently that we think there is a connection between them.

Even in common cases (like STRESS and STRAIN or P.D. and CURRENT), we prefer to say P and Q go together: we still look for *relationships* to codify our knowledge, but we treat P and Q as cousins rather than as parent and child.

And now Relativity tells us that *some* events can show a different order in time for different observers—and all observers are equally "right." The sketches of Fig. 31-40(e), below, show how various observers *at* an event P, *here-now*, must classify some other events (e.g., Q_1) as in the *absolute future*; some other events (e.g., Q_2) in the *absolute past*; and some events (e.g., Q_3) in the *absolute elsewhere* (as Eddington named it) where observers with different motions at P may disagree over the order of events P and Q.

[19] Note that the disagreement over simultaneity is not due to forgetting the time taken by light signals to bring the information to either observer. We treat the problem as if each observer had a whole gang of perfectly trained clockwatchers ranged along his coach to make observations without signal delays and then report at leisure. The observers compare notes (e.g. by radio). Then each has an obvious explanation of the other man's claim that he saw the light flash reach the ends of his own coach simultaneously: "Why, the silly fellow has set his clocks askew. He has a clock at each end of his coach, and when the light flash hit those end clocks they both showed the same instant of time—I saw that, too. But he is wrong in saying his end clocks are set in agreement: I can see that he has set his front-end clock back by my standard, and his hind-end clock ahead. *I* can see that the flash had to travel farther to reach his front end. And *my* clocks tell me it arrived there later, as *I* know it should. But since his clock is mis-set, early by mine, the lateness of arrival did not show on it. Those mistakes of his in setting his clocks just cover up the difference of transit-time for what I can see are different travel-distances to the ends of his coach." As in all such relativistic comparisons, *each observer blames the other for making exactly the same kind of mistake.*

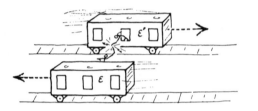

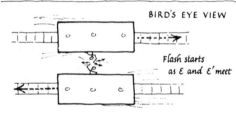

BIRD'S EYE VIEW

Flash starts as ε and ε′ meet

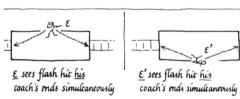

ε sees flash hit *his* coach's ends simultaneously

ε′ sees flash hit *his* coach's ends simultaneously

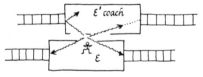

ε′ coach

ε

ε sees flash hit both ends of his coach simultaneously, but the ends of ε′ coach at different times. (similarly for ε′)

FIG. 31-39. THOUGHT-EXPERIMENT
To show that events that are simultaneous for one observer are not simultaneous for an observer moving with a different velocity.

PAIRS OF EVENTS

ON A TIME AND DISTANCE MAP

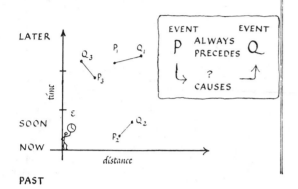

GALILEAN TIME AND DISTANCE MAP

for OBSERVER ε *and* MOVING OBSERVER ε'

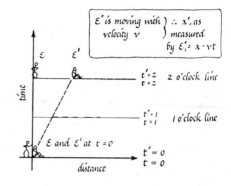

TWO OBSERVERS <u>MOVING VERY FAST RELATIVE TO EACH OTHER</u> RECORD EVENTS P & Q

IN GALILEAN WORLD

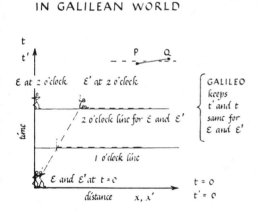

IN LORENTZ WORLD

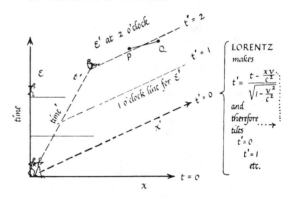

FIG. 31-40. CHARTS OF SPACE (ONE DIMENSION) AND TIME

(These fanciful sketches are highly restricted: all the events shown occur in one straight line, in a one-dimensional space, along an x-axis.

In the Lorentz picture, a very high relative velocity between ε and ε' is assumed. The distortion of the x' and t' system in the Lorentz picture shows the view taken by ε. Of course, ε' himself would take an "undistorted" view of his own system, but ε' would find the x and t system "distorted."

It is not possible to show the essential symmetry here; so the Lorentz picture should only be taken as a suggestion: taken literally, it would be misleading.)

(a) An event that occurs on the straight line (x-axis) is shown by a point on this chart. Distance *along* shows *where* the event occurs on the line. Distance *up* shows *when* it occurs. Event P precedes event Q in time. It may be sensible to say that P causes Q, for some types of event.

(b) A moving experimenter carries his origin for distance with him. On the Galilean system he uses the same time-scale as a stationary experimenter.

(c) With a Galilean transformation between two experimenters, the lines for each hour by the clock are the same for both observers, and parallel to the axis, $t = 0$.

(d) The Lorentz transformation between two experimenters *tilts* one coordinate system of space-&-time relative to the other (through a negligible angle, except when speed of ε' relative to ε approaches c).

Then an event Q that follows event P in time for one experimenter may precede P for another—but only if the events are so far apart that a light signal from one event could not travel to the place of the other event and reach it before the other event occurred there.

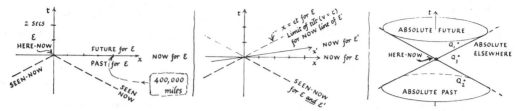

FIG. 31-40(e) [after Eddington]

Observer ε is at the origin; and so is ε′ who is moving fast along x-axis relative to ε. The line SEEN-NOW has equation $x = -ct$, and marks all events that ε (or ε′) sees at this instant NOW. ε, knowing the value of c, allows for travel-time and marks his axis of events that happen now along the x-axis. However, ε′ will make a different allowance from the same SEEN-NOW line and will mark a tilted "now" line as his x′-axis. The lines continuing SEEN-NOW in the forward direction of time mark the maximum tilt that ε′ could have for his NOW line—because ε′ can never have relative velocity greater than c; so his x′-axis can never tilt as much as those

"light-lines" which have slope c. Rotate the picture around the t-axis and the light-lines make a double cone. Suppose an event P occurs at the origin, HERE-NOW, and another event at Q. If Q is within the upper light-cone (Q_1), it is definitely in the future of P for all observers. Similarly, all events in the lower light-cone (Q_2) are in the absolute past, earlier than P for all observers. But Q_3 in the space between the cones may be in the future for ε and yet be in the past for an observer ε′ whose x′-axis tilts above it. So we label that intermediate region ABSOLUTE ELSEWHERE. If Q falls there, *neither P nor Q can cause the other*—they simply occur at different places.

So now we must be more careful. We may keep cause and effect in simple cases such as apples and stomach-ache, or alpha-particles and ions; but we must be wary with events so close in time, for their distance apart, that they fall in each other's ABSOLUTE ELSEWHERE.

In atomic physics you will meet other doubts concerning cause and effect. Radioactive changes appear to be a matter of pure chance—the future life-time of an individual atom being unpredictable. In the final chapter you will see that nature enforces partial unpredictability on all our knowledge, hedging individual atomic events with some unavoidable uncertainty, making it unwise to insist on exact "effects" from exact "causes."

The Lorentz Transformation as a Rotation

The sketches of Fig. 31-40 suggest we can throw light on the Lorentz transformation if we look at the effect of a simple rotation of the axes of a common x-, y-graph. Try the algebra, and find the "transformation" connecting the old coordinates of a point, x, y, with the new coordinates, x′, y′ of the *same* point, thus:

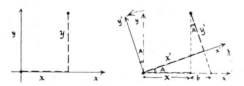

Refer a point in a plane to x-y-axes. Then rotate the axes through an angle A (around the z-axis). The point, remaining at its old position in space, has coordinates x′, y′ referred to the new axes. Use the symbol s for the *slope* of the new x-axis, so that s is tan A. Then, as the diagram shows

$$x' = (x + b) \cos A = (x + y \tan A) \cos A$$
$$= (x + sy)/\sec A = (x + sy)/\sqrt{(1 + \tan^2 A)}$$
$$\therefore \quad x' = (x + sy)/\sqrt{(1 + s^2)}$$

Similarly, $y' = (y - sx)/\sqrt{(1 + s^2)}$

This transformation for a simple rotation of axes shows a square root playing much the same role as in the Lorentz transformation. In fact we obtain the Lorentz form if we replace y by a time coordinate, thus: instead of y, use t multiplied by constant c and by i the square root of (−1). And instead of slope s use i(v/c). Then, with $y = ict$ and $y' = ict'$ and $s = iv/c$, the simple rotation-transformation *is* the Lorentz transformation. Try that. That shows how the Lorentz transformation can be regarded as a slicing of space-&-time with a different slant for different observers.

The Invariant "Interval" between Two Events

We can define the "interval" R between two events (x_1, t_1) and (x_2, t_2) by the Pythagorean form

$$R^2 = (x_1 - x_2)^2 + (ict_1 - ict_2)^2$$

Then we can also write the expression that gives R′, the "interval" for another observer who records the same two events at (x_1', t_1') and (x_2', t_2') on his coordinates. If we then use the Lorentz transformation to express R′ in terms of the first observer's coordinates, we find that R′ is the same as R. The Lorentz transformation keeps that "interval" invariant. That states the Relativity assumption—measured c is always the same—in a different way.

John A. Wheeler suggests a fable to illustrate the role of c. Suppose the inhabitants of an island do their surveying with rectangular coordinates, but measure *North-South* distances in *miles* and *East-West* ones in *feet*. Then a sudden, permanent shift of magnetic North through an angle A makes them turn their system of axes to the new direction. They again measure in miles along the new N′-S′ direction, and in feet E′-W′. They try to compute the distance R between two points by Pythagoras: $R^2 = (\Delta x)^2 + (\Delta y)^2$; and they find that R takes a different value with the new coordinates.

Then they find that they obtain the same value for R (and a useful one) with both sets of coordinates if they define R by: $R^2 = (\Delta x)^2 + (5280\,\Delta y)^2$.

Their "mysterious essential factor," 5280, corresponds to c in the relativistic "interval" in the paragraph above. Moral: c is not so much a mysterious limiting velocity as a unit-changing factor, which suggests that time and space are not utterly different: they form one continuum, with both of them measurable in meters.

Is There a Framework of Fixed Space?

Thus we have devised, in special Relativity, a new geometry and physics of space-&-time with our clocks and measuring scales (basic instruments of physics), conspiring, by their changes when we change observers, to present us with a universally constant velocity of light, to limit all moving matter to lesser speeds, to reveal physical laws in the same form for all observers moving with constant velocities; and thus to conceal from us forever any absolute motion through a fixed framework of space; in fact, to render meaningless the question whether such a framework exists.

HIGHER VALUES OF MATHEMATICS AS A LANGUAGE

Mathematical Form and Beauty

As a language, algebra may be very truthful or accurate, and even fruitful, but is it not doomed to remain dull, uninteresting prose and never rise to poetry? Most mathematicians will deny that doubt and claim there is a great beauty in mathematics. One can learn to enjoy its form and elegance as much as those of poetry. As an example, watch a pair of simultaneous equations being polished up into elegance. Start with

$$2x + 3y = 9$$
$$4x - 2y = 10.$$

Then with some juggling we can get rid of y and find $x = 3$; and then $y = 1$. But these are lopsided, individual equations. Let us make them more general, replacing the coefficients, 2, 3, 9, etc., by letters a, b, c, etc., thus

$$ax + by = c \qquad dx + ey = f$$

After heavier juggling we find $x = \dfrac{ec - fb}{ae - db}$. Then more juggling is needed to find y. These solutions enable us to solve the earlier equations and others like them by substituting the number coefficients for a, b, c, etc. But unless we had many equations to solve that would hardly pay; and we seem no nearer to poetry. But now let us be more systematic. We are dealing with x and y as much the same things; so we might emphasize the similarity

by calling them x_1 and x_2. To match that change, we use a_1, a_2, a_0 instead of a, b, c and write: $a_1 x_1 + a_2 x_2 = a_0$. But then we have the second equation's coefficients. We might call them a_1', etc., but even so the two equations do not look quite symmetrical. To be fairer still, we call the first lot a_1' etc. and the second lot a_1'' etc. Then:

$$a_1' x_1 + a_2' x_2 = a_0'$$
$$\text{and } a_1'' x_1 + a_2'' x_2 = a_0''$$

These look neat, but is their neatness much use?

Solve for x. We obtain $x_1 = \dfrac{a_0' a_2'' - a_0'' a_2'}{a_1' a_2'' - a_1'' a_2'}$. Here is a gain: we need not solve for x_2 or y. Symmetry will show us the answer straight away. Note that x_1 and x_2 (the old x and y) and their coefficients are only distinguished by the subscripts $_1$ and $_2$. If we interchange the subscripts $_1$ and $_2$ throughout, we get the same equations again, and therefore we must have the same solutions. We make that interchange in the solution above and $x_1 = \dfrac{a_0' a_2'' - a_0'' a_2'}{a_1' a_2'' - a_1'' a_2'}$ becomes $x_2 = \dfrac{a_0' a_1'' - a_0'' a_1'}{a_2' a_1'' - a_2'' a_1'}$. Now we have the answer for x_2 (the old y), free of charge. The economy of working may seem small; but think of the increased complexity if we had, say, five unknowns and five simultaneous equations. With this symmetrical system of writing, we just solve for one unknown, and then write down the other four solutions by symmetry. Here is *form* playing a part that is useful for economy and pleasant in appearance to the mathematical eye. More than that, the new form of equations and answers is general and universal—in a sense this is a case of covariance. This is the kind of symmetrical form that appealed to Maxwell and Einstein.

This is only a little way towards finding poetry in the language of mathematics—about as far as well-metered verse. The next stage would be to use symmetrical *methods* rather than symmetrical *forms*, e.g. "determinants." As the professional mathematician develops the careful arguments which back up his methods, he builds a structure of logic and form which to his eye is as beautiful as the finest poem.

Geometry and Science: Truth and General Relativity

Thus, mathematics goes far beyond working arithmetic and sausage-grinding algebra. It even abandons pert definitions and some of the restrictions of logic, to encourage full flowering of its growth; but yet its whole scheme is based on its own starting points; the views its founders take of numbers, points, parallel lines, vectors, ... Pure mathematics is an ivory-tower science. The results, being derived by good logic, are automatically true to the original assumptions and definitions. Whether the real world fits the assumptions seems at first a matter for experiment. We certainly must not trust the assumptions just because they seem reasonable and obvious. However, they may be more like definitions of procedure, in which case mathematics, still true to those definitions, might interpret any world in terms of them.

We used to think that when the mathematician had developed his world of space and numbers, we then had to do experiments to find out whether the real world agrees with him. For example, Euclid made assumptions regarding points and lines, etc. and proved, or argued out, a consistent geometry. On the face of it, by rough comparison with real circles and triangles drawn on paper or surveyed on land, the results of his system seemed true to nature. But, one felt, more and more precise experiments were needed to test whether Euclid had chosen the right assumptions to imitate nature exactly; whether, for example, the three angles of a triangle do make just 180 degrees.[20] Relativity-mechanics and astronomical thinking about the universe have raised serious questions about the most fitting choice of geometry. Mathematicians have long known that Euclid's version is only one of several devisable geometries which agree on a small scale but differ radically on a large scale in their physical and philosophical nature.

Special Relativity deals with cases where an observer is moving with *constant velocity* relative to apparatus or to another observer. Einstein then developed *General Relativity* to deal with measurement in systems that are *accelerating*.

What is General Relativity, and how does it affect our views of physics—and of geometry?

[20] It probably seems obvious to you that they do. This may be because you have swallowed Euclid's proof whole—authoritarian deduction. Or you may have assured yourself inductively by making a paper triangle, tearing off the corners and assembling them. Suppose, however, we lived on a huge globe, *without knowing it*. Small triangles, confined to the schoolroom would have a 180° sum. But a huge triangle would have a bigger sum. For example, one with a 90° apex at the N-pole would have right angles at its base on the equator.

Fig. 31-41.
(a) Tearing a paper triangle.   (b) Triangle on a sphere.

Einstein's Principle of Equivalence

Einstein was led to General Relativity by a single question: "Could an observer in a falling elevator or accelerating train really know he is accelerating?" Of course he would notice strange forces (as in the case of truck-and-track experiments to test $F = Ma$ in an accelerating railroad coach.° There strange forces act on the truck and make $F = Ma$ untrue). But could he decide by experiment between acceleration of his frame of reference and a new gravitational field? (If a carpenter builds a correctly tilted laboratory in the accelerating coach, the observer will again find $F = Ma$ holds, but he will find "*g*" different.)° Therefore, Einstein assumed that no local experiments—mechanical, electrical or optical—could decide: no experiments could tell an observer whether the forces he finds are due to his acceleration or to a local "gravitational" field. Then, Einstein said, *the laws of physics must take the same essential form for ALL observers*, even those who are accelerating. In other words, Einstein required all the laws of physics to be covariant for all transformations from one frame of reference (or laboratory) to another. That is the essential basis of General Relativity: all physical laws to keep the same form.

It was obvious long ago that for *mechanical behavior* a gravitational field and an accelerating frame of reference are equivalent. Einstein's great contribution was his assumption that they are *completely* equivalent, that even in optical and electrical experiments a gravitational field would have the same effect as an accelerated frame of reference. "This assertion supplied the long-sought-for link between gravitation and the rest of physics. . . ."[21]

Accelerating Local Observer ≡ "Gravitational Field"

The Principle of Equivalence influences our view of matter motion and geometry in several ways:

(1) *Local Physics for Accelerated Observers.* If the Principle of Equivalence is true, all the strange effects observed in an accelerating laboratory can be ascribed to an extra force-field. If the laboratory's acceleration is a meters/sec², we may treat the laboratory as at rest instead if we give every mass m kg an extra force $-ma$ newtons, presumably due to a force-field of strength $-a$ newtons/kg. Then, with this field included, the ordinary rules of mechanics should apply—or rather the Lorentz modification of Newtonian mechanics and Euclidean geometry, just as in Special Relativity.

° See Chapter 7, Problems 30 and 31.

[21] Sir Edmund Whittaker, in *From Euclid to Eddington* (Cambridge University Press, 1949): now in Dover paperback edition.

Examples:

(i) Experimenters in a railroad coach that is accelerating—or in a rocket that is being driven by its fuel—will find Newton's Laws of motion applying at low speeds, provided they add to all visible forces on each mass m the extra (backward) force, $-ma$, due to the equivalent force-field.[22] Objects moving through the laboratory at very high speeds would seem to have increased mass, etc., just as we always expect from Special Relativity.

(ii) An experimenter weighing himself on a spring scale in an elevator moving with downward acceleration a would obtain the scale reading that he would expect in a gravitational field of strength $(g - a)$. (See Ch. 7, Problem 10.)

(iii) In a freely falling box the force exerted by the equivalent force-field on a mass m would be mg upward. Since this would exactly balance the weight of the body, mg downward, everything would appear to be weightless. The same applies to experiments inside a rocket when its fuel has stopped driving it, or to experiments on any satellite pursuing an orbit around the Earth: the pull of the Earth's controlling gravity is not felt, because the whole laboratory is accelerating too.

(iv) In a rotating laboratory, adding an outward force-field of strength v^2/R would reduce the local mechanical behavior to that of a stationary lab.

(2) *Interpreting Gravity.* All (real) gravitational fields can be reinterpreted as local modifications of space-&-time by changing to appropriate accelerating axes so that the field disappears. This change gives us no help in mechanical calculations, but it leads to a new meaning for gravity, to be discussed in the next section.

(3) *"Removing Gravity."* If a gravitational field is really equivalent to an accelerating frame, we can remove it by giving our laboratory an appropriate acceleration. Common gravity, the pull of the Earth, pulls vertically down. It is equivalent to an accelera-

tion of our frame, g vertically up. If we then let our lab fall through our frame of reference with acceleration g vertically down, we observe no effects of gravity. Our lab has two accelerations, the "real" one of falling and the opposite one that replaces the gravitational field. The two just cancel and we have the equivalent of a *stationary lab* in *zero gravitational field.* That just means, "let the lab fall freely, and gravity is not felt in it." We do that physically when we travel in a space ship, or in a freely-falling elevator. Our accelerating framework removes all sign of the gravitational field of Earth or Sun[23] on a small local scale. Then we can leave a body to move with no forces and watch its path. We call its path in space-&-time a straight line and we expect to find simple mechanical laws obeyed. We have an inertial frame in our locality.

(4) *Artificial Gravity.* Conversely, by imposing a large real acceleration we can manufacture a strong force-field. If we trust the Principle of Equivalence we expect this force-field to treat matter in the same way as a very strong gravitational field. On this view, centrifuging increases available "g" many thousandfold.

(5) *Myth-and-Symbol Experiment.* To an observer with acceleration a every mass $m°$ seems to suffer an opposite force of size $m°a$, in addition to the pushes and pulls exerted on it by known agents. In a gravitational field of strength g every mass $m^†$ is pulled with a force $m^†g$. Here, we are using $m°$ for inertial mass, the m in $F = ma$, and $m^†$ for gravitational mass, the m in $F = GMm/d^2$. The Principle of Equivalence says that gravitational field of strength g can be replaced in effect by an opposite acceleration g of the observer.

$\therefore$ $m^†g$ must be the same as $m°g$ $\therefore$ $m^† \equiv m°$

The Principle of Equivalence requires gravitational mass and inertial mass to be the same; and the Myth-and-Symbol Experiment long ago told us that they are. As you will see in the discussion that follows, Einstein, in his development of General Relativity, gave a deeper meaning for this equality of the two kinds of mass.

General Relativity and Geometry

Over *small* regions of space-&-time, the Earth's gravity is practically uniform—and so is any other

[22] Over 200 years ago, the French philosopher and mathematician d'Alembert stated a general principle for solving problems that involve accelerated motion: *add* to all the known forces acting on an accelerating mass m an extra force $-ma$; then treat m as in equilibrium. By adding such "d'Alembert forces" to all the bodies of a complex system of masses in motion we can convert the *dynamical* problem of predicting forces or motion into a *statical* problem of forces in equilibrium. This is now common practice among professional physicists, but it is an artificial, sophisticated notion that is apt to be misleading; so we avoid it in elementary teaching. It is the basis of the "engineer's headache-cure" mentioned in Opinion III of centrifugal force, in Chapter 21.

[23] That is why the Sun's gravitational pull produces "no noticeable field" as we move with the Earth around its yearly orbit. (That phrase in the table of field values on p.116 was a quibble!) Only if inertial mass and gravitational mass failed to keep *exactly* the same proportion for different substances would any noticeable effect occur. Minute differences of such a kind are being looked for—if any are discovered, they will have a profound effect on our theory.

gravitational field. So we can "remove" gravity for local experiments by having our lab accelerate freely; and it will behave like an inertial frame with no gravitational field: an object left alone will stay at rest or move in a straight line; and with forces applied we shall find $F = ma$. However, on a grander scale, say all around the Earth or the Sun, we should have to use many different accelerations for our local labs to remove gravity. In fitting a straight line defined in one lab by Newton's Law I to its continuation in a neighboring lab, also accelerating freely, we should find we have to "bend" our straight line to make it fit. The demands of bending would get worse as we proceeded from lab to lab around the gravitating mass. How can we explain that? Instead of saying "we have found there is gravity here after all" we might say "Euclidean geometry does not quite fit the real world near the massive Earth or Sun." The second choice is taken in developing General Relativity. As in devising Special Relativity, Einstein looked for the simplest geometry to fit the new assumption that the laws of physics should *always* take the same form. He arrived at a General-Relativity geometry in which gravity disappears as a strange force reaching out from matter; instead, it appears as a distortion of space-&-time around matter.

"From time immemorial the physicist and the pure mathematician had worked on a certain agreement as to the shares which they were respectively to take in the study of nature. The mathematician was to come first and analyse the properties of space and time building up the primary sciences of geometry and kinematics (pure motion); then, when the stage had thus been prepared, the physicist was to come along with the dramatis personae—material bodies, magnets, electric charges, light and so forth—and the play was to begin. But in Einstein's revolutionary conception the characters created the stage as they walked about on it: geometry was no longer antecedent to physics but indissolubly fused with it into a single discipline. The properties of space in General Relativity depend on the material bodies and the energy that are present. . . ."[24]

Is this new geometry right and the old wrong? Let us return to our view of mathematics as the obedient servant. Could we not use *any* system of geometry to carry out our description of the physical world, stretching the world picture to fit the geometry, so to speak? Then our search would not be to find the *right* geometry but to choose the *simplest or most convenient* one which would describe the

world with least stretching.[25] If we do, we must realize that we *choose* our geometry but we *have* our universe; and if we ruthlessly make one fit the other by pushing and pulling and distorting, then we must take the consequences.

For example, if all the objects in our world consisted of some pieces of the elastic skin of an orange, the easiest geometrical model to fit them on would be a ball. But if we were brought up with an undying belief in plane geometry, we could press the peel down on a flat table and glue it to the surface, making it stretch where necessary to accommodate to the table. We might find the cells of the peel larger near the outer edge of our flattened piece, but we should announce that as a law of nature. We might find strange forces trying to make the middle of the patch bulge away from the table—again, a "law of nature." If we sought to simplify our view of nature, the peel's behavior would tempt us to use a spherical surface instead of a flat one, as our model of "surface-space." All this sounds fanciful, and it is; but just such a discussion on a three- or four-dimensional basis, instead of a two-dimensional one, has been used in General Relativity. The strange force of gravity may be a necessary result of trying to interpret nature with an unsuitable geometry—the system Euclid developed so beautifully. If we choose a different geometry, in which matter distorts the measurement system around it, then gravitation changes from a surprising set of forces to a mere matter of geometry. A cannon ball need no longer be regarded as being dragged by gravity in what the old geometry would call a "curve" in space. Instead, we may think of it as sailing serenely along what the new geometry considers a straight line in its space-&-time, as distorted by the neighboring Earth.

This would merely be a change of view (and as scientists we should hardly bother much about it), unless it could open our eyes to new knowledge or improve our comprehension of old knowledge. It can. On such a new geometrical view, the "curved" paths of freely moving bodies are inlaid in the new geometry of space-&-time and *all* projectiles, big and small, with given speed must follow the same path. Notice how the surprise of the Myth-and-Symbol fact disappears. The long-standing mystery of gravitational mass being equal to inertial mass is solved. Obviously a great property of nature, this equality was neglected for centuries until Einstein claimed it as a pattern property imposed on space-&-time by matter.

[24] Sir Edmund Whittaker, *From Euclid to Eddington*, *op.cit.*, p. 117.

[25] You can have your coffee served on any tray, but on some trays it wobbles less.

Even a light ray must follow a curve, just as much as a bullet moving at light speed. Near the Earth that curve would be imperceptible, but starlight streaming past the Sun should be deflected by an angle of about 0.0005 degrees, just measurable by modern instruments. Photographs taken during total eclipses show that stars very near the edge of the Sun seem shifted by about 0.0006°. On the traditional ("classical") view, the Sun has a gravitational field that appears to modify the straight-line law for light rays of the Euclidean geometrical scheme. On the General Relativity view, we replace the Sun's gravitational field by a crumpling of the local geometry from simple Euclidean form into a version where light seems to us to travel slower. Thus the light beam is curved slightly around as it passes the Sun—the reverse of the bending of light by hot air over a road, when it makes a mirage.

Finding this view of gravitation both simple and fruitful—when boiled down to simplest mathematical form—we would like to adopt it. In any ordinary laboratory experiments we find Euclid's geometry gives simple, accurate descriptions. But in astronomical cases with large gravitational fields we must either use a new geometry (in which the mesh of "straight lines" in space-&-time seems to us slightly crumpled) or else we must make some complicating changes in the laws of physics. As in Special Relativity, the modern fashion is to make the change in geometry. This enables us to polish up the laws of physics into simple forms which hold universally; and sometimes in doing that we can see the possibility of new knowledge.

In specifying gravitation on the new geometrical view, Einstein found that his simplest, most plausible form of law led to slightly different predictions from those produced by Newton's inverse-square law of gravitation. He did not "prove Newton's Law wrong" but offered a refining modification—though this involved a radical change in viewpoint. We must not think of either law as right because it is suggested by a great man or because it is enshrined in beautiful mathematics. We are offered it as a brilliant guess from a great mind unduly sensitive to the overtones of evidence from the real universe. We take it as a promising guess, even a likely one, but we then test it ruthlessly. The changes, from Newton's predictions to Einstein's, though fundamental in nature, are usually too small in effect to make any difference in laboratory experiments or even in most astronomical measurements. But there should be a noticeable effect in the rapid motion of the planet Mercury around its orbit. Newton pre-

Fig. 31-42. Motion of Planet Mercury

dicted a simple ellipse, with other planets producing perturbations which could be calculated and observed. General Relativity theory predicts an extra motion, a very slow slewing around of the long axis of the ellipse by 0.00119 degree per century. When Einstein predicted it, this tiny motion was already known, discovered long before by Leverrier. The measured value, 0.00117°/century was waiting to test the theory.

Accepting this view of gravity, astronomers can speculate on the geometry of all space and ask whether the universe is infinite or bounded by its own geometric curvature (as a sphere is). We may yet be able to make some test of this question.

There are still difficulties and doubts about General Relativity. Even as we use it confidently to deal with Mercury's motion, or the light from a massive star, we *may* have to anchor our calculations to *some* frame of reference, perhaps the remotest regions of space far from gravitating matter, or perhaps the center of gravity of our universe. So space as we treat it, *may* have some kind of absolute milestones. This doubt, this threat to a powerful theory, does not irritate the wise scientist: he keeps it in mind with hopes of an interesting future for his thoughts.

New Mathematics for Nuclear Physics

In atomic and nuclear physics, mathematics now takes a strong hand. Instead of sketching a model with sharp bullet-like electrons whirling round an equally sharp nucleus, we express our knowledge of atoms in mathematical forms for which no picture can be drawn. These forms use unorthodox rules of algebra, dreamed up for the purpose; and some show the usual mathematical trademark of waves. Yet, although they remain mathematical forms, they yield fruitful predictions, ranging from the strength of metal wires and chemical energies to the behavior of radioactive nuclei.

We now see mathematics, pure thought and argument, again offering to present physics in clearer forms which help our thinking; but now far from a servant, it is rather a Lord Chancellor standing behind the throne of ruling Science to advise on law. Or, we might describe mathematics as a master architect designing the building in which science can grow to its best.

Invariance is central to the theory of relativity as to all modern physics. The story told here introduces many of the important fundamental concepts of relativity theory.

8 Parable of the Surveyors

Edwin F. Taylor and John Archibald Wheeler

Excerpt from their book, *Spacetime Physics*, W. H. Freeman and Company Copyright © 1966.

Once upon a time there was a Daytime surveyor who measured off the king's lands. He took his directions of north and east from a magnetic compass needle. Eastward directions from the center of the town square he measured in meters (x in meters). Northward directions were sacred and were measured in a different unit, in miles (y in miles). His records were complete and accurate and were often consulted by the Daytimers.

Daytime surveyor uses magnetic north

Nighttimers used the services of another surveyor. His north and east directions were based on the North Star. He too measured distances eastward from the center of the town square in meters (x' in meters) and sacred distances north in miles (y' in miles). His records were complete and accurate. Every corner of a plot appeared in his book with its two coordinates, x' and y'.

Nighttime surveyor uses North Star north

One fall a student of surveying turned up with novel openmindedness. Contrary to all previous tradition he attended both of the rival schools operated by the two leaders of surveying. At the day school he learned from one expert his method of recording the location of the gates of the town and the corners of plots of land. At night school he learned the other method. As the days and nights passed the student puzzled more and more in an attempt to find some harmonious relationship between the rival ways of recording location. He carefully compared the records of the two surveyors on the locations of the town gates relative to the center of the town square:

Table 1. Two different sets of records for the same points.

Place	Daytime surveyor's axes oriented to magnetic north (x in meters; y in miles)		Nighttime surveyor's axes oriented to the North Star (x' in meters; y' in miles)	
Town square	0	0	0	0
Gate A	x_A	y_A	x'_A	y'_A
Gate B	x_B	y_B	x'_B	y'_B
Other gates	...	...	...	...

In defiance of tradition, the student took the daring and heretical step to convert northward measurements, previously expressed always in miles, into meters by multiplication with a constant conversion factor, k. He then discovered that the quantity $[(x_A)^2 + (ky_A)^2]^{1/2}$ based on Daytime measurements of the position of gate A had exactly the same numerical value as the quantity

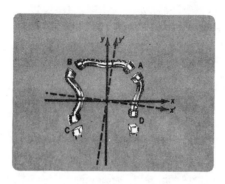

Fig. 1. The town and its gates, showing coordinate axes used by two different surveyors.

$[(x_A')^2 + (ky_A')^2]^{1/2}$ computed from the readings of the Nighttime surveyor for gate A. He tried the same comparison on the readings computed from the recorded positions of gate B, and found agreement here too. The student's excitement grew as he checked his scheme of comparison for all the other town gates and found everywhere agreement. He decided to give his discovery a name. He called the quantity

Discovery: invariance
of distance

(1)
$$[(x)^2 + (ky)^2]^{1/2}$$

the *distance* of the point (x, y) from the center of town. He said that he had discovered the *principle of the invariance of distance;* that one gets exactly the same distances from the Daytime coordinates as from the Nighttime coordinates, despite the fact that the two sets of surveyors' numbers are quite different.

This story illustrates the naive state of physics before the discovery of *special relativity* by Einstein of Bern, Lorentz of Leiden, and Poincaré of Paris. How naive?

1. Surveyors in this mythical kingdom measured northward distances in a sacred unit, the mile, different from the unit used in measuring eastward distances. Similarly, people studying physics measured time in a sacred unit, the second, different from the unit used in measuring space. No one thought of using the same unit for both, or of what one could learn by squaring and combining space and time coordinates when both were measured in meters. The conversion factor between seconds and meters, namely the speed of light, $c = 2.997925 \times 10^8$ meters per second, was regarded as a sacred number. It was not recognized as a mere conversion factor like the factor of conversion between miles and meters—a factor that arose out of historical accidents alone, with no deeper physical significance.

2. In the parable the northbound coordinates, y and y', as recorded by the two surveyors did not differ very much because the two directions of north were separated only by the small angle of 10 degrees. At first our mythical student thought the small differences between y and y' were due to surveying error alone. Analogously, people have thought of the time between the explosion of two firecrackers as the same, by whomever observed. Only in 1905 did we learn that the time difference between the second event and the first, or "reference event," really has dif-

ferent values, t and t', for observers in different states of motion. Think of one observer standing quietly in the laboratory. The other observer zooms by in a high-speed rocket. The rocket comes in through the front entry, goes down the middle of the long corridor and out the back door. The first firecracker goes off in the corridor ("reference event") then the other ("event A"). Both observers agree that the reference event establishes the zero of time and the origin for distance measurements. The second explosion occurs, for example, 5 seconds later than the first, as measured by laboratory clocks, and 12 meters further down the corridor. Then its time coordinate is $t_A = 5$ seconds and its position coordinate is $x_A = 12$ meters. Other explosions and events also take place down the length of the corridor. The readings of the two observers can be arranged as in Table 2.

One observer uses laboratory frame

Another observer uses rocket frame

Table 2. Space and time coordinates of the same events as seen by two observers in relative motion. For simplicity the y and z coordinates are zero, and the rocket is moving in the x direction.

Event	Coordinates as measured by observer who is	
	standing (x in meters; t in seconds)	moving by in rocket (x' in meters; t' in seconds)
Reference event	0 0	0 0
Event A	x_A t_A	x'_A t'_A
Event B	x_B t_B	x'_B t'_B
Other events	... ...	... ...

3. The mythical student's discovery of the concept of distance is matched by the Einstein-Poincaré discovery in 1905 of the idea of *interval*. The interval as calculated from the one observer's measurements

Discovery: invariance of interval

$$(2) \qquad \text{interval} = [(ct_A)^2 - (x_A)^2]^{1/2}$$

agrees with the interval as calculated from the other observer's measurements

$$(3) \qquad \text{interval} = [(ct_A')^2 - (x_A')^2]^{1/2}$$

even though the *separate coordinates* employed in the two calculations *do not* agree. The two observers will find different space and time coordinates for events A, B, C, ... relative to the same reference event, but when they calculate the Einstein *intervals* between these events, their results will agree. *The invariance of the interval*—its independence from the choice of the reference frame—forces one to recognize that time cannot be separated from space. Space and time are part of the single entity, *spacetime*. The geometry of spacetime is truly four-dimensional. In one way of speaking, the "direction of the time axis" depends upon the state of motion of the observer, just as the directions of the y axes employed by the surveyors depend upon their different standards of "north."

The rest of this chapter is an elaboration of the analogy between surveying in space and relating events to one another in spacetime. Table 3 is a preview of this elaboration. To recognize the unity of space and time one follows the procedure that makes a landscape take on meaning—he looks at it from several angles. This is the reason for comparing space and time coordinates of an event in two *different* reference frames in relative motion.

Table 3. Preview: Elaboration of the parable of the surveyors.

Parable of the surveyors: *geometry of space*	*Analogy to physics:* *geometry of spacetime*
The task of the surveyor is to locate the position of a point (gate A) using one of two coordinate systems that are rotated relative to one another.	The task of the physicist is to locate the position and time of an event (firecracker explosion A) using one of two reference frames which are in motion relative to one another.
The two coordinate systems: oriented to magnetic north and to North-Star north.	The two reference frames: the laboratory frame and the rocket frame.
For convenience all surveyors agree to make position measurements with respect to a common origin (the center of the town square).	For convenience all physicists agree to make position and time measurements with respect to a common reference event (explosion of the reference firecracker).
The analysis of the surveyors' results is simplified if x and y coordinates of a point are both measured in the same units, in meters.	The analysis of the physicists' results is simplified if the x and t coordinates of an event are both measured in the same units, in meters.
The *separate* coordinates x_A and y_A of gate A *do not* have the same values respectively in two coordinate systems that are rotated relative to one another.	The *separate* coordinates x_A and t_A of event A *do not* have the same values respectively in two reference frames that are in uniform motion relative to one another.
Invariance of distance. The *distance* $(x_A^2 + y_A^2)^{1/2}$ between gate A and the town square has the same value when calculated using measurements made with respect to either of two rotated coordinate systems (x_A and y_A both measured in meters).	*Invariance of the interval.* The *interval* $(t_A^2 - x_A^2)^{1/2}$ between event A and the reference event has the same value when calculated using measurements made with respect to either of two reference frames in relative motion (x_A and t_A both measured in meters).
Euclidean transformation. Using *Euclidean* geometry, the surveyor can solve the following problem: *Given* the Nighttime coordinates x_A' and y_A' of gate A and the relative inclination of respective coordinate axes, *find* the Daytime coordinates x_A and y_A of the same gate.	*Lorentz transformation.* Using *Lorentz* geometry, the physicist can solve the following problem: *Given* the rocket coordinates x_A' and t_A' of event A and the relative velocity between rocket and laboratory frames, *find* the laboratory coordinates x_A and t_A of the same event.

Measure time in meters The parable of the surveyors cautions us to use the same unit to measure both distance and time. So use meters for both. Time can be measured in meters. When a mirror is mounted at each end of a stick one-half meter long, a flash of light may be bounced back and forth between these two mirrors. Such a device is a *clock*. This clock may be said to "tick" each time the light flash arrives back at the first mirror. Between ticks the light flash has traveled a round-trip distance of 1 meter. Therefore the unit of time between ticks of this clock is called *1 meter of light-travel time* or more simply *1 meter of time*. (Show that 1 second is approximately equal to 3×10^8 meters of light-travel time.)

One purpose of the physicist is to sort out simple relations between events. To do this here he might as well choose a particular reference frame with respect to which the laws of physics have a simple form. Now, the force of gravity acts on everything near the earth. Its presence complicates the laws of motion as we know them from common experience. In order to eliminate this and other complications, we will, in the next section, focus attention on a freely falling reference frame near the earth. In this reference frame no gravitational forces will be felt. Such a gravitation-free reference frame will be called an *inertial reference frame*. Special relativity deals with the classical laws of physics expressed with respect to an inertial reference frame.

Simplify: Pick freely falling laboratory

The principles of special relativity are remarkably simple. They are very much simpler than the axioms of Euclid or the principles of operating an automobile. Yet both Euclid and the automobile have been mastered—perhaps with insufficient surprise—by generations of ordinary people. Some of the best minds of the twentieth century struggled with the concepts of relativity, not because nature is obscure, but simply because man finds it difficult to outgrow established ways of looking at nature. For us the battle has already been won. The concepts of relativity can now be expressed simply enough to make it easy to think correctly—thus "making the bad difficult and the good easy."† The problem of understanding relativity is no longer one of *learning* but one of *intuition*—a practiced way of seeing. With this way of seeing, a remarkable number of otherwise incomprehensible experimental results are seen to be perfectly natural.‡

---

†Einstein, in a similar connection, in a letter to the architect Le Corbusier.

‡For a comprehensive set of references to introductory literature concerning the special theory of relativity, together with several reprints of articles, see *Special Relativity Theory*, Selected Reprints, published for the American Association of Physics Teachers by the American Institute of Physics, 335 East 45th Street, New York 17, New York, 1963.

The father of the general theory of relativity and his associate illustrate one of the central ideas of the theory through the commonplace experience of riding in an elevator. (Note: The initials C. S. mean "coordinate system" in this selection.)

---

9 Outside and Inside the Elevator

Albert Einstein and Leopold Infeld

Excerpt from their book, *The Evolution of Physics,* 1938 and 1961.

The law of inertia marks the first great advance in physics; in fact, its real beginning. It was gained by the contemplation of an idealized experiment, a body moving forever with no friction nor any other external forces acting. From this example and later from many others, we recognized the importance of the idealized experiment created by thought. Here again, idealized experiments will be discussed. Although these may sound very fantastic they will, nevertheless, help us to understand as much about relativity as is possible by our simple methods.

We had previously the idealized experiments with a uniformly moving room. Here, for a change, we shall have a falling elevator.

Imagine a great elevator at the top of a skyscraper much higher than any real one. Suddenly the cable supporting the elevator breaks, and the elevator falls freely toward the ground. Observers in the elevator are performing experiments during the fall. In describing them, we need not bother about air resistance or friction, for we may disregard their existence under our idealized conditions. One of the observers takes a handkerchief and a watch from his pocket and drops them. What happens to these two bodies? For the outside observer, who is looking through the window of the elevator, both handkerchief and watch fall toward the ground in exactly the same way, with the same acceleration. We remember that the acceleration of a falling body is quite independent of its mass and that it was this fact which revealed the equality of gravitational and inertial mass (p. 37). We also remember that the equality of the two masses, gravitational and inertial, was quite accidental from the point of view of classical mechanics and played no role in its structure. Here, however, this equality reflected in the equal acceleration of all falling bodies is essential and forms the basis of our whole argument.

Let us return to our falling handkerchief and watch; for the outside observer they are both falling with the same acceleration. But so is the elevator, with its walls, ceiling, and floor. Therefore: the distance between the two bodies and the floor will not change. For the inside observer the two bodies remain exactly where they were when he let them go. The inside observer may ignore the gravitational field, since its source lies outside his CS. He finds that no forces inside the elevator act upon the two bodies, and so they are at rest, just as if they were in an inertial CS. Strange things happen in the elevator! If the observer pushes a body in any direction, up or down for instance, it always moves uniformly so long as it does not collide with the ceiling or the floor of the elevator. Briefly speaking, the laws of classical mechanics are valid for the observer inside the elevator. All bodies behave in the way expected by the law of inertia. Our new CS rigidly connected with the freely falling elevator differs from the inertial CS in only one respect. In an inertial CS, a moving body on which no forces are acting will move uniformly forever. The inertial CS as represented in classical physics is neither limited in space nor time. The case of the observer in our elevator is, however, different. The inertial character of his CS is limited in space and time. Sooner or later the uniformly moving body will collide with the wall of the elevator, destroying the uniform motion. Sooner or later the whole elevator will collide with the earth destroying the observers and their experiments. The CS is only a "pocket edition" of a real inertial CS.

This local character of the CS is quite essential. If our imaginary elevator were to reach from the North Pole to the Equator, with the handkerchief placed over the North Pole and the watch over the Equator, then, for the outside observer, the two bodies would not have the same acceleration; they would not be at rest relative to each other. Our whole argument would fail! The dimensions of the elevator must be limited so that the equality of acceleration of all bodies relative to the outside observer may be assumed.

With this restriction, the CS takes on an inertial character for the inside observer. We can at least indicate a CS in which all the physical laws are valid, even though it is limited in time and space. If we imagine another CS, another elevator moving uniformly, relative to the one falling freely, then both these CS will be locally inertial. All laws are exactly the same in both. The transition from one to the other is given by the Lorentz transformation.

Let us see in what way both the observers, outside and inside, describe what takes place in the elevator.

The outside observer notices the motion of the elevator and of all bodies in the elevator, and finds them in agreement with Newton's gravitational law. For him, the motion is not uniform, but accelerated, because of the action of the gravitational field of the earth.

However, a generation of physicists born and brought up in the elevator would reason quite differently. They would believe themselves in possession of an inertial system and would refer all laws of nature to their elevator, stating with justification that the laws take on a specially simple form in their CS. It would be natural for them to assume their elevator at rest and their CS the inertial one.

It is impossible to settle the differences between the outside and the inside observers. Each of them could claim the right to refer all events to his CS. Both descriptions of events could be made equally consistent.

We see from this example that a consistent description of physical phenomena in two different CS is possible, even if they are not moving uniformly, relative to each other. But for such a description we must take into account gravitation, building so to speak, the "bridge" which effects a transition from one CS to the other. The gravitational field exists for the outside observer; it does not for the inside observer. Accelerated motion of the elevator in the gravitational field exists for the outside observer, rest and absence of the gravitational field for the inside observer. But the "bridge," the gravitational field, making the description in both CS possible, rests on one very important pillar: the equivalence of gravitational and inertial mass. Without this clew, unnoticed in classical mechanics, our present argument would fail completely.

Now for a somewhat different idealized experiment. There is, let us assume, an inertial CS, in which the law of inertia is valid. We have already described what happens in an elevator resting in such an inertial CS. But we now change our picture. Someone outside has fastened a rope to the elevator and is pulling, with a constant force, in the direction indicated in our drawing. It is immaterial how this is done. Since the laws of mechanics are valid in this CS, the whole elevator moves with a constant acceleration in the direction of the motion. Again we shall listen to the explanation of

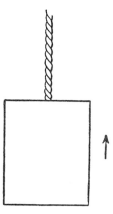

phenomena going on in the elevator and given by both the outside and inside observers.

The outside observer: My CS is an inertial one. The elevator moves with constant acceleration, because a constant force is acting. The observers inside are in absolute motion, for them the laws of mechanics are invalid. They do not find that bodies, on which no forces are acting, are at rest. If a body is left free, it soon collides with the floor of the elevator, since the floor moves upward toward the body. This happens exactly in the same way for a watch and for a handkerchief. It seems very strange to me that the observer inside the elevator must always be on the "floor" because as soon as he jumps, the floor will reach him again.

The inside observer: I do not see any reason for believing that my elevator is in absolute motion. I agree that my CS, rigidly connected with my elevator, is not really inertial, but I do not believe that it has anything to do with absolute motion. My watch, my handkerchief, and all bodies are falling because the whole elevator is in a gravitational field. I notice exactly the same kinds of motion as the man on the earth. He explains them very simply by the action of a gravitational field. The same holds good for me.

These two descriptions, one by the outside, the other by the inside, observer, are quite consistent, and there is no possibility of deciding which of them is right. We may assume either one of them for the description of phenomena in the elevator: either nonuniform motion and absence of a gravitational field with the outside observer, or rest and the presence of a gravitational field with the inside observer.

The outside observer may assume that the elevator is in "absolute" nonuniform motion. But a motion which is wiped out by the assumption of an acting gravitational field cannot be regarded as absolute motion.

There is, possibly, a way out of the ambiguity of two such different descriptions, and a decision in favor of one against the other could perhaps be made. Imagine that a light ray enters the elevator horizontally through a side window and reaches the opposite wall after a very short time. Again let us see how the path of the light would be predicted by the two observers.

The outside observer, believing in accelerated motion of the elevator, would argue: The light ray enters the window and moves horizontally, along a straight line and with a constant velocity, toward the opposite wall. But the elevator moves upward and during the time in which the light travels toward the wall, the elevator changes its position. Therefore, the ray will meet a point not exactly opposite its point of entrance, but a little below. The difference will be very slight, but it exists nevertheless, and the light ray travels, relative to the elevator, not along a straight, but along a

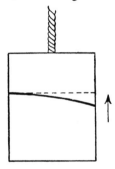

slightly curved line. The difference is due to the distance covered by the elevator during the time the ray is crossing the interior.

The inside observer, who believes in the gravitational field acting on all objects in his elevator, would say: there is no accelerated motion of the elevator, but only the action of the gravitational field. A beam of light is weightless and, therefore, will not be affected by the gravitational field. If sent in a horizontal direction, it will meet the wall at a point exactly opposite to that at which it entered.

It seems from this discussion that there is a possibility of deciding between these two opposite points of view as the phenomenon would be different for the two observers. If there is nothing illogical in either of the explanations just quoted, then our whole previous argument is destroyed, and we cannot describe all phenomena in two consistent ways, with and without a gravitational field.

But there is, fortunately, a grave fault in the reasoning of the inside observer, which saves our previous conclusion. He said: "A beam of light is weightless and, therefore, it will not be affected by the gravitational field." This cannot be right! A beam of light carries energy and energy has mass. But every inertial mass is attracted by the gravitational field as inertial and gravitational masses are equivalent. A beam of light will bend in a gravitational field exactly as a body would if thrown horizontally with a velocity equal to that of light. If the inside observer had reasoned correctly and had taken into account the bending of light rays in a gravitational field, then his results would have been exactly the same as those of an outside observer.

The gravitational field of the earth is, of course, too weak for the bending of light rays in it to be proved directly, by experiment. But the famous experiments performed during the solar eclipses show, conclusively though indirectly, the influence of a gravitational field on the path of a light ray.

It follows from these examples that there is a well-founded hope of formulating a relativistic physics. But for this we must first tackle the problem of gravitation.

We saw from the example of the elevator the consistency of the two descriptions. Nonuniform motion may, or may not, be assumed. We can eliminate "absolute" motion from our examples by a gravitational field. But then there is nothing absolute in the nonuniform motion. The gravitational field is able to wipe it out completely.

The ghosts of absolute motion and inertial CS can be expelled from physics and a new relativistic physics built. Our idealized experiments show how the problem of the general relativity theory is closely connected with that of gravitation and why the equivalence of gravitational and inertial mass is so essential for this connection. It is clear that the solution of the gravitational problem in the general theory of relativity must differ from the Newtonian one. The laws of gravitation must, just as all laws of nature, be formulated for all possible CS, whereas the laws of classical mechanics, as formulated by Newton, are valid only in inertial CS.

What lessons can be learned from the life and philosophy of a "high-school drop-out" named Albert Einstein? Martin Klein, a physicist and historian of science, discusses the possibility of inadequacies in our present education policies.

10   Einstein and some Civilized Discontents

Martin Klein

Article from the journal, *Physics Today*, January 1965.

The French novelist Stendhal began his most brilliant novel with this sentence: "On May 15, 1796, General Bonaparte made his entrance into Milan at the head of that youthful army which had just crossed the bridge of Lodi, and taught the world that after so many centuries Caesar and Alexander had a successor." In its military context, the quotation is irrelevant here, but it can be paraphrased a bit: almost exactly a century later Milan saw the arrival of another young foreigner who would soon teach the world that after so many centuries Galileo and Newton had a successor. It would, however, have taken superhuman insight to recognize the future intellectual conqueror in the boy of fifteen who had just crossed the Alps from Munich. For this boy, Albert Einstein, whose name was to become a symbol for profound scientific insight, had left Munich as what we would now call a high-school dropout.

He had been a slow child; he learned to speak at a much later age than the average, and he had shown no special ability in elementary school —except perhaps a talent for day-dreaming. The education offered at his secondary school in Munich, one of the highly praised classical gymnasia, did not appeal to him. The rigid, mechanical methods of the school appealed to him even less. He had already begun to develop his own intellectual pursuits, but the stimulus for them had not come from school. The mystery hidden in the compass given to him when he was five, the clarity and beauty of Euclidean geometry, discovered by devouring an old geometry text at the age of twelve—it was these things that set him on his own road of independent study and thought. The drill at school merely served to keep him from his own interests. When his father, a small and unsuccessful manufacturer, moved his business and his family from Munich to Milan, Albert Einstein was left behind to finish his schooling and acquire the diploma he would need to insure his future. After some months, however, Einstein was fed up with school, and resolved to leave. His leaving was assisted by the way in which his teachers reacted to his attitude toward school. "You will never amount to anything, Einstein," one of them said, and another actually suggested that Einstein leave school because his very presence in the classroom destroyed the respect of the students. This suggestion was gratefully accepted by Einstein, since it fit so well with his own decisions, and he set off to join his family in Milan. The next months were spent gloriously loafing, and hiking around northern Italy, enjoying the many contrasts with his homeland. With no diploma, and no prospects, he seemed a very model dropout.

It is sobering to think that no teacher had sensed his potentialities. Perhaps it suggests why I have chosen this subject in talking to this gathering of physics teachers seriously devoted to improving education in physics, and devoted in particular to a program aimed at the gifted student of our science—at his early detection and proper treatment. For what I really want to do is to highlight some aspects of Einstein's career and thought that stand in sharp contrast to a number of our accepted ideas on education and on the scientific career. The first matter we must reckon with is Einstein's own education and the way it affected him; but let me carry the story a little further before raising some questions.

Einstein had dropped out of school, but he had not lost his love for science. Since his family's resources, or lack of them, would make it necessary for him to become self-supporting, he decided to go on with his scientific studies in an official way. He, therefore, presented himself for admission at the renowned Swiss Federal Institute of Technology in Zürich. Since he had no high-school diploma he was given an entrance examination—and he failed. He had to attend a Swiss high school for a year in order to make up his deficiencies in almost everything except mathematics and physics, the subjects of his own private study. And then, when he was finally admitted to the Polytechnic Institute, did he settle down and assume what we would consider to be his rightful place at the head of the class? Not at all. Despite the fact that the courses were now almost all in mathematics and physics, Einstein cut most of the lectures. He did enjoy working in the laboratory, but he spent most of his time in his room studying the original works of the masters of nineteenth-century physics, and pondering what they set forth.

The lectures on advanced mathematics did not hold him, because in those days he saw no need or use for higher mathematics as a tool for grasping the structure of nature. Besides, mathematics appeared to be split into so many branches, each of which could absorb all one's time and energy, that he feared he could never have the insight to decide on one of them, the fundamental one. He would then be in the position of Buridan's ass, who died of hunger because he could not decide which bundle of hay he should eat.

Physics presented no such problems to Einstein, even then. As he wrote many years later: "True enough, physics was also divided into separate fields, each of which could devour a short working life without having satisfied the hunger for deeper knowledge. . . . But in physics I soon learned to scent out the paths that led to the depths, and to disregard everything else, all the many things that clutter up the mind, and divert it from the essential. The hitch in this was, of course, the fact that one had to cram all this stuff into one's mind for the examination, whether one liked it or not."

That was indeed the rub. Einstein had reconciled himself to being only an average scholar at the Polytechnic. He knew that he did not have and could not, or perhaps would not, acquire the traits of the outstanding student: the easy facility in comprehension, the willingness to concentrate one's energies on all the required subjects, and the orderliness to take good notes and work them over properly. Fortunately, however, the Swiss system required only two examinations. Even more fortunately Einstein had a close friend, Marcel Grossmann, who possessed just the qualities that Einstein lacked, and who generously shared his excellent systematic notes with his non-conforming comrade. So Einstein was able to follow his own line of study, and still succeed in the exams by doing some appropriate cramming from Grossmann's notes. This success left more

photo by Lotte Jacobi

than a bad taste in his mouth. As he put it, "It had such a deterring effect upon me that, after I had passed the final examination, I found the consideration of any scientific problems distasteful to me for an entire year." And he went on to say, "It is little short of a miracle that modern methods of instruction have not already completely strangled the holy curiosity of inquiry, because what this delicate little plant needs most, apart from initial stimulation, is freedom; without that it is surely destroyed . . . I believe that one could even deprive a healthy beast of prey of its voraciousness, if one could force it with a whip to eat continuously whether it were hungry or not. . . ."

This is strong language. Should we take it personally? Could it be meant for us, for the teachers responsible for an educational system of achievement tests, preliminary college boards, college boards, national scholarships, grade point averages, graduate record exams, PhD qualifying exams—a system that starts earlier and earlier and ends later and later in our students' careers? Could this system be dulling the appetites of our young intellectual tigers? Is it possible that our students need more time to day-dream rather than more hours in the school day? That the relentless pressure of our educational system makes everything only a step toward something else and nothing an end in itself and an object of pleasure and contemplation?

For almost two years after his graduation from the Polytechnic in 1900 Einstein seemed to be headed for no more success than his earlier history as a dropout might have suggested. He applied for an assistantship, but it went to someone else. During this period he managed to subsist on the odd jobs of the learned world: he substituted for a Swiss high-school teacher who was doing his two months of military service, he helped the professor of astronomy with some calculations, he tutored at a boys' school. Finally, in the spring of 1902, Einstein's good friend Marcel Grossmann, "the irreproachable student", came to his rescue. Grossmann's father recommended Einstein to the director of the Swiss Patent Office at Berne, and after a searching examination he was appointed to a position as patent examiner. He held this position for over seven years and often referred to it in later years as "a kind of salvation". It freed him from financial worries; he found the work rather interesting; and sometimes it served as a stimulus to his scientific imagination. And besides, it occupied only eight hours of the day, so that there was plenty of time left free for pondering the riddles of the universe.

In his spare time during those seven years at Berne, the young patent examiner wrought a series of scientific miracles: no weaker word is adequate. He did nothing less than to lay out the main lines along which twentieth-century theoretical physics has developed. A very brief list will have to suffice. He began by working out the subject of statistical mechanics quite independently and without knowing of the work of J. Willard Gibbs. He also took this subject seriously in a way that neither Gibbs nor Boltzmann had ever done, since he used it to give the theoretical basis for a final proof of the atomic nature of matter. His reflections on the problems of the Maxwell-Lorentz electrodynamics led him to create the special theory of relativity. Before he left Berne he had formulated the principle of equivalence and was struggling with the prob-

lems of gravitation which he later solved with the general theory of relativity. And, as if these were not enough, Einstein introduced another new idea into physics, one that even he described as "very revolutionary", the idea that light consists of particles of energy. Following a line of reasoning related to but quite distinct from Planck's, Einstein not only introduced the light quantum hypothesis, but proceeded almost at once to explore its implications for phenomena as diverse as photochemistry and the temperature dependence of the specific heat of solids.

What is more, Einstein did all this completely on his own, with no academic connections whatsoever, and with essentially no contact with the elders of his profession. Years later he remarked to Leopold Infeld that until he was almost thirty he had never seen a real theoretical physicist. To which, of course, we should add the phrase (as Infeld almost did aloud, and as Einstein would never have done), "except in the mirror!"

I suppose that some of us might be tempted to wonder what Einstein might have done during those seven years, if he had been able to work "under really favorable conditions", full time, at a major university, instead of being restricted to spare-time activity while earning his living as a minor civil servant. We should resist the temptation: our speculations would be not only fruitless, but completely unfounded. For not only did Einstein not regret his lack of an academic post in these years, he actually considered it a real advantage. "For an academic career puts a young man into a kind of embarrassing position," he wrote shortly before his death, "by requiring him to produce scientific publications in impressive quantity—a seduction into superficiality which only strong characters are able to withstand. Most practical occupations, however, are of such a nature that a man of normal ability is able to accomplish what is expected of him. His day-to-day existence does not depend on any special illuminations. If he has deeper scientific interests he may plunge into his favorite problems in addition to doing his required work. He need not be oppressed by the fear that his efforts may lead to no results. I owed it to Marcel Grossmann that I was in such a fortunate position."

These were no casual remarks: forty years earlier Einstein had told Max Born not to worry about placing a gifted student in an academic position. Let him be a cobbler or a locksmith; if he really has a love for science in his blood and if he's really worth anything, he will make his own way. (Of course, Einstein then gave what

help he could in placing the young man.) Einstein was even a little reluctant about accepting a research professorship at Berlin, partly because Prussian rigidity and academic bourgeois life were not to his Bohemian taste. But he was also reluctant because he knew very well that such a research professor was expected to be a sort of prize hen, and he did not want to guarantee that he would lay any more golden eggs.

It will not have escaped your notice that Einstein's views on research and the nature of a scientific career differ sharply from those which are standard in the scientific community. No doubt some of this difference in attitude reflects only Einstein's uniquely solitary nature. It is hard to imagine anyone else seriously suggesting as he did, that a position as lighthouse keeper might be suitable for a scientist. Most scientists feel the need to test their ideas on their peers, and often to form these ideas in the give and take of discussions, as among their most urgent needs. One may still question the necessity of as many meetings as we find announced in *Physics Today*, and one may question even more insistently the necessity of reporting on each and publishing its proceedings as if it were the first Solvay Congress itself.

More serious is the attitude that every young man of scientific ability can claim the right to a position as prize hen. "Doing research" has become the hallowed activity in the academic world, and, as Jacques Barzun has put it, "To suggest that practice, or teaching, or reflection might be preferred is blasphemy." I do not need to re-emphasize Einstein's remark on the publish-or-perish policy that corrupts one aspect of academic life. I would, however, like to remark parenthetically that I am always astonished when college administrators and department heads claim that it is terribly difficult, virtually impossible, to judge the quality of a man's teaching, but never doubt their ability to evaluate the results of his research. This is astonishing because any honest undergraduate can give a rather canny and usually accurate appraisal of the teaching he is subjected to, but judging the quality of a scientific paper generally increases in difficulty with the originality of the work reported. Einstein's hypothesis of light quanta, for example, was considered as wildly off the mark, as at best a pardonable excess in an otherwise sound thinker, even by Planck a decade after it was introduced.

The way in which physics is taught is deeply influenced by our views of how and why physics is done. Einstein, who was skeptical about the professionalization of research, was unswerving in his pursuit of fundamental understanding; he was a natural philosopher in the fullest sense of that old term, and he had no great respect for those who treated science as a game to be played for one's personal satisfaction, or those who solved problems to demonstrate and maintain their intellectual virtuosity. If physics is viewed in Einstein's way, it follows that it should be taught as a drama of ideas and not as a battery of techniques. It follows too that there should be an emphasis on the evolution of ideas, on the history of our attempts to understand the physical world, so that our students acquire some perspective and realize that, in Einstein's words, "the present position of science can have no lasting significance." Do we keep this liberal view of our science, or is it lost in what we call necessary preparation for graduate work and research?

One last theme that cannot be ignored when we speak of Einstein is that of the scientist as citizen. Einstein's active and courageous role in public affairs is widely known, and it absorbed a substantial fraction of his efforts for forty years. He stepped onto the public stage early and in characteristic style. In October 1914, two months after the outbreak of the First World War, a document was issued in Berlin bearing the grandiose title, Manifesto to the Civilized World; it carried the signatures of almost a hundred of Germany's most prominent scientists, artists, men of letters, clergymen, etc. This manifesto proclaimed its signers' full support of Germany's war effort, denounced the opponents of the fatherland, and defiantly asserted that German militarism and German culture formed an inseparable unity.

Not all German intellectuals approved this chauvinistic document, but among the very few who were willing to sign a sharply worded answer, calling for an end to war and an international organization, was Albert Einstein. The highly unpopular stand that he took in 1914 expressed a deeply felt conviction, one on which he acted throughout his life, regardless of the consequences to himself. During the succeeding decades Einstein devoted a great deal of his energy to the causes in which he believed, lending his name to many organizations which he felt could further these causes. Contrary to the view held in some circles, however, Einstein carefully considered each signature that he inscribed on a petition, each political use that he made of the name that had become renowned for scientific reasons, and often refused his support to organizations that attempted to solicit it.

His public statements became even more frequent and more outspoken in the years after the Second World War, as he put all his weight behind the effort to achieve a world government and to abolish war once and for all. Einstein was among those who have been trying to impress upon the world the very real likelihood that another war would destroy civilization and perhaps humanity as well. He was not overly optimistic

about his efforts, but they had to be made. He also felt that he had to speak out, loudly and clearly, during the McCarthy era, urging intellectuals to adopt the method of civil disobedience as practiced earlier by Gandhi (and later by Martin Luther King). As he wrote in an open letter, "Every intellectual who is called before one of the committees ought to refuse to testify; i.e., he must be prepared for jail and economic ruin, in short, for the sacrifice of his personal welfare in the interest of the cultural welfare of his country." If such a program were not adopted then, wrote Einstein, "the intellectuals of this country deserve nothing better than the slavery which is intended for them."

It is quite evident that Einstein approached political and social questions as a man who considered himself outside the Establishment. He had a very strong sense of responsibility to his conscience, but he did not feel obliged to accept all the restrictions that society expects of a "responsible spokesman". This approach is neither possible nor appropriate for today's leading scientists who are constantly serving as scientific statesmen—as advisers to the AEC, or the Department of Defense, or major corporations, or even the President. Such men are in no position to adopt Einstein's critical stance, even if they wanted to. At this time, when science requires and receives such large-scale support, it seems that we have all given more hostages to fortune than we may realize.

One of Einstein's last public statements was made in answer to a request that he comment on the situation of scientists in America. He wrote: "Instead of trying to analyze the problem I should like to express my feeling in a short remark. If I were a young man again and had to decide how to make a living, I would not try to become a scientist or scholar or teacher. I would rather choose to be a plumber or a peddler, in the hope of finding that modest degree of independence still available under present circumstances."

We may wonder how literally he meant this to be taken, but we cannot help feeling the force of the affront to our entire institutionalized life of the intellect.

As we pride ourselves on the success of physics and physicists in today's world, let us not forget that it was just that success and the way in which it was achieved that was repudiated by Einstein. And let us not forget to ask why: it may tell us something worth knowing about ourselves and our society.

photo by Alfred Eisenstaedt

We visit, in this brief passage, an elementary science class hearing for the first time about the Bohr theory of the atom.

11 The Teacher and the Bohr Theory of the Atom

Charles Percy Snow

An excerpt from his novel *The Search,* published in 1934 and 1958.

Then one day, just before we broke up for Christmas, Luard came into the class-room almost brightly.

"We're not going into the laboratory this morning," he said. "I'm going to talk to you, my friends." He used to say "my friends" whenever he was lashing us with his tongue, but now it sounded half in earnest. "Forget everything you know, will you? That is, if you know anything at all." He sat on the desk swinging his legs.

"Now, what do you think all the stuff in the world is made of? Every bit of us, you and me, the chairs in this room, the air, everything. No one knows? Well, perhaps that's not surprising, even for nincompoops like you. Because no one *did* know a year or two ago. But now we're beginning to think we *do*. That's what I want to tell you. You won't understand, of course. But it'll amuse me to tell you, and it won't hurt you, I suppose—and anyway I'm going to."

Someone dropped a ruler just then, and afterwards the room was very quiet. Luard took no notice and went on: "Well, if you took a piece of lead, and halved it, and halved the half, and went on like that, where do you think you'd come to in the end? Do you think it would be lead for ever? Do you think you could go down right to the infinitely small and still have tiny pieces of lead? It doesn't matter what you think. My friends, you couldn't. If you went on long enough, you'd come to an atom of lead, an atom, do you hear, an atom, and if you split that up, you wouldn't have lead any more. What do you think you would have? The answer to that is one of the oddest things you'll ever hear in your life. If you split up an atom of lead, you'd get—pieces of positive and negative electricity. Just that. Just positive and negative electricity. That's all matter is. That's all you are. Just positive and negative electricity—and, of course, an immortal soul." At the time I was too busy attending to his story to observe anything else; but in the picture I have formed later of Luard, I give him here the twitch of a smile. "And whether you started with lead or anything else it wouldn't matter. That's all you'd come to in the end. Positive and negative electricity. How do things differ then? Well, the atoms are all positive and negative electricity and they're all made on the same pattern, but they vary among themselves, do you see? Every atom has a bit of positive electricity in the middle of it—the nucleus, they call it—and every atom has bits of negative electricity going round the nucleus—like planets round the sun. But the nucleus is bigger in some atoms than others, bigger in lead than it is in carbon, and there are more bits of negative electricity in some atoms than others. It's as though you had different solar systems, made from the same sort of materials, some with bigger suns than others, some with a lot more planets. That's all the difference. That's where a diamond's different from a bit of lead. That's at the bottom of the whole of this world of ours." He stopped and cleaned his pince-nez, and talked as he swung them:

"There you are, that's the way things are going. Two people have found out about the atoms: one's an Englishman, Rutherford, and the other's a Dane called Bohr. And I tell you, my friends, they're great men. Greater even than Mr. Miles"—I flushed. I had come top of the form and this was his way of congratulating me—"incredible as that may seem. Great men, my friends, and perhaps, when you're older, by the side of them your painted heroes, your Cæsars and Napoleons, will seem like cocks crowing on a dungheap."

I went home and read everything I could discover about atoms. Popular exposition was comparatively slow at that time, however, and Rutherford's nucleus, let alone Bohr's atom, which could only have been published a few months before Luard's lesson, had not yet got into my Encyclopædia. I learned something of electrons and got some idea of size; I was fascinated by the tininess of the electron and the immensity of the great stars: I became caught up in light-years, made time-tables of a journey to the nearest star (in the

Encyclopædia there was an enthralling picture of an express train going off into space at the speed of light, taking years to get to the stars). Scale began to impress me, the infinitesimal electronic distances and the vastness of Aldebaran began to dance round in my head; and the time of an electronic journey round the nucleus compared itself with the time it takes for light to travel across the Milky Way. Distance and time, the infinitely great and the infinitely small, electron and star, went reeling round my mind.

It must have been soon after this that I let myself seep in the fantasies that come to many imaginative children nowadays. Why should not the electron contain worlds smaller than itself, carrying perhaps inconceivably minute replicas of ourselves? 'They wouldn't know they're small. They wouldn't know of us,' I thought, and felt serious and profound. And why should not our world be just a part of an electron in some cosmic atom, itself a part of some gargantuan world? The speculations gave me a pleasant sense of philosophic agoraphobia until I was about sixteen and then I had had enough of them.

Luard, who had set me alight by half an hour's talk, did not repeat himself. Chemistry lessons relapsed once more into exercises meaningless to me, definitions of acids and bases which I learned resentfully, and, as we got further up the school, descriptions of the properties of gases, which always began "colourless, transparent, non-poisonous." Luard, who had once burst into enthusiasm, droned out the definitions or left us to a text-book while he sat by himself at the end of the laboratory. Once or twice there would be a moment of fire; he told us about phlogiston—"that should be a lesson to you, my friends, to remember that you can always fall back on tradition if only you're dishonest enough" and Faraday—"there never will be a better scientist than he was; and Davy tried to keep him out of the Royal Society because he had been a laboratory assistant. Davy was the type of all the jumped-up second-raters of all time."

Educated as we are in classical physics, we may
be unprepared to comprehend the world of quantum
mechanics. This book tries to introduce us to this
new view of the world.

---

12   The New Landscape of Science

Banesh Hoffmann

Chapter from his book, *The Strange Story of the Quantum*, 1959.

LET US now gather the loose threads of our thoughts and see
what pattern they form when knit together.

We seem to glimpse an eerie shadow world lying beneath
our world of space and time; a weird and cryptic world which
somehow rules us. Its laws seem mathematically precise, and
its events appear to unfold with strict causality.

To pry into the secrets of this world we make experiments.
But experiments are a clumsy instrument, afflicted with a fatal
indeterminacy which destroys causality. And because our
mental images are formed thus clumsily, we may not hope to
fashion mental pictures in space and time of what transpires
within this deeper world. Abstract mathematics alone may try
to paint its likeness.

With indeterminacy corrupting experiment and dissolving
causality, all seems lost. We must wonder how there can be a
rational science. We must wonder how there can be anything at all but chaos. But though the detailed workings of the
indeterminacy lie hidden from us, we find therein an astounding uniformity. Despite the inescapable indeterminacy of
experiment, we find a definite, authentic residue of exactitude
and determinacy. Compared with the detailed determinacy
claimed by classical science, it is a meager residue indeed. But
it is precious exactitude none the less, on which to build a
science of natural law.

The very nature of the exactitude seems a paradox, for it is
an exactitude of probabilities; an exactitude, indeed, of wave-
like, interfering probabilities. But probabilities are potent

things—if only they are applied to large numbers. Let us see what strong reliance may be placed upon them.

When we toss a coin, the result may not be predicted, for it is a matter of chance. Yet it is not entirely undetermined. We know it must be one of only two possibilities. And, more important even than that, if we toss ten thousand coins we know we may safely predict that about half will come down heads. Of course we might be wrong once in a very long while. Of course we are taking a small risk in making such a prediction. But let us face the issue squarely, for we really place far more confidence in the certainty of probabilities than we sometimes like to admit to ourselves when thinking of them abstractly. If someone offered to pay two dollars every time a coin turned up heads provided we paid one dollar for every tails, would we really hesitate to accept his offer? If we did hesitate, it would not be because we mistrusted the probabilities. On the contrary, it would be because we trusted them so well we smelled fraud in an offer too attractive to be honest. Roulette casinos rely on probabilities for their gambling profits, trusting to chance that, in the long run, zero or double zero will come up as frequently as any other number and thus guarantee them a steady percentage of the total transactions. Now and again the luck runs against them and they go broke for the evening. But that is because chance is still capricious when only a few hundred spins are made. Insurance companies also rely on probabilities, but deal with far larger numbers. One does not hear of their ever going broke. They make a handsome living out of chance, for when precise probabilities can be found, chance, in the long run, becomes practical certainty. Even classical science built an elaborate and brilliantly successful theory of gases upon the seeming quicksands of probability.

In the new world of the atom we find both precise probabilities and enormous numbers, probabilities that follow exact mathematical laws, and vast, incredible numbers compared with which the multitude of persons carrying insurance is as nothing. Scientists have determined the weight of a single electron. Would a million electrons weigh as much as a feather, do you think? A million is not large enough. Nor even a billion. Well, surely a million billion then. No. Not even a billion billion electrons would outweigh the feather. Nor yet a million billion billion. Not till we have a billion billion billion can we talk of their weight in such everyday terms. Quantum mechanics having discovered precise and wonderful laws governing the probabilities, it is with numbers such as these that science overcomes its handicap of basic indeterminacy. It is by this means that science boldly predicts. Though now humbly confessing itself powerless to foretell the exact behavior of individual electrons, or photons, or other fundamental entities, it yet can tell with enormous confidence how such great multitudes of them must behave precisely.

But for all this mass precision, we are only human if, on first hearing of the breakdown of determinacy in fundamental science, we look back longingly to the good old classical days, when waves were waves and particles particles, when the workings of nature could be readily visualized, and the future was predictable in every individual detail, at least in theory. But the good old days were not such happy days as nostalgic, rose-tinted retrospect would make them seem. Too many contradictions flourished unresolved. Too many well-attested facts played havoc with their pretensions. Those were but days of scientific childhood. There is no going back to them as they were.

Nor may we stop with the world we have just described, if we are to round out our story faithfully. To stifle nostalgia, we pictured a world of causal law lying beneath our world of space and time. While important scientists seem to feel that such a world should exist, many others, pointing out that it is not demonstrable, regard it therefore as a bit of homely mysticism added more for the sake of comfort than of cold logic.

It is difficult to decide where science ends and mysticism begins. As soon as we begin to make even the most elementary theories we are open to the charge of indulging in metaphysics. Yet theories, however provisional, are the very lifeblood of scientific progress. We simply cannot escape metaphysics, though we can perhaps overindulge, as well as have too little. Nor is it feasible always to distinguish good metaphysics from bad, for the "bad" may lead to progress where the "good" would tend to stifle it. When Columbus made his historic voyage he believed he was on his westward way to Japan. Even when he reached land he thought it was part of Asia; nor did he live to learn otherwise. Would Columbus have embarked upon his hazardous journey had he known what was the true westward distance of Japan? Quantum mechanics itself came partly from the queer hunches of such men as Maxwell and Bohr and de Broglie. In talking of the meaning of quantum mechanics, physicists indulge in more or less mysticism according to their individual tastes. Just as different artists instinctively paint different likenesses of the same model, so do scientists allow their different personalities to color their interpretations of quantum mechanics. Our story would not be complete did we not tell of the austere conception of quantum mechanics hinted at above, and also in our parable of the coin and the principle of perversity, for it is a view held by many physicists.

These physicists are satisfied with the sign-language rules, the extraordinary precision of the probabilities, and the strange, wavelike laws which they obey. They realize the impossibility of following the detailed workings of an indeterminacy through which such bountiful precision and law so unaccountably seep. They recall such incidents as the vain attempts to build models of the ether, and their own former naïve beliefs regarding momentum and position, now so rudely shattered. And, recalling them, they are properly cautious. They point to such things as the sign-language rules, or the probabilities and the exquisite mathematical laws in multidimensional fictional space which govern them and which have so eminently proved themselves in the acid test of experiment. And they say that these are all we may hope and reasonably expect to know; that science, which deals with experiments, should not probe too deeply beneath those experiments for such things as cannot be demonstrated even in theory.

The great mathematician John von Neumann, who accomplished the Herculean labor of cleaning up the mathematical foundations of the quantum theory, has even proved mathematically that the quantum theory is a complete system in itself, needing no secret aid from a deeper, hidden world, and offering no evidence whatsoever that such a world exists. Let us then be content to accept the world as it presents itself to us through our experiments, however strange it may seem. This and this alone is the image of the world of science. After castigating the classical theorists for their unwarranted assumptions, however seemingly innocent, would it not be foolish and foolhardy to invent that hidden world of exact causality of which we once thought so fondly, a world which by its very nature must lie beyond the reach of our experiments? Or, indeed, to invent anything else which cannot be demonstrated, such as the detailed occurrences under the Heisenberg microscope and all other pieces of comforting imagery wherein we picture a wavicle as an old-fashioned particle preliminary to proving it not one?

All that talk of exactitude somehow seeping through the indeterminacy was only so much talk. We must cleanse our minds of previous pictorial notions and start afresh, taking the laws of quantum mechanics themselves as the basis and the complete outline of modern physics, the full delineation of the quantum world beyond which there is nothing that may properly belong to physical science. As for the idea of strict causality, not only does science, after all these years, suddenly find it an unnecessary concept, it even demonstrates that according to the quantum theory strict causality is fundamentally and intrinsically undemonstrable. Therefore, strict causality is no longer a legitimate scientific concept, and must be cast out from the official domain of present-day science. As Dirac has written, *"The only object of theoretical physics is to calculate results that can be compared with experiment, and it is quite unnecessary that any satisfying description of the whole course of the phenomena should be given."* The italics here are his. One cannot escape the feeling that it might have been more appropriate to italicize the second part of the statement rather than the first!

Here, then, is a more restricted pattern which, paradoxically, is at once a more cautious and a bolder view of the world of quantum physics; cautious in not venturing beyond what is well established, and bold in accepting and being well content with the result. Because it does not indulge too freely in speculation it is a proper view of present-day quantum physics, and it seems to be the sort of view held by the greatest number. Yet, as we said, there are many shades of opinion, and it is sometimes difficult to decide what are the precise views of particular individuals.

Some men feel that all this is a transitional stage through which science will ultimately pass to better things—and they hope soon. Others, accepting it with a certain discomfort, have tried to temper its awkwardness by such devices as the introduction of new types of logic. Some have suggested that the observer creates the result of his observation by the act of observation, somewhat as in the parable of the tossed coin. Many nonscientists, but few scientists, have seen in the new ideas the embodiment of free will in the inanimate world, and have rejoiced. Some, more cautious, have seen merely a revived possibility of free will in ourselves now that our physical processes are freed from the shackles of strict causality. One could continue endlessly the list of these speculations, all testifying to the devastating potency of Planck's quantum of action h, a quantity so incredibly minute as to seem utterly inconsequential to the uninitiated.

That some prefer to swallow their quantum mechanics plain while others gag unless it be strongly seasoned with imagery and metaphysics is a matter of individual taste behind which lie certain fundamental facts which may not be disputed; hard, uncompromising, and at present inescapable facts of experiment and bitter experience, agreed upon by all and directly opposed to the classical way of thinking:

There is simply no satisfactory way at all of picturing the fundamental atomic processes of nature in terms of space and time and causality.

The result of an experiment on an individual atomic particle generally cannot be predicted. Only a list of various possible results may be known beforehand.

Nevertheless, the statistical result of performing the same individual experiment over and over again an enormous number of times may be predicted with virtual certainty.

For example, though we can show there is absolutely no contradiction involved, we cannot visualize how an electron which is enough of a wave to pass through two holes in a screen and interfere with itself can suddenly become enough of a particle to produce a single scintillation. Neither can we predict where it will scintillate, though we can say it may do so only in certain regions but not in others. Nevertheless when, instead of a single electron, we send through a rich and abundant stream we can predict with detailed precision the intricate interference pattern that will build up, even to the relative brightness of its various parts.

Our inability to predict the individual result, an inability which, despite the evidence, the classical view was unable to tolerate, is not only a fundamental but actually a plausible characteristic of quantum mechanics. So long as quantum mechanics is accepted as wholly valid, so long must we accept this inability as intrinsically unavoidable. Should a way ever be found to overcome this inability, that event would mark the end of the reign of quantum mechanics as a fundamental pattern of nature. A new, and deeper, theory would have to be found to replace it, and quantum mechanics would have to be retired, to become a theory emeritus with the revered, if faintly irreverent title "classical."

Now that we are accustomed, a little, to the bizarre new ideas we may at last look briefly into the quantum mechanical significance of something which at first sight seems trivial and inconsequential, namely, that electrons are so similar we cannot tell one from another. This is true also of other atomic particles, but for simplicity let us talk about electrons, with the understanding that the discussion is not thereby confined to them alone.

Imagine, then, an electron on this page and another on the opposite page. Take a good look at them. You cannot tell them apart. Now blink your eyes and take another look at them. They are still there, one on this page and one on that. But how do you know they did not change places just at the moment your eyes were closed? You think it most unlikely? Does it not always rain on just those days when you go out and leave the windows open? Does it not always happen that your shoelace breaks on just those days when you are in a special hurry? Remember these electrons are identical twins and apt to be mischievous. Surely you know better than to argue that the electron interchange was unlikely. You certainly could not prove it one way or another.

Perhaps you are still unconvinced. Let us put it a little differently, then. Suppose the electrons collided and bounced off one another. Then you certainly could not tell which one was which after the collision.

You still think so? You think you could keep your eyes glued on them so they could not fool you? But, my dear sir, that is classical. That is old-fashioned. We cannot keep a continual watch in the quantum world. The best we can do is keep up a bombardment of photons. And with each impact the electrons jump we know not how. For all we know they could be changing places all the time. At the moment of impact especially the danger of deception is surely enormous. Let us then agree that we can never be sure of the identity of each electron.

Now suppose we wish to write down quantum equations for the two electrons. In the present state of our theories, we are obliged to deal with them first as individuals, saying that certain mathematical co-ordinates belong to the first and certain others to the second. This is dishonest though. It goes beyond permissible information, for it allows each electron to preserve its identity, whereas electrons should belong to the nameless masses. Somehow we must remedy our initial error. Somehow we must repress the electrons and remove from them their unwarranted individuality. This reduces to a simple question of mathematical symmetries. We must so remold our equations that interchanging the electrons has no physically detectable effect on the answers they yield.

Imposing this nonindividuality is a grave mathematical restriction, strongly influencing the behavior of the electrons. Of the possible ways of imposing it, two are specially simple mathematically, and it happens that just these two are physically of interest. One of them implies a behavior which is actually observed in the case of photons, and α particles, and other atomic particles. The other method of imposing nonindividuality turns out to mean that the particles will shun one another; in fact, it gives precisely the mysterious exclusion principle of Pauli.

This is indeed a remarkable result, and an outstanding triumph for quantum mechanics. It takes on added significance when we learn that all those atomic particles which do not obey the Pauli principle are found to behave like the photons and α particles. It is about as far as anyone has gone toward an understanding of the deeper significance of the exclusion principle. Yet it remains a confession of failure, for instead of having nonindividuality from the start we begin with individuality and then deny it. The Pauli principle lies far deeper than this. It lies at the very heart of inscrutable Nature. Someday, perhaps, we shall have a more profound theory in which the exclusion principle will find its rightful place. Meanwhile we must be content with our present veiled insight.

The mathematical removal of individuality warps our equations and causes extraordinary effects which cannot be properly explained in pictorial terms. It may be interpreted as bringing into being strange forces called exchange forces, but these forces, though already appearing in other connections in quantum mechanics, have no counterpart at all in classical physics.

We might have suspected some such forces were involved. It would have been incredibly naïve to have believed that so stringent an ordinance against overcrowding as the exclusion principle could be imposed without some measure of force, however well disguised.

Is it so sure that these exchange forces cannot be properly explained in pictorial terms? After all, with force is associated energy. And with energy is associated frequency according to Planck's basic quantum law. With frequency we may associate some sort of oscillation. Perhaps, then, if we think not of the exchange forces themselves but of the oscillations associated with them we may be able to picture the mechanism through which these forces exist. This is a promising idea. But if it is clarity we seek we shall be greatly disappointed in it.

It is true there is an oscillation involved here, but what a fantastic oscillation it is: a rhythmic interchange of the electrons' identities. The electrons do not physically change places by leaping the intervening space. That would be too simple. Rather, there is a smooth ebb and flow of individuality between them. For example, if we start with electron A here and electron B on the opposite page, then later on we would here have some such mixture as sixty per cent A and forty per cent B, with forty per cent A and sixty per cent B over there. Later still it would be all B here and all A there, the electrons then having definitely exchanged identities. The flow would now reverse, and the strange oscillation continue indefinitely. It is with such a pulsation of identity that the exchange forces of the exclusion principle are associated. There is another type of exchange which can affect even a single electron, the electron being analogously pictured as oscillating in this curious, disembodied way between two different positions.

Perhaps it is easier to accept such curious pulsations if we think of the electrons more as waves than as particles, for then we can imagine the electron waves becoming tangled up with each other. Mathematically this can be readily perceived, but it does not lend itself well to visualization. If we stay with the particle aspect of the electrons we find it hard to imagine what a 60 per cent–40 per cent mixture of A and B would look like if we observed it. We cannot observe it, though. The act of observation would so jolt the electrons that we would find either pure A or else pure B, but never a combination, the percentages being just probabilities of finding either one. It is really our parable of the tossed coin all over again. In mid-air the coin fluctuates rhythmically from pure heads to pure tails through all intermediate mixtures. When it lands on the table, which is to say when we observe it, there is a jolt which yields only heads or tails.

Though we can at least meet objections, exchange remains an elusive and difficult concept. It is still a strange and awe-inspiring thought that you and I are thus rhythmically exchanging particles with one another, and with the earth and the beasts of the earth, and the sun and the moon and the stars, to the uttermost galaxy.

A striking instance of the power of exchange is seen in chemical valence, for it is essentially by means of these mysterious forces that atoms cling together, their outer electrons busily shuttling identity and position back and forth to weave a bond that knits the atoms into molecules.

Such are the fascinating concepts that emerged from the quantum mechanical revolution. The days of tumult shook science to its deepest foundations. They brought a new charter to science, and perhaps even cast a new light on the significance of the scientific method itself. The physics that survived the revolution was vastly changed, and strangely so, its whole outlook drastically altered. Where once it confidently sought a clear-cut mechanical model of nature for all to behold, it now contented itself with abstract, esoteric forms which may not be clearly focused by the unmathematical eye of the imagination. Is it as strongly confident as once it seemed to be in younger days, or has internal upheaval undermined its health and robbed it of its powers? Has quantum mechanics been an advance or a retreat?

If it has been a retreat in any sense at all, it has been a strategic retreat from the suffocating determinism of classical physics, which channeled and all but surrounded the advancing forces of science. Whether or not science, later in its quest, may once more encounter a deep causality, the determinism of the nineteenth century, for all the great discoveries it sired, was rapidly becoming an impediment to progress. When Planck first discovered the infinitesimal existence of the quantum, it seemed there could be no proper place for it anywhere in the whole broad domain of physical science. Yet in a brief quarter century, so powerful did it prove, it thrust itself into every nook and cranny, its influence growing to such undreamed-of proportions that the whole aspect of science was utterly transformed. With explosive violence it finally thrust through the restraining walls of determinism, releasing the pent-up forces of scientific progress to pour into the untouched fertile plains beyond, there to reap an untold harvest of discovery while still retaining the use of those splendid edifices it had created within the classical domain. The older theories were made more secure than ever, their triumphs unimpaired and their failures mitigated, for now their validity was established wherever the influence of the quantum might momentarily be neglected. Their failures were no longer disquieting perplexities which threatened to undermine the whole structure and bring it toppling down. With proper diagnosis the classical structures could be saved for special purposes, and their very weaknesses turned to good account as strong corroborations of the newer ideas; ideas which transcended the old without destroying their limited effectiveness.

True, the newer theory baffled the untutored imagination, and was formidably abstract as no physical theory had ever been before. But this was a small price to pay for its extraordinary accomplishments. Newton's theory too had once seemed almost incredible, as also had that of Maxwell, and strange though quantum mechanics might appear, it was firmly founded on fundamental experiment. Here at long last was a theory which could embrace that primitive, salient fact of our material universe, that simple, everyday fact on which the Maxwellian theory so spectacularly foundered, the enduring stability of the different elements and of their physical and chemical properties. Nor was the new theory too rigid in this regard, but could equally well embrace the fact of radioactive transformation. Here at last was a theory which could yield the precise details of the enormously intricate data of spectroscopy. The photoelectric effect and a host of kindred phenomena succumbed to the new ideas, as too did the wavelike interference effects which formerly seemed to contradict them. With the aid of relativity, the spin of the electron was incorporated with remarkable felicity and success. Pauli's exclusion principle took on a broader significance, and through it the science of chemistry acquired a new theoretical basis amounting almost to a new science, theoretical chemistry, capable of solving problems hitherto beyond the reach of the theorist. The theory of metallic magnetism was brilliantly transformed, and staggering difficulties in the theory of the flow of electricity through metals were removed as if by magic thanks to quantum mechanics, and especially to Pauli's exclusion principle. The atomic nucleus was to yield up invaluable secrets to the new quantum physics, as will be told; secrets which could not be revealed at all to the classical theory, since that theory was too primitive to comprehend them; secrets so abstruse they may not even be uttered except in quantum terms. Our understanding of the nature of the tremendous forces residing in the atomic nucleus, incomplete though it be, would be meager indeed without the quantum theory to guide our search and encourage our comprehension in these most intriguing and mysterious regions of the universe. This is no more than a glimpse of the unparalleled achievements of quantum mechanics. The wealth of accomplishment and corroborative evidence is simply staggering.

"Daddy, do scientists really know what they are talking about?"

To still an inquiring child one is sometimes driven to regrettable extremes. Was our affirmative answer honest in this particular instance?

Certainly it was honest enough in its context, immediately following the two other questions. But what of this same question now, standing alone? Do scientists really know what they are talking about?

If we allowed the poets and philosophers and priests to decide, they would assuredly decide, on lofty grounds, against the physicists—quite irrespective of quantum mechanics. But on sufficiently lofty grounds the poets, philosophers, and priests themselves may scarcely claim they know whereof they talk, and in some instances, far from lofty, science has caught both them and itself in outright error.

True, the universe is more than a collection of objective experimental data; more than the complexus of theories, abstractions, and special assumptions devised to hold the data together; more, indeed, than any construct modeled on this cold objectivity. For there is a deeper, more subjective world, a world of sensation and emotion, of aesthetic, moral, and religious values as yet beyond the grasp of objective science. And towering majestically over all, inscrutable and inescapable, is the awful mystery of Existence itself, to confound the mind with an eternal enigma.

But let us descend from these to more mundane levels, for then the quantum physicist may make a truly impressive case; a case, moreover, backed by innumerable interlocking experiments forming a proof of stupendous cogency. Where else could one find a proof so overwhelming? How could one doubt the validity of so victorious a system? Men are hanged on evidence which, by comparison, must seem small and inconsequential beyond measure. Surely, then, the quantum physicists know what they are talking about. Surely their present theories are proper theories of the workings of the universe. Surely physical nature cannot be markedly different from what has at last so painfully been revealed.

And yet, if this is our belief, surely our whole story has been told in vain. Here, for instance, is a confident utterance of the year 1889:

"The wave theory of light is from the point of view of human beings a certainty."

It was no irresponsible visionary who made this bold assertion, no fifth-rate incompetent whose views might be lightly laughed away. It was the very man whose classic experiments, more than those of any other, established the electrical character of the waves of light; none other than the great Heinrich Hertz himself, whose own seemingly incidental observation contained the seed from which there later was to spring the revitalized particle theory.

Did not the classical physicists point to overwhelming evidence in support of their theories, theories which now seem to us so incomplete and superficial? Did they not generally believe that physics was near its end, its main problems solved and its basis fully revealed, with only a little sweeping up and polishing left to occupy succeeding generations? And did they not believe these things even while they were aware of such unsolved puzzles as the violet catastrophe, and the photoelectric effect, and radioactive disintegration?

The experimental proofs of science are not ultimate proofs. Experiment, that final arbiter of science, has something of the aspect of an oracle, its precise factual pronouncements couched in muffled language of deceptive import. While to Bohr such a thing as the Balmer ladder meant orbits and jumps, to Schrödinger it meant a smeared-out essence of ψ; neither view is accepted at this moment. Even the measurement of the speed of light in water, that seemingly clear-cut experiment specifically conceived to decide between wave and particle, yielded a truth whose import was misconstrued. Science abounds with similar instances. Each change of theory demonstrates anew the uncertain certainty of experiment. One would be bold indeed to assert that science at last has reached an ultimate theory, that the quantum theory as we know it now will survive with only superficial alteration. It may be so, but we are unable to prove it, and certainly precedent would seem to be against it. The quantum physicist does not know whether he knows what he is talking about. But this at least he does know, that his talk, however incorrect it may ultimately prove to be, is at present immeasurably superior to that of his classical forebears, and better founded in fact than ever before. And that is surely something well worth knowing.

Never had fundamental science seen an era so explosively triumphant. With such revolutionary concepts as relativity and the quantum theory developing simultaneously, physics experienced a turmoil of upheaval and transformation without parallel in its history. The majestic motions of the heavens and the innermost tremblings of the atoms alike came under the searching scrutiny of the new theories. Man's concepts of time and space, of matter and radiation, energy, momentum, and causality, even of science and of the universe itself, all were transmuted under the electrifying impact of the double revolution. Here in our story we have followed the frenzied fortunes of the quantum during those fabulous years, from its first hesitant conception in the minds of gifted men, through precarious early years of infancy, to a temporary lodgment in the primitive theory of Bohr, there to prepare for a bewildering and spectacular leap into maturity that was to turn the orderly landscape of science into a scene of utmost confusion. Gradually, from the confusion we saw a new landscape emerge, barely recognizable, serene, and immeasurably extended, and once more orderly and neat as befits the landscape of science.

The new ideas, when first they came, were wholly repugnant to the older scientists whose minds were firmly set in traditional ways. In those days even the flexible minds of the younger men found them startling. Yet now the physicists of the new generation, like infants incomprehensibly enjoying their cod-liver oil, lap up these quantum ideas with hearty appetite, untroubled by the misgivings and gnawing doubts which so sorely plagued their elders. Thus to the already burdensome list of scientific corroborations and proofs may now be added this crowning testimony out of the mouths of babes and sucklings. The quantum has arrived. The tale is told. Let the final curtain fall.

But ere the curtain falls we of the audience thrust forward, not yet satisfied. We are not specialists in atomic physics. We are but plain men who daily go about our appointed tasks, and of an evening peer hesitantly over the shoulder of the scientific theorist to glimpse the enchanted pageant that passes before his mind. Is all this business of wavicles and lack of causality in space and time something which the theorist can now accept with serenity? Can we ourselves ever learn to welcome it with any deep feeling of acceptance? When so alien a world has been revealed to us we cannot but shrink from its vast unfriendliness. It is a world far removed from our everyday experience.

It offers no simple comfort. It beckons us without warmth. We are saddened that science should have taken this curious, unhappy turn, ever away from the beliefs we most fondly cherish. Surely, we console ourselves, it is but a temporary aberration. Surely science will someday find the tenuous road back to normalcy, and ordinary men will once more understand its message, simple and clear, and untroubled by abstract paradox.

But we must remember that men have always felt thus when a bold new idea has arisen, be the idea right or wrong. When men first proclaimed the earth was not flat, did they not propose a paradox as devilish and devastating as any we have met in our tale of the quantum? How utterly fantastic must such a belief at first have appeared to most people; this belief which is now so readily and blindly accepted by children, against the clearest evidence of their immediate senses, that they are quick to ridicule the solitary crank who still may claim the earth is flat; their only concern, if any, is for the welfare of the poor people on the other side of this our round earth who, they so vividly reason, are fated to live out their lives walking on their heads. Let us pray that political wisdom and heaven-sent luck be granted us so that our children's children may be able as readily to accept the quantum horrors of today and laugh at the fears and misgivings of their benighted ancestors, those poor souls who still believed in old-fashioned waves and particles, and the necessity for national sovereignty, and all the other superstitions of an outworn age.

It is not on the basis of our routine feelings that we should try here to weigh the value and significance of the quantum revolution. It is rather on the basis of its innate logic.

"What!" you will exclaim. "Its innate logic? Surely that is the last thing we could grant it. We have to concede its overwhelming experimental support. But innate logic, a sort of aura to compel our belief, experiment or no experiment? No, that is too much. The new ideas are not innately acceptable, nor will talking ever make them so. Experiment forced them on us, but we cannot feel their inevitability. We accept them only laboriously, after much obstinate struggle. We shall never see their deeper meaning as in a flash of revelation. Though Nature be for them, our whole nature is against them. Innate logic? No! Just bitter medicine."

But there is yet a possibility. Perhaps there is after all some innate logic in the quantum theory. Perhaps we may yet see in it a profoundly simple revelation, by whose light the ideas of the older science may appear as laughable as the doctrine that the earth is flat. We have but to remind ourselves that our ideas of space and time came to us through our everyday experience and were gradually refined by the careful experiment of the scientist. As experiment became more precise, space and time began to assume a new aspect. Even the relatively superficial experiment of Michelson and Morley, back in 1887, ultimately led to the shattering of some of our concepts of space and time by the theory of relativity. Nowadays, through the deeper techniques of the modern physicist we find that space and time as we know them so familiarly, and even space and time as relativity knows them, simply do not fit the more profound pattern of existence revealed by atomic experiment.

What, after all, are these mystic entities space and time? We tend to take them for granted. We imagine space to be so smooth and precise we can define within it such a thing as a point—something having no size at all but only a continuing location. Now, this is all very well in abstract thought. Indeed, it seems almost an unavoidable necessity. Yet if we examine it in the light of the quantum discoveries, do we not find the beginning of a doubt? For how would we try to fix such a disembodied location in actual physical space as distinct from the purely mental image of space we have within our minds? What is the smallest, most delicate instrument we could use in order to locate it? Certainly not our finger. That could suffice to point out a house, or a pebble, or even, with difficulty, a particular grain of sand. But for a point it is far too gross.

What of the point of a needle, then? Better. But far from adequate. Look at the needle point under a microscope and the reason is clear, for it there appears as a pitted, tortured landscape, shapeless and useless. What then? We must try smaller and ever smaller, finer and ever finer indicators. But try as we will we cannot continue indefinitely. The ultimate point will always elude us. For in the end we shall come to such things as individual electrons, or nuclei, or photons, and beyond these, in the present state of science, we cannot go. What has become, then, of our idea of the location of a point? Has it not somehow dissolved away amid the swirling wavicles? True, we have said that we may know the exact position of a wavicle if we will sacrifice all knowledge of its motion. Yet even here there happen to be theoretical reasons connected with Compton's experiment which limit the precision with which this position may be known. Even supposing the position could be known with the utmost exactitude, would we then have a point such as we have in mind? No. For a point has a continuing location, while our location would be evanescent. We would still have merely a sort of abstract wavicle rather than an abstract point. Whether we think of an electron as a wavicle, or whether we think of it as a particle buffeted by the photons under a Heisenberg microscope, we find that the physical notion of a precise, continuing location escapes us. Though we have reached the present theoretical limit of refinement we have not yet found location. Indeed, we seem to be further from it than when we so hopefully started out. Space is not so simple a concept as we had naïvely thought.

It is much as if we sought to observe a detail in a newspaper photograph. We look at the picture more closely but the tantalizing detail still escapes us. Annoyed, we bring a magnifying glass to bear upon it, and lo! our eager optimism is shattered. We find ourselves far worse off than before. What seemed to be an eye has now dissolved away into a meaningless jumble of splotches of black and white. The detail we had imagined simply was not there. Yet from a distance the picture still looks perfect.

Perhaps it is the same with space, and with time too. Instinctively we feel they have infinite detail. But when we bring to bear on them our most refined techniques of observation and precise measurement we find that the infinite detail we had imagined has somehow vanished away. It is not space and time that are basic, but the fundamental particles of matter or energy themselves. Without these we could not have formed even the picture we instinctively have of a smooth, unblemished, faultless, and infinitely detailed space and time. These electrons and the other fundamental particles, they do not exist in space and time. It is space and time that exist because of them. These particles—wavicles, as we must regard them if we wish to mix in our inappropriate, anthropomorphic fancies of space and time—these fundamental particles precede and transcend the concepts of space and time. They are deeper and more fundamental, more primitive and primordial. It is out of them in the untold aggregate that we build our spatial and temporal concepts, much as out of the multitude of seemingly haphazard dots and splotches of the newspaper photograph we build in our minds a smooth, unblemished portrait; much as from the swift succession of quite motionless pictures projected on a motion-picture screen we build in our minds the illusion of smooth, continuous motion.

Perhaps it is this which the quantum theory is striving to express. Perhaps it is this which makes it seem so paradoxical. If space and time are not the fundamental stuff of the universe but merely particular average, statistical effects of crowds of more fundamental entities lying deeper down, it is no longer strange that these fundamental entities, when imagined as existing in space and time, should exhibit such ill-matched properties as those of wave and particle. There may, after all, be some innate logic in the paradoxes of quantum physics.

This idea of average effects which do not belong to the individual is nothing new to science. Temperature, so real and definite that we can read it with a simple thermometer, is merely a statistical effect of chaotic molecular motions. Nor are we at all troubled that it should be so. The air pressure in our automobile tires is but the statistical effect of a ceaseless bombardment by tireless air molecules. A single molecule has neither temperature nor pressure in any ordinary sense of those terms. Ordinary temperature and pressure are crowd effects. When we try to examine them too closely, by observing an individual molecule, they simply vanish away. Take the smooth flow of water. It too vanishes away when we examine a single water molecule. It is no more than a potent myth created out of the myriad motions of water molecules in enormous numbers.

So too may it well be with space and time themselves, though this is something far more difficult to imagine even tentatively. As the individual water molecules lack the everyday qualities of temperature, pressure, and fluidity, as single letters of the alphabet lack the quality of poetry, so perhaps may the fundamental particles of the universe individually lack the quality of existing in space and time; the very space and time which the particles themselves, in the enormous aggregate, falsely present to us as entities so pre-eminently fundamental we can hardly conceive of any existence at all without them. See how it all fits in now. The quantum paradoxes are of our own making, for we have tried to follow the motions of individual particles through space and time, while all along these individual particles have no existence in space and time. It is space and time that exist through the particles. An individual particle is not in two places at once. It is in no place at all. Would we feel amazed and upset that a thought could be in two places at once? A thought, if we imagine it as something outside our brain, has no quality of location. If we did wish to locate it hypothetically, for any particular reason, we would expect it to transcend the ordinary limitations of space and time. It is only because we have all along regarded matter as existing in space and time that we find it so hard to renounce this idea for the individual particles. But once we do renounce it the paradoxes vanish away and the message of the quantum suddenly becomes clear: space and time are not fundamental.

Speculation? Certainly. But so is all theorizing. While nothing so drastic has yet been really incorporated into the mathematical fabric of quantum mechanics, this may well be because of the formidable technical and emotional problems involved. Meanwhile quantum theorists find themselves more and more strongly thrust toward some such speculation. It would solve so many problems. But nobody knows how to set about giving it proper mathematical expression. If something such as this shall prove to be the true nature of space and time, then relativity and the quantum theory as they now stand would appear to be quite irreconcilable. For relativity, as a field theory, must look on space and time as basic entities, while the quantum theory, for all its present technical inability to emancipate itself from the space-time tyranny, tends very strongly against that view. Yet there is a deal of truth in both relativity and the present quantum theory, and neither can wholly succumb to the other. Where the two theories meet there is a vital ferment. A process of cross-fertilization is under way. Out of it someday will spring a new and far more potent theory, bearing hereditary traces of its two illustrious ancestors, which will ultimately fall heir to all their rich possessions and spread itself to bring their separate domains under a single rule. What will then survive of our present ideas no one can say. Already we have seen waves and particles and causality and space and time all undermined. Let us hasten to bring the curtain down in a rush lest something really serious should happen.

An account of how physical theory has developed
in the past and how it might be expected to develop
in the future.

---

13 The Evolution of the Physicist's Picture of Nature

Paul A. M. Dirac

Popular article published in 1963.

In this article I should like to discuss the development of general physical theory: how it developed in the past and how one may expect it to develop in the future. One can look on this continual development as a process of evolution, a process that has been going on for several centuries.

The first main step in this process of evolution was brought about by Newton. Before Newton, people looked on the world as being essentially two-dimensional—the two dimensions in which one can walk about—and the up-and-down dimension seemed to be something essentially different. Newton showed how one can look on the up-and-down direction as being symmetrical with the other two directions, by bringing in gravitational forces and showing how they take their place in physical theory. One can say that Newton enabled us to pass from a picture with two-dimensional symmetry to a picture with three-dimensional symmetry.

Einstein made another step in the same direction, showing how one can pass from a picture with three-dimensional symmetry to a picture with four-dimensional symmetry. Einstein brought in time and showed how it plays a role that is in many ways symmetrical with the three space dimensions. However, this symmetry is not quite perfect. With

Einstein's picture one is led to think of the world from a four-dimensional point of view, but the four dimensions are not completely symmetrical. There are some directions in the four-dimensional picture that are different from others: directions that are called null directions, along which a ray of light can move; hence the four-dimensional picture is not completely symmetrical. Still, there is a great deal of symmetry among the four dimensions. The only lack of symmetry, so far as concerns the equations of physics, is in the appearance of a minus sign in the equations with respect to the time dimension as compared with the three space dimensions [see top equation on page 8].

We have, then, the development from the three-dimensional picture of the world to the four-dimensional picture. The reader will probably not be happy with this situation, because the world still appears three-dimensional to his consciousness. How can one bring this appearance into the four-dimensional picture that Einstein requires the physicist to have?

What appears to our consciousness is really a three-dimensional section of the four-dimensional picture. We must take a three-dimensional section to give us what appears to our consciousness at one time; at a later time we shall have a

different three-dimensional section. The task of the physicist consists largely of relating events in one of these sections to events in another section referring to a later time. Thus the picture with four-dimensional symmetry does not give us the whole situation. This becomes particularly important when one takes into account the developments that have been brought about by quantum theory. Quantum theory has taught us that we have to take the process of observation into account, and observations usually require us to bring in the three-dimensional sections of the four-dimensional picture of the universe.

The special theory of relativity, which Einstein introduced, requires us to put all the laws of physics into a form that displays four-dimensional symmetry. But when we use these laws to get results about observations, we have to bring in something additional to the four-dimensional symmetry, namely the three-dimensional sections that describe our consciousness of the universe at a certain time.

Einstein made another most important contribution to the development of our physical picture: he put forward the general theory of relativity, which requires us to suppose that the space of physics is curved. Before this physicists had always worked with a flat space, the three-dimensional flat space of Newton which was then extended to the four-dimensional flat space of special relativity. General relativity made a really important contribution to the evolution of our physical picture by requiring us to go over to curved space. The general requirements of this theory mean that all the laws of physics can be formulated in curved four-dimensional space, and that they show symmetry among the four dimensions. But again, when we want to bring in observations, as we must if we look at things from the point of view of quantum theory, we have to refer to a section of this four-dimensional space. With the four-dimensional space curved, any section that we make in it also has to be curved, because in general we cannot give a meaning to a flat section in a curved space. This leads us to a picture in which we have to take curved three-dimensional sections in the curved four-dimensional space and discuss observations in these sections.

During the past few years people have been trying to apply quantum ideas to

gravitation as well as to the other phenomena of physics, and this has led to a rather unexpected development, namely that when one looks at gravitational theory from the point of view of the sections, one finds that there are some degrees of freedom that drop out of the theory. The gravitational field is a tensor field with 10 components. One finds that six of the components are adequate for describing everything of physical importance and the other four can be dropped out of the equations. One cannot, however, pick out the six important components from the complete set of 10 in any way that does not destroy the four-dimensional symmetry. Thus if one insists on preserving four-dimensional symmetry in the equations, one cannot adapt the theory of gravitation to a discussion of measurements in the way quantum theory requires without being forced to a more complicated description than is needed by the physical situation. This result has led me to doubt how fundamental the four-dimensional requirement in physics is. A few decades ago it seemed quite certain that one had

to express the whole of physics in four-dimensional form. But now it seems that four-dimensional symmetry is not of such overriding importance, since the description of nature sometimes gets simplified when one departs from it.

Now I should like to proceed to the developments that have been brought about by quantum theory. Quantum theory is the discussion of very small things, and it has formed the main subject of physics for the past 60 years. During this period physicists have been amassing quite a lot of experimental information and developing a theory to correspond to it, and this combination of theory and experiment has led to important developments in the physicist's picture of the world.

The quantum first made its appearance when Planck discovered the need to suppose that the energy of electromagnetic waves can exist only in multiples of a certain unit, depending on the frequency of the waves, in order to explain the law of black-body radiation. Then Einstein discovered the same unit of energy occurring in the photoelectric effect. In this early work on quantum theory one simply had to accept the unit of energy without being able to incorporate it into a physical picture.

The first new picture that appeared was Bohr's picture of the atom. It was a picture in which we had electrons moving about in certain well-defined orbits and occasionally making a jump from one orbit to another. We could not picture how the jump took place. We just had to accept it as a kind of discontinuity. Bohr's picture of the atom worked only for special examples, essentially when there was only one electron that was of importance for the problem under consideration. Thus the picture was an incomplete and primitive one.

The big advance in the quantum theory came in 1925, with the discovery of quantum mechanics. This advance was brought about independently by two men, Heisenberg first and Schrödinger soon afterward, working from different points of view. Heisenberg worked keeping close to the experimental evidence about spectra that was being amassed at that time, and he found out how the experimental information could be fitted into a scheme that is now known as matrix mechanics. All the experimental data of spectroscopy fitted beautifully into the scheme of matrix mechanics, and this led to quite a different picture of the atomic world. Schrödinger worked from a more mathematical point of view, trying to find a beautiful theory for describ-

ISAAC NEWTON (1642–1727), with his law of gravitation, changed the physicist's picture of nature from one with two-dimensional symmetry to one with three-dimensional symmetry. This drawing of him was made in 1760 by James Macardel from a painting by Enoch Seeman.

ing atomic events, and was helped by De Broglie's ideas of waves associated with particles. He was able to extend De Broglie's ideas and to get a very beautiful equation, known as Schrödinger's wave equation, for describing atomic processes. Schrödinger got this equation by pure thought, looking for some beautiful generalization of De Broglie's ideas, and not by keeping close to the experimental development of the subject in the way Heisenberg did.

I might tell you the story I heard from Schrödinger of how, when he first got the idea for this equation, he immediately applied it to the behavior of the electron in the hydrogen atom, and then he got results that did not agree with experiment. The disagreement arose because at that time it was not known that the electron has a spin. That, of course, was a great disappointment to Schrödinger, and it caused him to abandon the work for some months. Then he noticed that if he applied the theory in a more approximate way, not taking into account the refinements required by relativity, to this rough approximation his work was in agreement with observation. He published his first paper with only this rough approximation, and in that way Schrödinger's wave equation was presented to the world. Afterward, of course, when people found out how to take into account correctly the spin of the electron, the discrepancy between the results of applying Schrödinger's relativistic equation and the experiments was completely cleared up.

I think there is a moral to this story, namely that it is more important to have beauty in one's equations than to have them fit experiment. If Schrödinger had been more confident of his work, he could have published it some months earlier, and he could have published a more accurate equation. That equation is now known as the Klein-Gordon equation, although it was really discovered by Schrödinger, and in fact was discovered by Schrödinger before he discovered his nonrelativistic treatment of the hydrogen atom. It seems that if one is working from the point of view of getting beauty in one's equations, and if one has really a sound insight, one is on a sure line of progress. If there is not complete agreement between the results of one's work and experiment, one should not allow oneself to be too discouraged, because the discrepancy may well be due to minor features that are not properly taken into account and that will get cleared up with further development of the theory.

ALBERT EINSTEIN (1879-1955), with his special theory of relativity, changed the physicist's picture from one with three-dimensional symmetry to one with four-dimensional symmetry. This photograph of him and his wife and their daughter Margot was made in 1929.

That is how quantum mechanics was discovered. It led to a drastic change in the physicist's picture of the world, perhaps the biggest that has yet taken place. This change comes from our having to give up the deterministic picture we had always taken for granted. We are led to a theory that does not predict with certainty what is going to happen in the future but gives us information only about the probability of occurrence of various events. This giving up of determinacy has been a very controversial subject, and some people do not like it at all. Einstein in particular never liked it.

Although Einstein was one of the great contributors to the development of quantum mechanics, he still was always rather hostile to the form that quantum mechanics evolved into during his lifetime and that it still retains.

The hostility some people have to the giving up of the deterministic picture can be centered on a much discussed paper by Einstein, Podolsky and Rosen dealing with the difficulty one has in forming a consistent picture that still gives results according to the rules of quantum mechanics. The rules of quantum mechanics are quite definite. People

NIELS BOHR (1885–1962) introduced the idea that the electron moved about the nucleus in well-defined orbits. This photograph was made in 1922, nine years after the publication of his paper.

MAX PLANCK (1858–1947) introduced the idea that electromagnetic radiation consists of quanta, or particles. This photograph was made in 1913, 13 years after his original paper was published.

know how to calculate results and how to compare the results of their calculations with experiment. Everyone is agreed on the formalism. It works so well that nobody can afford to disagree with it. But still the picture that we are to set up behind this formalism is a subject of controversy.

I should like to suggest that one not worry too much about this controversy. I feel very strongly that the stage physics has reached at the present day is not the final stage. It is just one stage in the evolution of our picture of nature, and we should expect this process of evolution to continue in the future, as biological evolution continues into the future. The present stage of physical theory is merely a steppingstone toward the better stages we shall have in the future. One can be quite sure that there will be better stages simply because of the difficulties that occur in the physics of today.

I should now like to dwell a bit on the difficulties in the physics of the present day. The reader who is not an expert in the subject might get the idea that because of all these difficulties physical theory is in pretty poor shape and that the quantum theory is not much good. I should like to correct this impression by saying that quantum theory is an extremely good theory. It gives wonderful agreement with observation over a wide range of phenomena. There is no doubt that it is a good theory, and the only reason physicists talk so much about

the difficulties in it is that it is precisely the difficulties that are interesting. The successes of the theory are all taken for granted. One does not get anywhere simply by going over the successes again and again, whereas by talking over the difficulties people can hope to make some progress.

The difficulties in quantum theory are of two kinds. I might call them Class One difficulties and Class Two difficulties. Class One difficulties are the difficulties I have already mentioned: How can one form a consistent picture behind the rules for the present quantum theory? These Class One difficulties do not really worry the physicist. If the physicist knows how to calculate results and compare them with experiment, he is quite happy if the results agree with his experiments, and that is all he needs. It is only the philosopher, wanting to have a satisfying description of nature, who is bothered by Class One difficulties.

There are, in addition to the Class One difficulties, the Class Two difficulties, which stem from the fact that the present laws of quantum theory are not always adequate to give any results. If one pushes the laws to extreme conditions—to phenomena involving very high energies or very small distances—one sometimes gets results that are ambiguous or not really sensible at all. Then it is clear that one has reached the limits of application of the theory and that some further development is needed. The Class Two difficulties are important even for

the physicist, because they put a limitation on how far he can use the rules of quantum theory to get results comparable with experiment.

I should like to say a little more about the Class One difficulties. I feel that one should not be bothered with them too much, because they are difficulties that refer to the present stage in the development of our physical picture and are almost certain to change with future development. There is one strong reason, I think, why one can be quite confident that these difficulties will change. There are some fundamental constants in nature: the charge on the electron (designated e), Planck's constant divided by 2π (designated h) and the velocity of light (c). From these fundamental constants one can construct a number that has no dimensions: the number hc/e^2. That number is found by experiment to have the value 137, or something very close to 137. Now, there is no known reason why it should have this value rather than some other number. Various people have put forward ideas about it, but there is no accepted theory. Still, one can be fairly sure that someday physicists will solve the problem and explain why the number has this value. There will be a physics in the future that works when hc/e^2 has the value 137 and that will not work when it has any other value.

The physics of the future, of course, cannot have the three quantities h, e and c all as fundamental quantities. Only two of them can be fundamental, and the third must be derived from those two. It is almost certain that c will be one of the two fundamental ones. The velocity of light, c, is so important in the four-dimensional picture, and it plays such a fundamental role in the special theory of relativity, correlating our units of space and time, that it has to be fundamental. Then we are faced with the fact that of the two quantities h and e, one will be fundamental and one will be derived. If h is fundamental, e will have to be explained in some way in terms of the square root of h, and it seems most unlikely that any fundamental theory can give e in terms of a square root, since square roots do not occur in basic equations. It is much more likely that e will be the fundamental quantity and that h will be explained in terms of e^2. Then there will be no square root in the basic equations. I think one is on safe ground if one makes the guess that in the physical picture we shall have at some future stage e and c will be fundamental quantities and h will be derived.

If h is a derived quantity instead of a fundamental one, our whole set of ideas about uncertainty will be altered: h is the fundamental quantity that occurs in the Heisenberg uncertainty relation connecting the amount of uncertainty in a position and in a momentum. This uncertainty relation cannot play a fundamental role in a theory in which h itself is not a fundamental quantity. I think one can make a safe guess that uncertainty relations in their present form will not survive in the physics of the future.

Of course there will not be a return to the determinism of classical physical theory. Evolution does not go backward. It will have to go forward. There will have to be some new development that is quite unexpected, that we cannot make a guess about, which will take us still further from classical ideas but which will alter completely the discussion of uncertainty relations. And when this new development occurs, people will find it all rather futile to have had so much of a discussion on the role of observation in the theory, because they will have then a much better point of view from which to look at things. So I shall say that if we can find a way to describe the uncertainty relations and the indeterminacy of present quantum mechanics that is satisfying to our philosophical ideas, we can count ourselves lucky. But if we cannot find such a way, it is nothing to be really disturbed about. We simply have to take into account that we are at a transitional stage

and that perhaps it is quite impossible to get a satisfactory picture for this stage.

I have disposed of the Class One difficulties by saying that they are really not so important, that if one can make progress with them one can count oneself lucky, and that if one cannot it is nothing to be genuinely disturbed about. The Class Two difficulties are the really serious ones. They arise primarily from the fact that when we apply our quantum theory to fields in the way we have to if we are to make it agree with special relativity, interpreting it in terms of the three-dimensional sections I have mentioned, we have equations that at first look all right. But when one tries to solve them, one finds that they do not have any solutions. At this point we ought to say that we do not have a theory. But physicists are very ingenious about it, and they have found a way to make progress in spite of this obstacle. They find that when they try to solve the equations, the trouble is that certain quantities that ought to be finite are actually infinite. One gets integrals that diverge instead of converging to something definite. Physicists have found that there is a

way to handle these infinities according to certain rules, which makes it possible to get definite results. This method is known as the renormalization method.

I shall merely explain the idea in words. We start out with a theory involving equations. In these equations there occur certain parameters: the charge of the electron, e, the mass of the electron, m, and things of a similar nature. One then finds that these quantities, which appear in the original equations, are not equal to the measured values of the charge and the mass of the electron. The measured values differ from these by certain correcting terms—$\triangle e$, $\triangle m$ and so on—so that the total charge is $e + \triangle e$ and the total mass $m + \triangle m$. These changes in charge and mass are brought about through the interaction of our elementary particle with other things. Then one says that $e + \triangle e$ and $m + \triangle m$, being the observed things, are the important things. The original e and m are just mathematical parameters; they are unobservable and therefore just tools one can discard when one has got far enough to bring in the things that one can com-

LOUIS DE BROGLIE (1892–) put forward the idea that particles are associated with waves. This photograph was made in 1929, five years after the appearance of his paper.

pare with observation. This would be a quite correct way to proceed if $\triangle e$ and $\triangle m$ were small (or even if they were not so small but finite) corrections. According to the actual theory, however, $\triangle e$ and $\triangle m$ are infinitely great. In spite of that fact one can still use the formalism and get results in terms of $e + \triangle e$ and $m + \triangle m$, which one can interpret by saying that the original e and m have to be minus infinity of a suitable amount to compensate for the $\triangle e$ and $\triangle m$ that are infinitely great. One can use the theory to get results that can be compared with experiment, in particular for electrodynamics. The surprising thing is that in the case of electrodynamics one gets results that are in extremely good agreement with experiment. The agreement applies to many significant figures—the kind of accuracy that previously one had only in astronomy. It is because of this good agreement that physicists do attach some value to the renormalization theory, in spite of its illogical character.

It seems to be quite impossible to put this theory on a mathematically sound basis. At one time physical theory was all built on mathematics that was inherently

sound. I do not say that physicists always use sound mathematics; they often use unsound steps in their calculations. But previously when they did so it was simply because of, one might say, laziness. They wanted to get results as quickly as possible without doing unnecessary work. It was always possible for the pure mathematician to come along and make the theory sound by bringing in further steps, and perhaps by introducing quite a lot of cumbersome notation and other things that are desirable from a mathematical point of view in order to get everything expressed rigorously but do not contribute to the physical ideas. The earlier mathematics could always be made sound in that way, but in the renormalization theory we have a theory that has defied all the attempts of the mathematician to make it sound. I am inclined to suspect that the renormalization theory is something that will not survive in the future, and that the remarkable agreement between its results and experiment should be looked on as a fluke.

This is perhaps not altogether surprising, because there have been similar flukes in the past. In fact, Bohr's elec-

tron-orbit theory was found to give very good agreement with observation as long as one confined oneself to one-electron problems. I think people will now say that this agreement was a fluke, because the basic ideas of Bohr's orbit theory have been superseded by something radically different. I believe the successes of the renormalization theory will be on the same footing as the successes of the Bohr orbit theory applied to one-electron problems.

The renormalization theory has removed some of these Class Two difficulties, if one can accept the illogical character of discarding infinities, but it does not remove all of them. There are a good many problems left over concerning particles other than those that come into electrodynamics: the new particles—mesons of various kinds and neutrinos. There the theory is still in a primitive stage. It is fairly certain that there will have to be drastic changes in our fundamental ideas before these problems can be solved.

One of the problems is the one I have already mentioned about accounting for the number 137. Other problems are how to introduce the fundamental length to physics in some natural way, how to explain the ratios of the masses of the elementary particles and how to explain their other properties. I believe separate ideas will be needed to solve these distinct problems and that they will be solved one at a time through successive stages in the future evolution of physics. At this point I find myself in disagreement with most physicists. They are inclined to think one master idea will be discovered that will solve all these problems together. I think it is asking too much to hope that anyone will be able to solve all these problems together. One should separate them one from another as much as possible and try to tackle them separately. And I believe the future development of physics will consist of solving them one at a time, and that after any one of them has been solved there will still be a great mystery about how to attack further ones.

I might perhaps discuss some ideas I have had about how one can possibly attack some of these problems. None of these ideas has been worked out very far, and I do not have much hope for any one of them. But I think they are worth mentioning briefly.

One of these ideas is to introduce something corresponding to the luminiferous ether, which was so popular among the physicists of the 19th century. I said earlier that physics does not evolve back-

$$ds^2 = c^2dt^2 - dx^2 - dy^2 - dz^2$$

FOUR-DIMENSIONAL SYMMETRY introduced by the special theory of relativity is not quite perfect. This equation is the expression for the invariant distance in four-dimensional space-time. The symbol s is the invariant distance; c, the speed of light; t, time; x, y and z, the three spatial dimensions. The d's are differentials. The lack of complete symmetry lies in the fact that the contribution from the time direction (c^2dt^2) does not have the same sign as the contributions from the three spatial directions ($-dx^2$, $-dy^2$ and $-dz^2$).

$$\left(\frac{ih}{2\pi c}\frac{\partial}{\partial t} + \frac{e^2}{cr}\right)^2 \psi = \left[m^2c^2 - \frac{h^2}{4\pi^2}\left(\frac{\partial^2}{\partial x^2} + \frac{\partial^2}{\partial y^2} + \frac{\partial^2}{\partial z^2}\right)\right]\psi$$

SCHRÖDINGER'S FIRST WAVE EQUATION did not fit experimental results because it did not take into account the spin of the electron, which was not known at the time. The equation is a generalization of De Broglie's equation for the motion of a free electron. The symbol e represents the charge on the electron; i, the square root of minus one; h, Planck's constant; r, the distance from the nucleus; ψ, Schrödinger's wave function; m, the mass of the electron. The symbols resembling sixes turned backward are partial derivatives.

$$\left(E + \frac{e^2}{r}\right)\psi = -\frac{h^2}{8\pi^2 m}\left(\frac{\partial^2}{\partial x^2} + \frac{\partial^2}{\partial y^2} + \frac{\partial^2}{\partial z^2}\right)\psi$$

SCHRÖDINGER'S SECOND WAVE EQUATION is an approximation to the original equation, which does not take into account the refinements that are required by relativity.

ward. When I talk about reintroducing the ether, I do not mean to go back to the picture of the ether that one had in the 19th century, but I do mean to introduce a new picture of the ether that will conform to our present ideas of quantum theory. The objection to the old idea of the ether was that if you suppose it to be a fluid filling up the whole of space, in any place it has a definite velocity, which destroys the four-dimensional symmetry required by Einstein's special principle of relativity. Einstein's special relativity killed this idea of the ether.

But with our present quantum theory we no longer have to attach a definite velocity to any given physical thing, because the velocity is subject to uncertainty relations. The smaller the mass of the thing we are interested in, the more important are the uncertainty relations. Now, the ether will certainly have very little mass, so that uncertainty relations for it will be extremely important. The velocity of the ether at some particular place should therefore not be pictured as definite, because it will be subject to uncertainty relations and so may be anything over a wide range of values. In that way one can get over the difficulties of reconciling the existence of an ether with the special theory of relativity.

There is one important change this will make in our picture of a vacuum. We would like to think of a vacuum as a region in which we have complete symmetry between the four dimensions of space-time as required by special relativity. If there is an ether subject to uncertainty relations, it will not be possible to have this symmetry accurately. We can suppose that the velocity of the ether is equally likely to be anything within a wide range of values that would give the symmetry only approximately. We cannot in any precise way proceed to the limit of allowing all values for the velocity between plus and minus the velocity of light, which we would have to do in order to make the symmetry accurate. Thus the vacuum becomes a state that is unattainable. I do not think that this is a physical objection to the theory. It would mean that the vacuum is a state we can approach very closely. There is no limit as to how closely we can approach it, but we can never attain it. I believe that would be quite satisfactory to the experimental physicist. It would, however, mean a departure from the notion of the vacuum that we have in the quantum theory, where we start off with the vacuum state having exactly the symmetry required by special relativity.

That is one idea for the development of physics in the future that would

ERWIN SCHRÖDINGER (1887–1961) devised his wave equation by extending De Broglie's idea that waves are associated with particles to the electrons moving around the nucleus. This photograph was made in 1929, four years after he had published his second equation.

change our picture of the vacuum, but change it in a way that is not unacceptable to the experimental physicist. It has proved difficult to continue with the theory, because one would need to set up mathematically the uncertainty relations for the ether and so far some satisfactory theory along these lines has not been discovered. If it could be developed satisfactorily, it would give rise to a new kind of field in physical theory, which might help in explaining some of the elementary particles.

Another possible picture I should like to mention concerns the question of why all the electric charges that are observed in nature should be multiples of one elementary unit, e. Why does one not have a continuous distribution of charge occurring in nature? The picture I propose goes back to the idea of Faraday lines of force and involves a development of this idea. The Faraday

lines of force are a way of picturing electric fields. If we have an electric field in any region of space, then according to Faraday we can draw a set of lines that have the direction of the electric field. The closeness of the lines to one another gives a measure of the strength of the field—they are close where the field is strong and less close where the field is weak. The Faraday lines of force give us a good picture of the electric field in classical theory.

When we go over to quantum theory, we bring a kind of discreteness into our basic picture. We can suppose that the continuous distribution of Faraday lines of force that we have in the classical picture is replaced by just a few discrete lines of force with no lines of force between them.

Now, the lines of force in the Faraday picture end where there are charges. Therefore with these quantized Faraday lines of force it would be reasonable to suppose the charge associated with each line, which has to lie at the end if the line of force has an end, is always the same (apart from its sign), and is always just the electronic charge, − e or + e. This leads us to a picture of discrete Faraday lines of force, each associated with a charge, − e or + e. There is a direction attached to each line, so that the ends of a line that has two ends are not the same, and there is a charge + e at one end and a charge − e at the other. We may have lines of force extending to infinity, of course, and then there is no charge.

If we suppose that these discrete Faraday lines of force are something basic in physics and lie at the bottom of our picture of the electromagnetic field, we shall have an explanation of why charges always occur in multiples of e. This happens because if we have any particle with some lines of force ending on it, the number of these lines must be a whole number. In that way we get a picture that is qualitatively quite reasonable.

We suppose these lines of force can move about. Some of them, forming closed loops or simply extending from minus infinity to infinity, will correspond to electromagnetic waves. Others will have ends, and the ends of these lines will be the charges. We may have a line of force sometimes breaking. When that happens, we have two ends appearing, and there must be charges at the two ends. This process—the breaking of a line of force—would be the picture for the creation of an electron (e) and a positron (e+). It would be quite a reasonable picture, and if one could develop it, it would provide a theory in which e appears as a basic quantity. I have not yet found any reasonable system of equations of motion for these lines of force, and so I just put forward the idea as a possible physical picture we might have in the future.

There is one very attractive feature in this picture. It will quite alter the discussion of renormalization. The renormalization we have in our present quantum electrodynamics comes from starting off with what people call a bare electron—an electron without a charge

on it. At a certain stage in the theory one brings in the charge and puts it on the electron, thereby making the electron interact with the electromagnetic field. This brings a perturbation into the equations and causes a change in the mass of the electron, the $\triangle m$, which is to be added to the previous mass of the electron. The procedure is rather roundabout because it starts off with the unphysical concept of the bare electron. Probably in the improved physical picture we shall have in the future the bare electron will not exist at all.

Now, that state of affairs is just what we have with the discrete lines of force. We can picture the lines of force as strings, and then the electron in the picture is the end of a string. The string itself is the Coulomb force around the electron. A bare electron means an electron without the Coulomb force around it. That is inconceivable with this picture, just as it is inconceivable to think of the end of a piece of string without thinking of the string itself. This, I think, is the kind of way in which we should try to develop our physical picture—to bring in ideas that make inconceivable the things we do not want to have. Again we have a picture that looks reasonable, but I have not found the proper equations for developing it.

I might mention a third picture with which I have been dealing lately. It involves departing from the picture of the electron as a point and thinking of it as a kind of sphere with a finite size. Of course, it is really quite an old idea to picture the electron as a sphere, but previously one had the difficulty of discussing a sphere that is subject to acceleration and to irregular motion. It will get distorted, and how is one to deal with the distortions? I propose that one should allow the electron to have, in general, an arbitrary shape and size. There will be some shapes and sizes in which it has less energy than in others, and it will tend to assume a spherical shape with a certain size in which the electron has the least energy.

This picture of the extended electron has been stimulated by the discovery of the mu meson, or muon, one of the new particles of physics. The muon has the surprising property of being almost identical with the electron except in one particular, namely, its mass is some 200 times greater than the mass of the electron. Apart from this disparity in mass the muon is remarkably similar to the electron, having, to an extremely high degree of accuracy, the same spin and the same magnetic moment in proportion to its mass as the electron does. This

WERNER HEISENBERG (1901–) introduced matrix mechanics, which, like the Schrödinger theory, accounted for the motions of the electron. This photograph was made in 1929.

leads to the suggestion that the muon should be looked on as an excited electron. If the electron is a point, picturing how it can be excited becomes quite awkward. But if the electron is the most stable state for an object of finite size, the muon might just be the next most stable state in which the object undergoes a kind of oscillation. That is an idea I have been working on recently. There are difficulties in the development of this idea, in particular the difficulty of bringing in the correct spin.

I have mentioned three possible ways in which one might think of developing our physical picture. No doubt there will be others that other people will think of. One hopes that sooner or later someone will find an idea that really fits and leads to a big development. I am rather pessimistic about it and am inclined to think none of them will be good enough. The future evolution of basic physics—that is to say, a development that will really solve one of the fundamental problems, such as bringing in the fundamental length or calculating the ratio of the masses—may require some much more drastic change in our physical picture. This would mean that in our present attempts to think of a new physical picture we are setting our imaginations to work in terms of inadequate physical concepts. If that is really the case, how can we hope to make progress in the future?

There is one other line along which one can still proceed by theoretical means. It seems to be one of the fundamental features of nature that fundamental physical laws are described in terms of a mathematical theory of great beauty and power, needing quite a high standard of mathematics for one to understand it. You may wonder: Why is nature constructed along these lines? One can only answer that our present knowledge seems to show that nature is so constructed. We simply have to accept it. One could perhaps describe the situation by saying that God is a mathematician of a very high order, and He used very advanced mathematics in constructing the universe. Our feeble attempts at mathematics enable us to understand a bit of the universe, and as we proceed to develop higher and higher mathematics we can hope to understand the universe better.

This view provides us with another way in which we can hope to make advances in our theories. Just by studying mathematics we can hope to make a guess at the kind of mathematics that will come into the physics of the future.

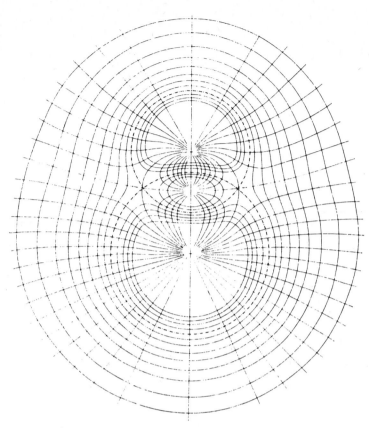

LINES OF FORCE in an electromagnetic field, if they are assumed to be discrete in the quantum theory, suggest why electric charges always occur in multiples of the charge of the electron. In Dirac's view, when a line of force has two ends, there is a particle with charge − e, perhaps an electron, at one end and a particle with charge + e, perhaps a positron, at the other end. When a closed line of force is broken, an electron-positron pair materializes.

A good many people are working on the mathematical basis of quantum theory, trying to understand the theory better and to make it more powerful and more beautiful. If someone can hit on the right lines along which to make this development, it may lead to a future advance in which people will first discover the equations and then, after examining them, gradually learn how to apply them. To some extent that corresponds with the line of development that occurred with Schrödinger's discovery of his wave equation. Schrödinger discovered the equation simply by looking for an equation with mathematical beauty. When the equation was first discovered, people saw that it fitted in certain ways, but the general principles according to which one should apply it were worked out only some two or three years later. It may well be that the next advance in physics will come about along these lines: people first discovering the equations and then needing a few years of development in order to find the physical ideas behind the equations. My own belief is that this is a more likely line of progress than trying to guess at physical pictures.

Of course, it may be that even this line of progress will fail, and then the only line left is the experimental one. Experimental physicists are continuing their work quite independently of theory, collecting a vast storehouse of information. Sooner or later there will be a new Heisenberg who will be able to pick out the important features of this information and see how to use them in a way similar to that in which Heisenberg used the experimental knowledge of spectra to build his matrix mechanics. It is inevitable that physics will develop ultimately along these lines, but we may have to wait quite a long time if people do not get bright ideas for developing the theoretical side.

Infeld reminisces what it was like to work at
Cambridge University in England with two great,
but very different, theoretical physicists.

14   Dirac and Born

Leopold Infeld

Excerpt from *Quest*.

The greatest theoretical physicist in Cambridge was P. A. M. Dirac, one of the outstanding scientists of our generation, then a young man about thirty. He still occupies the chair of mathematics, the genealogy of which can be traced directly to Newton.

I knew nothing of Dirac, except that he was a great mathematical physicist. His papers, appearing chiefly in the *Proceedings of the Royal Society*, were written with wonderful clarity and great imagination. His name is usually linked with those of Heisenberg and Schroedinger as the creators of quantum mechanics. Dirac's book *The Principles of Quantum Mechanics* is regarded as the bible of modern physics. It is deep, simple, lucid and original. It can only be compared in its importance and maturity to Newton's *Principia*. Admired by everyone as a genius, as a great star in the firmament of English physics, he created a legend around him. His thin figure with its long hands, walking in heat and cold without overcoat or hat, was a familiar one to Cambridge students. His loneliness and shyness were famous among physicists. Only a few men could penetrate his solitude. One of the fellows, a well-known physicist, told me:

"I still find it very difficult to talk with Dirac. If I need his advice I try to formulate my question as briefly as possible. He looks for five minutes at the ceiling, five minutes at the windows, and then says 'Yes' or 'No.' And he is always right."

Once—according to a story which I heard—Dirac was lecturing in the United States and the chairman called for questions after the lecture. One of the audience said:

"I did not understand this and this in your arguments."

Dirac sat quietly, as though the man had not spoken. A disagreeable silence ensued, and the chairman turned to Dirac uncertainly:

"Would you not be kind enough, Professor Dirac, to answer this question?"

To which Dirac replied: "It was not a question; it was a statement."

Another story also refers to his stay in the United States. He lived in an apartment with a famous French physicist and they invariably talked English to each other. Once the French physicist, finding it difficult to explain something in English, asked Dirac, who is half English and half French:

"Do you speak French?"

"Yes. French is my mother's tongue," answered Dirac in an unusually long sentence. The French professor burst out:

"And you say this to me now, having allowed me to speak my bad, painful English for weeks! Why did you not tell me this before?"

"You did not ask me before," was Dirac's answer.

But a few scientists who knew Dirac better, who managed after years of acquaintance to talk to him, were full of praise of his gentle attitude toward everyone. They believed that his solitude was a result of shyness and could be broken in time by careful aggressiveness and persistence.

These idiosyncrasies made it difficult to work with Dirac. The result has been that Dirac has not created a school by personal contact. He has created a school by his papers, by his book, but not by collaboration. He is one of the very few scientists who could work even on a lonely island if he had a library and could perhaps even do without books and journals.

When I visited Dirac for the first time I did not know how difficult it was to talk to him as I did not then know anyone who could have warned me.

I went along the narrow wooden stairs in St John's College and knocked at the door of Dirac's room. He opened it silently and with a friendly gesture indicated an armchair. I sat down and waited for Dirac to start the conversation. Complete silence. I began by warning my host that I spoke very little English. A friendly smile but again no answer. I had to go further:

"I talked with Professor Fowler. He told me that I am supposed to work with you. He suggested that I work on the internal conversion effect of positrons."

No answer. I waited for some time and tried a direct question:
"Do you have any objection to my working on this subject?"
"No."
At least I had got a word out of Dirac.

Then I spoke of the problem, took out my pen in order to write a formula. Without saying a word Dirac got up and brought paper. But my pen refused to write. Silently Dirac took out his pencil and handed it to me. Again I asked him a direct question to which I received an answer in five words which took me two days to digest. The conversation was finished. I made an attempt to prolong it.

"Do you mind if I bother you sometimes when I come across difficulties?"
"No."

I left Dirac's room, surprised and depressed. He was not forbidding, and I should have had no disagreeable feeling had I known what everyone in Cambridge knew. If he seemed peculiar to Englishmen, how much more so he seemed to a Pole who had polished his smooth tongue in Lwow cafés! One of Dirac's principles is:

"One must not start a sentence before one knows how to finish it."

Someone in Cambridge generalized this ironically:

"One must not start a life before one knows how to finish it."

It is difficult to make friends in England. The process is slow and it takes time for one to graduate from pleasantries about the weather to personal themes. But for me it was exactly right. I was safe because nobody on the island would suddenly ask me: "Have you been married?" No conversation would even approach my personal problems. The gossipy atmosphere of Lwow's cafés belonged to the past. How we worked for hours, analyzing the actions and reactions of others, inventing talks and situations, imitating their voices, mocking their weaknesses, lifting gossip to an art and cultivating it for its own sake! I was glad of an end to these pleasures. The only remarks which one is likely to hear from an Englishman, on the subject of another's personality, are:

"He is very nice."

"He is quite nice."

Or, in the worst case:

"I believe that he is all right."

From these few variations, but much more from the subtle way in which they are spoken, one can gain a very fair picture after some practice. But the poverty of words kills the conversation after two minutes.

The first month I met scarcely anyone. The problem on which I worked required tedious calculations rather than a search for new ideas. I had never enjoyed this kind of work, but I determined to learn its technique. I worked hard. In the morning I went to a small dusty library in the Cavendish Laboratory. Every time I entered this building I became sentimental. If someone had asked me, "What is the most important place in the world?" I would have answered: "The Cavendish Laboratory." Here Maxwell and J. J. Thomson worked. From here, in the last years under Rutherford's leadership, ideas and experiments emerged which changed our picture of the external world. Nearly all the great physicists of the world have lectured in this shabby old auditorium which is, by the way, the worst I have ever seen.

I studied hard all day until late at night, interrupted only by a movie which took the place of the missing English conversation. I knew that I must bring results back to Poland. I knew what happened to anyone who returned empty-handed after a year on a fellowship. I had heard conversations on the subject and I needed only to change the names about to have a complete picture:

A: I saw Infeld today; he is back already. What did he do in England?

B: We have just searched carefully through the science abstracts. He didn't publish anything during the whole year.

A: What? He couldn't squeeze out even one brief paper in twelve months, when he had nothing else to do and had the best help in the world?

B: I'm sure he didn't. He is finished now. I am really very sorry for him. Loria ought to have known better than to make a fool of himself by recommending Infeld for a Rockefeller fellowship.

A: We can have fun when Loria comes here. We'll ask him what his
protégé did in England. Loria is very talkative. Let's give him a
good opportunity.

B: Yes. It will be quite amusing. What about innocently asking
Infeld to give a lecture about Cambridge and his work there? It
will be fun to see him dodging the subject of his own work.

This is the way academic failure was discussed in Poland. I
should have little right to object. Bitter competition and lack
of opportunity create this atmosphere.

When I came to Cambridge, before the academic year began,
I learned that Professor Born would lecture there for a year. His
name, too, is well known to every physicist. He was as famous
for the distinguished work which he did in theoretical physics
as for the school which he created. Born was a professor in Goettingen, the strongest mathematical center of the world before it
was destroyed by Hitler. Many mathematicians and physicists
from all over the world went to Goettingen to do research in the
place associated with the shining names of Gauss in the past and
Hilbert in the present. Dirac had had a fellowship in Goettingen
and Heisenberg obtained his docentship there. Some of the most
important papers in quantum mechanics were written in collaboration by Born and Heisenberg. Born was the first to present
the probability interpretation of quantum mechanics, introducing ideas which penetrated deeply into philosophy and are
linked with the much-discussed problem of determinism and
indeterminism.

I also knew that Born had recently published an interesting
note in *Nature*, concerning the generalization of Maxwell's
theory of electricity, and had announced a paper, dealing at
length with this problem which would appear shortly in the
Proceedings of the Royal Society.

Being of Jewish blood, Professor Born had to leave Germany
and immediately received five offers, from which he chose the
invitation to Cambridge. For the first term he announced a course
on the theory on which he was working.

I attended his lectures. The audience consisted of graduate
students and fellows from other colleges, chiefly research work-

ers. Born spoke English with a heavy German accent. He was about fifty, with gray hair and a tense, intelligent face with eyes in which the suffering expression was intensified by fatigue. In the beginning I did not understand his lectures fully. The whole general theory seemed to be sketchy, a program rather than a finished piece of work.

His lectures and papers revealed the difference between the German and English style in scientific work, as far as general comparisons of this kind make any sense at all. It was in the tradition of the German school to publish results quickly. Papers appeared in German journals six weeks after they were sent to the editor. Characteristic of this spirit of competition and priority quarrels was a story which Loria told me of a professor of his in Germany, a most distinguished man. This professor had attacked someone's work, and it turned out that he had read the paper too quickly; his attack was unjustified, and he simply had not taken the trouble to understand what the author said. When this was pointed out to him he was genuinely sorry that he had published a paper containing a severe and unjust criticism. But he consoled himself with the remark: "Better a wrong paper than no paper at all."

The English style of work is quieter and more dignified. No one is interested in quick publishing, and it matters much less to an Englishman when someone else achieves the same results and publishes them a few days earlier. It takes six months to print a paper in the *Proceedings of the Royal Society*. Priority quarrels and stealing of ideas are practically unknown in England. The attitude is: "Better no paper at all than a wrong paper."

In the beginning, as I have said, I was not greatly impressed with Born's results. But later, when he came to the concrete problem of generalizing Maxwell's equations, I found the subject exciting, closely related to the problems on which I had worked before. In general terms the idea was:

Maxwell's theory is the theory of the electromagnetic field, and it forms one of the most important chapters in theoretical physics. Its great achievement lies in the introduction of the concept of the *field*. It explains a wide region of experimental facts but, like every theory, it has its limitations. Maxwell's theory does not explain why elementary particles like electrons exist, and it does not bind the properties of the field to those of matter.

After the discovery of elementary particles it was clear that Maxwell's theory, like all our theories, captures only part of the truth. And again, as always in physics, attempts were made to cover, through modifications and generalizations, a wider range of facts. Born succeeded in generalizing Maxwell's equations and replacing them by new ones. As their first approximation these new equations gave the old laws confirmed by experiments. But in addition they gave a new solution representing an elementary particle, the electron. Its physical properties were determined to some extent by the new laws governing the field. The aim of this new theory was to form a bridge between two hitherto isolated and unreconciled concepts: field and matter. Born called it the Unitary Field Theory, the name indicating the union of these two fundamental concepts.

After one of his lectures I asked Born whether he would lend me a copy of his manuscript. He gave it to me with the assurance that he would be very happy if I would help him. I wanted to understand a point which had not been clear to me during the lecture and which seemed to me to be an essential step. Born's new theory allowed the construction of an elementary particle, the electron, with a finite mass. Here lay the essential difference between Born's new and Maxwell's old theories. A whole chain of argument led to this theoretical determination of the mass of the electron. I suspected that something was wrong in this derivation. On the evening of the day I received the paper the point suddenly became clear to me. I knew that the mass of the electron was wrongly evaluated in Born's paper and I knew how to find the right value. My whole argument seemed simple and convincing to me. I could hardly wait to tell it to Born, sure that he would see my point immediately. The next day I went to him after his lecture and said:

"I read your paper; the mass of the electron is wrong."

Born's face looked even more tense than usual. He said:

"This is very interesting. Show me why."

Two of his audience were still present in the lecture room. I took a piece of chalk and wrote a relativistic formula for the mass density. Born interrupted me angrily:

"This problem has nothing to do with relativity theory. I don't like such a formal approach. I find nothing wrong with the way I introduced the mass." Then he turned toward the two students who were listening to our stormy discussion.

"What do you think of my derivation?"

They nodded their heads in full approval. I put down the piece of chalk and did not even try to defend my point.

Born felt a little uneasy. Leaving the lecture room, he said:

"I shall think it over."

I was annoyed at Born's behavior as well as at my own and was, for one afternoon, disgusted with Cambridge. I thought: "Here I met two great physicists. One of them does not talk. I could as easily read his papers in Poland as here. The other talks, but he is rude." I scrutinized my argument carefully but could find nothing wrong with it. I made some further progress and found that new and interesting consequences could be drawn if the "free densities" were introduced relativistically. A different interpretation of the unitary theory could be achieved which would deepen its physical meaning.

The next day I went again to Born's lecture. He stood at the door before the lecture room. When I passed him he said to me:

"I am waiting for you. You were quite right. We will talk it over after the lecture. You must not mind my being rude. Everyone who has worked with me knows it. I have a resistance against accepting something from outside. I get angry and swear but always accept after a time if it is right."

Our collaboration had begun with a quarrel, but a day later complete peace and understanding had been restored. I told Born about my new interpretation connecting more closely and clearly, through the "free densities," the field and particle aspects. He immediately accepted these ideas with enthusiasm. Our collaboration grew closer. We discussed, worked together after lectures, in Born's home or mine. Soon our relationship became informal and friendly.

I ceased to work on my old problem. After three months of my stay in Cambridge we published together two notes in *Nature*, and a long paper, in which the foundations of the New Unitary Field Theory were laid down more deeply and carefully than before, was ready for publication in the *Proceedings of the Royal Society*.

For the first time in my life I had close contact with a famous, distinguished physicist, and I learned much through our relationship. Born came to my home on his bicycle whenever he wished to communicate with me, and I visited him, unannounced, whenever I felt like it. The atmosphere of his home was a combination of high intellectual level with heavy Germany pedantry. In the hall there was a wooden gadget announcing which of the members of the family were out and which were in.

I marveled at the way in which he managed his heavy correspondence, answering letters with incredible dispatch, at the same time looking through scientific papers. His tremendous collection of reprints was well ordered; even the reprints from cranks and lunatics were kept, under the heading "Idiots." Born functioned like an entire institution, combining vivid imagination with splendid organization. He worked quickly and in a restless mood. As in the case of nearly all scientists, not only the result was important but the fact that he had achieved it. This is human, and scientists are human. The only scientist I have ever met for whom this personal aspect of work is of no concern at all is Einstein. Perhaps to find complete freedom from human weakness we must look up to the highest level achieved by the human race. There was something childish and attractive in Born's eagerness to go ahead quickly, in his restlessness and his moods, which changed suddenly from high enthusiasm to deep depression. Sometimes when I would come with a new idea he would say rudely, "I think it is rubbish," but he never minded if I applied the same phrase to some of his ideas. But the great, the celebrated Born was as happy and as pleased as a young student at words of praise and encouragement. In his enthusiastic attitude, in the vividness of his mind, the impulsiveness with which he grasped and rejected ideas, lay his great charm. Near his bed he had always a pencil and a piece of paper on which to scribble his inspirations, to avoid turning them over and over in his mind during sleepless nights.

Once I asked Born how he came to study theoretical physics. I was interested to know at what age the first impulse to choose a definite path in life crystalizes. Born told me his story. His father was a medical man, a university professor, famous and rich. When he died he left his son plenty of money and good advice. The money was sufficient, in normal times, to assure his son's independence. The advice was simply to listen during his first student year to many lectures on many subjects and to make a choice only at the end of the first year. So young Born went to the university at Breslau, listened to lectures on law, literature, biology, music, economics, astronomy. He liked the astronomy lectures the most. Perhaps not so much for the lectures themselves as for the old Gothic building in which they were held. But he soon discovered that to understand astronomy one must know mathematics. He asked where the best mathematicians in the world were to be found and was told "Goettingen." So he went to Goettingen, where he finished his studies as a theoretical physicist, habilitated and finally became a professor.

"At that time, before the war," he added, "I could have done whatever I wanted with my life since I did not even know what the struggle for existence meant. I believe I could have become a successful writer or a pianist. But I found the work in theoretical physics more pleasant and more exciting than anything else."

Through our work I gained confidence in myself, a confidence that was strengthened by Born's assurance that ours was one of the pleasantest collaborations he had ever known. Loyally he stressed my contributions in his lectures and pointed out my share in our collaboration. I was happy in the excitement of obtaining new results and in the conviction that I was working on essential problems, the importance of which I certainly exaggerated. Having new ideas, turning blankness into understanding, suddenly finding the right solution after weeks or months of painful doubt, creates perhaps the highest emotion man can experience. Every scientist knows this feeling of ecstasy even if his achievements are small. But this pure feeling of *Eureka* is mixed with overtones of very human, selfish emotions: "*I* found it; *I* will have an important paper; it will help me in my career." I was fully aware of the presence of these overtones in my own consciousness.

Erwin Schrödinger developed some of the basic equations of modern atomic theory. This article considers a book in which Schrödinger discusses the repercussions of the quantum theory.

---

15   I am this Whole World: Erwin Schrödinger

Jeremy Bernstein

Chapter from Bernstein's book, *A Comprehensible World: On Modern Science and its Origins*, published in 1961.

THERE is a parlor game often played by my colleagues in physics. It consists of trying to decide whether the physicists of the extraordinary generation that produced the modern quantum theory, in the late twenties, were intrinsically more gifted than our present generation or whether they simply had the good fortune to be at the height of their creative powers (for physicists, with some notable exceptions, this lies between the ages of twenty-five and thirty-five at a time when there was a state of acute and total crisis in physics—a crisis brought about by the fact that existing physics simply did not account for what was known about the atom. In brief, if our generation had been alive at that time, could we have invented the quantum theory?

It is a question that will never be answered. But there is no doubt that the group of men who *did* invent the theory was absolutely remarkable. Aside from Max Planck and Einstein (it was Planck who invented the notion of the quantum—the idea that energy was always emitted and absorbed in distinct units, or quanta, and not continuously, like water flowing from a tap—and it was Einstein who pointed out how Planck's idea could be extended and used to explain a variety of mysteries about matter and radiation that physicists were contending with), who did their important work before 1925, the list includes Niels Bohr, who conceived the theory that the orbits of electrons around atoms were quantized (electrons, according to the Bohr theory, can move only in special elliptical paths— "Bohr orbits"—around the nucleus and not in any path, as the older physics would have predicted) ; Prince Louis de Broglie, a French aristocrat who conjectured in his doctoral thesis that both light and matter had particle and wave aspects; Werner Heisenberg, who made the first breakthrough that led to the mathematical formulation of the quantum theory, from which the Bohr orbits can be derived, and whose "uncertainty relations" set the limitations on measurements of atomic systems; P. A. M. Dirac, who made basic contributions to the mathematics of the theory and who showed how it could be reconciled with Einstein's theory of relativity; Wolfgang Pauli, whose "exclusion principle" led to an explanation of why there is a periodic table of chemical elements; Max Born and Pascual Jordan, who contributed to the interpretation of the theory; and, finally, Erwin Schrödinger, whose Schrödinger Equation is in many ways the basic equation of the quantum theory, and is to the new physics what Newton's laws of motion were to the physics that went before it.

While Heisenberg, Pauli, and Dirac were all in their early twenties when they did their work, de Broglie and Bohr were older, as was Schrödinger, who was born in Vienna in 1887. In 1926, he published the paper in which his equation was formulated. Oddly, just a few years before, he had decided to give up physics altogether for philosophy. Philipp Frank, who had been a classmate of Schrödinger's in Vienna, once told me that just before Schrödinger began his work on the quantum theory he had been working on a psychological theory of color perception. Schrödinger himself writes in the preface of his last book, *My View of the World* (Cambridge), published posthumously (he died in 1961), "In 1918, when I was thirty-one, I had good reason to expect a chair of theoretical physics at Czernowitz. . . . I was prepared to do a good job lecturing on theoretical physics . . . but for the rest, to devote myself to philosophy, being deeply imbued at the time with the writings of Spinoza, Schopenhauer, Ernst Mach, Richard Semon, and Richard Avenarius. My guardian angel intervened: Czernowitz soon no longer belonged to Austria. So nothing came of it. I had to stick to theoretical physics, and, to my astonishment, something occasionally emerged from it."

The early quantum theoreticians were a small group, mainly Europeans, who knew each other well. There was among them a sense of collaborating on one of the most important discoveries in the history of physics. In his *Science and the Common Understanding,* Robert Oppenheimer wrote, "Our understanding of atomic physics, of what we call the quantum theory of atomic systems, had its origins at the turn of the century and its great synthesis and resolutions in the nineteen-twenties. It was a heroic time. It was not the doing of any one man; it involved the collaboration of scores of scientists from many different lands, though from first to last the deeply creative and subtle and critical spirit of Niels Bohr guided, restrained, deepened, and finally transmuted the enterprise. It was a period of patient work in the laboratory, of crucial experiments and daring action, of many false starts and many untenable conjectures. It was a time of earnest correspondence and hurried conjectures, of debate, criticism, and brilliant mathematical improvisation. For those who participated, it was a time of creation; there was terror as well as exaltation in their new insight. It will probably not be recorded very completely as history. As history, its recreation would call for an art as high as the story of Oedipus or the story of Cromwell, yet in a realm of action so remote from our common experience that it is unlikely to be known to any poet or any historian."

However, as the outlines of the theory became clearer, a sharp division of opinion arose as to the ultimate significance of it. Indeed, de Broglie, Einstein, and Schrödinger came to feel that even though the theory illuminated vast stretches of physics and chemistry ("All of chemistry and most of physics," Dirac wrote), there was fundamentally something unsatisfactory about it. The basic problem that troubled them was that the theory abandons causation of the kind that had been the goal of the classical physics of Newton and his successors: In the quantum theory, one cannot ask what one single electron in a single atom will do at a given time; the theory only describes the most probable behavior of an electron in a large collection of electrons. The theory is fundamentally statistical and deals solely with probabilities. The Schrödinger Equation enables one to work out the mathematical expressions for these probabilities and to determine how the probabilities will change in time, but according to the accepted interpretation it does not provide a step-by-step description of the motion of, say, a single electron in an atom, in the way that Newtonian mechanics projects the trajectory of a planet moving around the sun.

To most physicists, these limitations are a fundamental limitation, in principle, on the type of information that can be gathered by carrying out measurements of atomic systems. These limitations, which were first analyzed by Heisenberg and Bohr, are summarized in the Heisenberg uncertainty relations, which state, generally speaking, that the very process of making most measurements of an atomic system disturbs the system's behavior so greatly that it is put into a state qualitatively different from the one it was in before the measurement. (For example, to measure the position of an electron in an atom, one must illuminate the electron with light of very short wave length. This light carries so much momentum that the process of illuminating the electron knocks it clear out of the atom, so a second measurement of the position of the electron in the atom is impossible. "We murder to dissect," as Wordsworth has said.) The observer—or, really, his measuring apparatus—has an essential influence on the observed. The physicists who have objected to the quantum theory feel that this limitation indicates the incompleteness of the theory and that there must exist a deeper explanation that would yield the same universal agreement with experiment that the quantum theory does but that would allow a completely deterministic description of atomic events. Naturally, the burden of finding such a theory rests upon those who feel that it must exist; so far, despite the repeated efforts of people like de Broglie, Einstein, and Schrödinger, no such theory has been forthcoming.

Schrödinger, who was a brilliant writer of both scientific texts and popular scientific essays, summarized his distaste for the quantum theory in an essay entitled *Are There Quantum Jumps?* published in 1952: "I have been trying to produce a mood that makes one wonder what parts of contemporary science will still be of interest to more than historians two thousand years hence. There have been ingenious constructs of the human mind that gave an exceedingly accurate description of observed facts and have yet lost all interest except to historians. I am thinking of the theory of epicycles. [This theory was used, especially by the Alexandrian astronomer Ptolemy, to account for the extremely complicated planetary motions that had been observed; it postulated that they were compounded of innumerable simple circular motions. Reduced to the simplest terms, a planet was presumed to move in a small circle around a point that moved in a large circle around the earth. The theory was replaced by the assumption, conceived by Copernicus and Kepler, that the planets move in elliptical orbits around the sun.] I confess to the heretical view that their modern counterpart in physical theory are the quantum jumps." In his introduction to *My View of the World,* Schrödinger puts his belief even more strongly: "There is one complaint which I shall not escape. Not a word is said here of acausality, wave mechanics, indeterminacy relations, complementarity, an expanding universe, continuous creation, etc. Why doesn't he talk about what he knows instead of trespassing on the professional philosopher's preserves? *Ne sutor supra crepidam.* On this I can cheerfully justify myself: because I do not think that these things have as much connection as is currently supposed with a philosophical view of the world." There is a story that after Schrödinger lectured, in the twenties, at the Institute of Theoretical Physics, in Copenhagen, in which Bohr was teaching, on the implications of his equation, a vigorous debate took place, in the course of which Schrödinger remarked that if he had known that the whole thing would be taken so seriously he never would have invented it in the first place.

Schrödinger was too great a scientist not to recognize the significance of the all but universal success of the quantum theory—it accounts not only for "all of chemistry and most of physics" but even for astronomy; it can be used, for example, to make very precise computations of the energy generated in the nuclear reactions that go on in the sun and other stars. Indeed, Schrödinger's popular master-piece, *What Is Life?* deals with the impact of quantum ideas on biology and above all on the molecular processes that underlie the laws of heredity. The two striking fea-tures of the hereditary mechanism are its stability and its changeability—the existence of mutations, which allow for the evolution of a biological species. The characteristics that are inherited by a child from its mother and father are all contained in several large organic molecules—the genes. Genes are maintained at a fairly high temperature, 98°F., in the human body, which means that they are subject to constant thermal agitation. The question is how does this molecule retain its identity through generation after gen-eration. Schrödinger states the problem brilliantly: "Let me throw the truly amazing situation into relief once again. Several members of the Habsburg dynasty have a peculiar disfigurement of the lower lip ('Habsburger Lippe'). Its inheritance has been studied carefully and published, complete with historical portraits, by the Im-perial Academy of Vienna, under the auspices of the fam-ily. . . . Fixing our attention on the portraits of a member of the family in the sixteenth century and of his descend-ant, living in the nineteenth, we may safely assume that the material gene structure responsible for the abnormal feature has been carried on from generation to generation through the centuries, faithfully reproduced at every one of the not very numerous cell divisions that lie between. . . . The gene has been kept at a temperature around 98°F. during all that time. How are we to understand that it has remained unperturbed by the disordering tendency of the heat motion for centuries?"

According to the quantum theory, the stability of any chemical molecule has a natural explanation. The mole-cule is in a definite energy state. To go from one state to another the molecule must absorb just the right amount of energy. If too little energy is supplied, the molecule will not make the transition. This situation differs completely from that envisaged by classical physics, in which the change of state can be achieved by absorbing any energy. It can be shown that the thermal agitations that go on in the human body do not in general supply enough energy to cause such a transition, but mutations can take place in those rare thermal processes in which enough energy is available to alter the gene.

What Is Life? was published in 1944. Since then the field of molecular biology has become one of the most active and exciting in all science. A good deal of what Schrödinger said is now dated. But the book has had an enormous influence on physicists and biologists in that it hints how the two disciplines join together at their base. Schrödinger, who received the Nobel Prize jointly with Dirac, in 1933, succeeded Max Planck at the University of Berlin in 1927. When Hitler came to power, Schrödinger, although not a Jew, was deeply affected by the political climate. Philipp Frank has told me that Schrödinger attempted to intervene in a Storm Trooper raid on a Jewish ghetto and would have been beaten to death if one of the troopers, who had studied physics, had not recognized him as Germany's most recent Nobel Laureate and persuaded his colleagues to let him go. Shortly afterward, Schrödinger went to England, then back to Austria, then to Belgium, when Austria fell, and finally to the Dublin Institute for Advanced Studies, where he remained until he returned to Vienna, in 1956. By the end of his life, he must have mastered as much general culture—scientific and nonscientific—as it is possible for any single person to absorb in this age of technical specialization. He read widely in several languages, and wrote perceptively about the relation between science and the humanities and about Greek science, in which he was particularly interested. He even wrote poetry, which, I am told, was extremely romantic.

(The pictures of Schrödinger as a young man give him a Byronic look.) What kind of personal metaphysics would such a man derive from his reading and experience? In *My View of the World,* he leaves a partial answer.

My View of the World consists of two long essays—one written in 1925, just before the discovery of the Schrödinger Equation, and one written in 1960, just before his death. In both essays he reveals himself as a mystic deeply influenced by the philosophy of the Vedas. In 1925 he writes, "This life of yours which you are living is not merely a piece of the entire existence, but is in a certain sense the *whole;* only this whole is not so constituted that it can be surveyed in one single glance. This, as we know, is what the Brahmins express in that sacred, mystic formula which is yet really so simple and so clear: *Tat tvam asi,* this is you. Or, again, in such words as 'I am in the east and in the west. I am below and above, *I am this whole world,'*" and in the later essay he returns to this theme. He does not attempt to derive or justify his convictions with scientific argument. In fact, as he stresses in his preface, he feels that modern science, his own work included, is not relevant to the search for the underlying metaphysical and moral truths by which one lives. For him, they must be intuitively, almost mystically arrived at. He writes, "It is the vision of this truth (of which the individual is seldom conscious in his actions) which underlies all morally valuable activity. It brings a man of nobility not only to risk his life for an end which he recognizes or believes to be good but—in rare cases—to lay it down in full serenity, even when there is no prospect of saving his own person. It guides the hand of the well-doer—this perhaps even more rarely—when, without hope of future reward, he gives to relieve a stranger's suffering what he cannot spare without suffering himself."

In 1960, I had the chance to visit Schrödinger in Vienna. I was studying at the Boltzmann Institute for

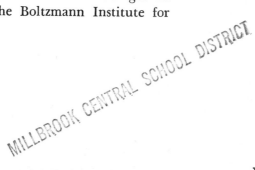

Theoretical Physics, whose director, Walter Thirring, is the son of Hans Thirring, a distinguished Austrian physicist, also a classmate of Schrödinger. Schrödinger had been very ill and he rarely appeared at the Institute. But he enjoyed maintaining his contact with physics and the young physicists who were working under Walter Thirring. Thirring took a small group of us to visit Schrödinger. He lived in an old-fashioned Viennese apartment house, with a rickety elevator and dimly lit hallways. The Schrödinger living room–library was piled to the ceiling with books, and Schrödinger was in the process of writing the second of the two essays in *My View of the World*. Physically he was extremely frail, but his intellectual vigor was intact. He told us some of the lessons that modern scientists might learn from the Greeks. In particular, he stressed the recurrent theme of the writings of his later years—that modern science may be as far from revealing the underlying laws of the natural universe as was the science of ancient Greece. It was clear from watching and listening to him that the flame that illuminated his intellectual curiosity throughout his long life still burned brightly at the end of it.

16 The Fundamental Idea of Wave Mechanics

Erwin Schrödinger

Schrödinger's Nobel Prize lecture given in December 1933.

On passing through an optical instrument, such as a telescope or a camera lens, a ray of light is subjected to a change in direction at each refracting or reflecting surface. The path of the rays can be constructed if we know the two simple laws which govern the changes in direction: the law of refraction which was discovered by Snellius a few hundred years ago, and the law of reflection with which Archimedes was familiar more than 2,000 years ago. As a simple example, Fig. 1 shows a ray A–B which is subjected to refraction at each of the four boundary surfaces of two lenses in accordance with the law of Snellius.

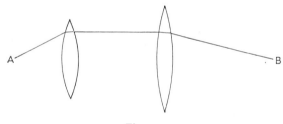

Fig. 1.

Fermat defined the total path of a ray of light from a much more general point of view. In different media, light propagates with different velocities, and the radiation path gives the appearance as if the light must arrive at its destination *as quickly as possible*. (Incidentally, it is permissible here to consider *any two* points along the ray as the starting- and end-points.) The least deviation from the path actually taken would mean a delay. This is the famous Fermat *principle of the shortest light time*, which in a marvellous manner determines the entire fate of a ray of light by a single statement and also includes the more general case, when the nature of the medium varies not suddenly at individual surfaces, but gradually from place to place. The atmosphere of the earth provides an example. The more deeply a ray of light penetrates into it from outside, the more slowly it progresses in an increasingly denser air. Although the differences in the speed of propagation are infinitesimal, Fermat's principle in these circumstances demands that the light ray should curve earthward (see Fig. 2), so that it remains a little longer in the higher «faster» layers and reaches its destination more quickly than by the shorter straight path (broken line in the figure; disregard the square,

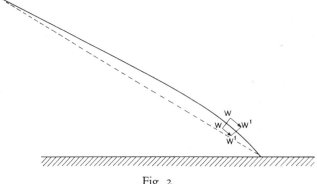

Fig. 2.

WWW¹W¹ for the time being). I think, hardly any of you will have failed to observe that the sun when it is deep on the horizon appears to be not circular but flattened: its vertical diameter looks to be shortened. This is a result of the curvature of the rays.

According to the wave theory of light, the light rays, strictly speaking, have only fictitious significance. They are not the physical paths of some particles of light, but are a mathematical device, the so-called orthogonal trajectories of wave surfaces, imaginary guide lines as it were, which point in the direction normal to the wave surface in which the latter advances (cf. Fig. 3 which shows the simplest case of concentric spherical wave surfaces and accordingly rectilinear rays, whereas Fig. 4 illustrates the case of curved

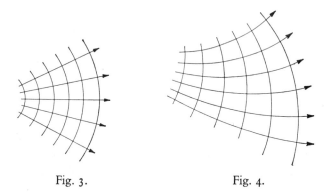

Fig. 3.   Fig. 4.

rays). It is surprising that a general principle as important as Fermat's relates directly to these mathematical guide lines, and not to the wave surfaces, and one might be inclined for this reason to consider it a mere mathematical curiosity. Far from it. It becomes properly understandable only from the point of view of wave theory and ceases to be a divine miracle. From the wave point of view, the so-called *curvature* of the light ray is far more readily understandable as a *swerving* of the wave surface, which must obviously occur when neighbouring parts of a wave surface advance at different speeds; in exactly the same manner as a company of soldiers marching forward will carry out the order «right incline» by the men taking steps of varying lengths, the right-wing man the smallest, and the left-wing man the longest. In atmospheric refraction of radiation for example (Fig. 2) the section of wave surface WW must necessarily swerve to the right towards W^1W^1 because its left half is located in slightly higher, thinner air and thus advances more rapidly than the right part at lower point. (In passing, I wish to refer to one point at which the *Snellius'* view fails. A horizontally emitted light ray should remain horizontal because the refraction index does not vary in the horizontal direction. In truth, a horizontal ray curves more strongly than any other, which is an obvious consequence of the theory of a swerving wave front.) On detailed examination the Fermat principle is found to be completely *tantamount* to the trivial and obvious statement that–given local distribution of light velocities–the wave front must swerve in the manner indicated. I cannot prove this here, but shall attempt to make it plausible. I would again ask you to visualize a rank of soldiers marching forward. To ensure that the line remains dressed, let the men be connected by a long rod which each holds firmly in his hand. No orders as to direction are given; the only order is: let each man march or run as fast as he can. If the nature of the ground varies slowly from place to place, it will be now the right wing, now the left that advances more quickly, and changes in direction will occur spontaneously. After some time has elapsed, it will be seen that the entire path travelled is not rectilinear, but somehow curved. That this curved path is exactly that by which the destination attained at any moment could be attained *most rapidly* according to the nature of the terrain, is at least quite plausible, since each of the men did his best. It will also be seen that the swerving also occurs invariably in the direction in which the terrain is worse, so that it will come to look in the end as if the men had intentionally «bypassed» a place where they would advance slowly.

The Fermat principle thus appears to be the *trivial quintessence* of the wave theory. It was therefore a memorable occasion when Hamilton made the discovery that the true movement of mass points in a field of forces (e.g. of a planet on its orbit around the sun or of a stone thrown in the gravitational field of the earth) is also governed by a very similar general principle, which carries and has made famous the name of its discoverer since then. Admittedly, the Hamilton principle does not say exactly that the mass point chooses the quickest way, but it does say something *so* similar – the analogy with the principle of the shortest travelling time of light is *so* close, that one was faced with a puzzle. It seemed as if Nature had realized one and the same law twice by entirely different means: first in the case of light, by means of a fairly obvious play of rays; and again in the case of the mass points, which was anything but obvious, unless somehow wave nature were to be attributed to them also. And this, it seemed impossible to do. Because the «mass points» on which the laws of mechanics had really been confirmed experimentally at that time were only the large, visible, sometimes *very* large bodies, the planets, for which a thing like «wave nature» appeared to be out of the question.

The smallest, elementary components of matter which we today, much more specifically, call «mass points», were purely hypothetical at the time. It was only after the discovery of radioactivity that constant refinements of methods of measurement permitted the properties of these particles to be studied in detail, and now permit the paths of such particles to be photographed and to be measured very exactly (stereophotogrammetrically) by the brilliant method of C. T. R. Wilson. As far as the measurements extend they confirm that the same mechanical laws are valid for particles as for large bodies, planets, etc. However, it was found that neither the molecule nor the individual atom can be considered as the «ultimate component»: but even the atom is a system of highly complex structure. Images are formed in our minds of the structure of atoms *consisting of* particles, images which seem to have a certain similarity with the planetary system. It was only natural that the attempt should at first be made to consider as valid the same laws of motion that had proved themselves so amazingly satisfactory on a large scale. In other words, Hamilton's mechanics, which, as I said above, culminates in the Hamilton principle, were applied also to the «inner life» of the atom. That there is a very close analogy between Hamilton's principle and Fermat's optical principle had meanwhile become all but forgotten. If it was remembered, it was considered to be nothing more than a curious trait of the mathematical theory.

Now, it is very difficult, without further going into details, to convey a proper conception of the success or failure of these classical-mechanical images of the atom. On the one hand, Hamilton's principle in particular proved to be the most faithful and reliable guide, which was simply indispensable; on the other hand one had to suffer, to do justice to the facts, the rough interference of entirely new incomprehensible postulates, of the so-called quantum conditions and quantum postulates. Strident disharmony in the symphony of classical mechanics—yet strangely familiar—played as it were on the same instrument. In mathematical terms we can formulate this as follows: whereas the Hamilton principle merely postulates that a given integral must be a minimum, without the numerical value of the minimum being established by this postulate, it is now demanded that the numerical value of the minimum should be restricted to integral multiples of a universal natural constant, Planck's quantum of action. This incidentally. The situation was fairly desperate. Had the old mechanics failed completely, it would not have been so bad. The way would then have been free to the development of a new system of mechanics. As it was, one was faced with the difficult task of saving the *soul* of the old system, whose inspiration clearly held sway in this microcosm, while at the same time flattering it as it were into accepting the quantum conditions not as gross interference but as issuing from its own innermost essence.

The way out lay just in the possibility, already indicated above, of attributing to the Hamilton principle, also, the operation of a wave mechanism on which the point-mechanical processes are essentially based, just as one had long become accustomed to doing in the case of phenomena relating to light and of the Fermat principle which governs them. Admittedly, the individual path of a mass point loses its proper physical significance and becomes as fictitious as the individual isolated ray of light. The essence of the theory, the minimum principle, however, remains not only intact, but reveals its true and simple meaning only under the wave-like aspect, as already explained. Strictly speaking, the new theory is in fact not *new*, it is a completely organic development, one might almost be tempted to say a more elaborate exposition, of the old theory.

How was it then that this new more « elaborate » exposition led to notably different results; what enabled it, when applied to the atom, to obviate difficulties which the old theory could not solve? What enabled it to render gross interference acceptable or even to make it its own?

Again, these matters can best be illustrated by analogy with optics. Quite properly, indeed, I previously called the Fermat principle the quintessence of the wave theory of light: nevertheless, it cannot render dispensible a more exact study of the wave process itself. The so-called refraction and interference phenomena of light can only be understood if we trace the wave process in detail because what matters is not only the eventual destination of the wave, but also whether at a given moment it arrives there with a wave peak or a wave trough. In the older, coarser experimental arrangements, these phenomena occurred as small details only and escaped observation. Once they were noticed and were interpreted correctly, by means of waves, it was easy to devise experiments in which the wave nature of light finds expression not only in small details, but on a very large scale in the entire character of the phenomenon.

Allow me to illustrate this by two examples, first, the example of an optical instrument, such as telescope, microscope, etc. The object is to obtain a sharp image, i.e. it is desired that all rays issuing from a point should be re-united in a point, the so-called focus (cf. Fig. 5 a). It was at first believed that it was only geometrical-optical difficulties which prevented this: they are indeed considerable. Later it was found that even in the best designed instru-

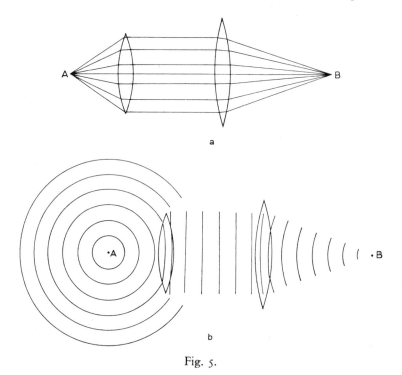

a

b

Fig. 5.

ments focussing of the rays was considerably inferior than would be expected if each ray exactly obeyed the Fermat principle independently of the neighbouring rays. The light which issues from a point and is received by the instrument is reunited behind the instrument not in a single point any more, but is distributed over a small circular area, a so-called diffraction disc, which, otherwise, is in most cases a circle only because the apertures and lens contours are generally circular. For, the cause of the phenomenon which we call *diffraction* is that not all the spherical waves issuing from the object point can be accommodated by the instrument. The lens edges and any apertures merely cut out a part of the wave surfaces (cf. Fig. 5b) and–if you will permit me to use a more suggestive expression–the injured margins resist rigid unification in a point and produce the somewhat blurred or vague image. The degree of blurring is closely associated with the *wavelength* of the light and is completely inevitable because of this deep-seated theoretical relationship. Hardly noticed at first, it governs and restricts the performance of the modern microscope which has mastered all other errors of reproduction. The images obtained of structures not much coarser or even still finer than the wavelengths of light are only remotely or not at all similar to the original.

A second, even simpler example is the shadow of an opaque object cast on a screen by a small point light source. In order to construct the shape of the shadow, each light ray must be traced and it must be established whether or not the opaque object prevents it from reaching the screen. The *margin* of the shadow is formed by those light rays which only just brush past the edge of the body. Experience has shown that the shadow.margin is not absolutely sharp even with a point-shaped light source and a sharply defined shadow-casting object. The reason for this is the same as in the first example. The wave front is as it were bisected by the body (cf. Fig. 6) and the traces of this injury result in blurring of the margin of the shadow which would be incomprehensible if the individual light rays were independent entities advancing independently of one another without reference to their neighbours.

This phenomenon – which is also called diffraction – is not as a rule very noticeable with large bodies. But if the shadow-casting body is very small at least in one dimension, diffraction finds expression firstly in that no proper shadow is formed at all, and secondly – much more strikingly – in that the small body itself becomes as it were its own source of light and radiates light in all directions (preferentially to be sure, at small angles relative to the inci-

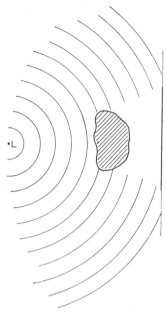

Fig. 6.

dent light). All of you are undoubtedly familiar with the so-called « motes of dust » in a light beam falling into a dark room. Fine blades of grass and spiders' webs on the crest of a hill with the sun behind it, or the errant locks of hair of a man standing with the sun behind often light up mysteriously by diffracted light, and the visibility of smoke and mist is based on it. It comes not really from the body itself, but from its immediate surroundings, an area in which it causes considerable interference with the incident wave fronts. It is interesting, and important for what follows, to observe that the area of interference always and in every direction has at least the extent of one or a few wavelengths, no matter how small the disturbing particle may be. Once again, therefore, we observe a close relationship between the phenomenon of diffraction and wavelength. This is perhaps best illustrated by reference to another wave process, i.e. sound. Because of the much greater wavelength, which is of the order of centimetres and metres, shadow formation recedes in the case of sound, and diffraction plays a major, and practically important, part: we can easily *hear* a man calling from behind a high wall or around the corner of a solid house, even if we cannot *see* him.

Let us return from optics to mechanics and explore the analogy to its fullest extent. In optics the *old* system of mechanics corresponds to intellectually operating with isolated mutually independent light rays. The new undulatory mechanics corresponds to the wave theory of light. What is gained by changing from the old view to the new is that the diffraction phenomena can be accommodated or, better expressed, what is gained is something that is strictly analogous to the diffraction phenomena of light and which on the whole must be very unimportant, otherwise the old view of mechanics would not have given full satisfaction so long. It is, however, easy to surmise that the neglected phenomenon may in some circumstances make itself very much felt, will entirely dominate the mechanical process, and will face the old system with insoluble riddles, if *the entire mechanical system is comparable in extent with the wavelengths of the «waves of matter»* which play the same part in mechanical processes as that played by the light waves in optical processes.

This is the reason why in these minute systems, the atoms, the old view was bound to fail, which though remaining intact as a close approximation for gross mechanical processes, but is no longer adequate for the delicate interplay in areas of the order of magnitude of one or a few wavelengths. It was astounding to observe the manner in which all those strange additional requirements developed spontaneously from the new undulatory view, whereas they had to be forced upon the old view to adapt them to the inner life of the atom and to provide some explanation of the observed facts.

Thus, the salient point of the whole matter is that the diameters of the atoms and the wavelength of the hypothetical material waves are of approximately the same order of magnitude. And now you are bound to ask whether it must be considered mere chance that in our continued analysis of the structure of matter we should come upon the order of magnitude of the wavelength at this of all points, or whether this is to some extent comprehensible. Further, you may ask, how we know that this is so, since the material waves are an entirely new requirement of this theory, unknown anywhere else. Or is it simply that this is an *assumption* which had to be made?

The agreement between the orders of magnitude is no mere chance, nor is any special assumption about it necessary; it follows automatically from the theory in the following remarkable manner. That the heavy *nucleus* of the atom is very much smaller than the atom and may therefore be considered as a point centre of attraction in the argument which follows may be considered as experimentally established by the experiments on the scattering of alpha rays done by Rutherford and Chadwick. Instead of the *electrons* we introduce hypothetical waves, whose wavelengths are left entirely open, because we know nothing about them yet. This leaves a letter, say *a*, indicating a still unknown figure, in our calculation. We are, however, used to this in such calculations and it does not prevent us from calculating that the nucleus of the atom must produce a kind of diffraction phenomenon in these waves, similarly as a minute dust particle does in light waves. Analogously, it follows that there is a close relationship between the extent of the area of interference with which the nucleus surrounds itself and the wavelength, and that the two are of the same order of magnitude. What this is, we have had to leave open; but the most important step now follows: *we identify the area of interference, the diffraction halo, with the atom; we assert that the atom in reality is merely the diffraction phenomenon of an electron wave captured as it were by the nucleus of the atom.* It is no longer a matter of chance that the size of the atom and the wavelength are of the same order of magnitude: it is a matter of course. We know the numerical value of neither, because we still have in our calculation the *one* unknown constant, which we called *a*. There are two possible ways of determining it, which provide a mutual check on one another. First, we can so select it that the manifestations of life of the atom, above all the spectrum lines emitted, come out correctly quantitatively; these can after all be measured very accurately. Secondly, we can select *a* in a manner such that the diffraction halo acquires the size required for the atom. These two determinations of *a* (of which the second is admittedly far more imprecise because « size of the atom » is no clearly defined term) *are in complete agreement with one another.* Thirdly, and lastly, we can remark that the constant remaining unknown, physically speaking, does not in fact have the dimension of a length, but of an action, i.e. energy $\times$ time. It is then an obvious step to substitute for it the numerical value of Planck's universal quantum of action, which is accurately known from the laws of heat radiation. It will be seen that *we return*, with the full, now considerable accuracy, *to the first* (most accurate) *determination.*

Quantitatively speaking, the theory therefore manages with a minimum of new assumptions. It contains a single available constant, to which a numerical value familiar from the older quantum theory must be given, first to attribute to the diffraction halos the right size so that they can be reasonably identified with the atoms, and secondly, to evaluate quantitatively and correctly all the manifestations of life of the atom, the light radiated by it, the ionization energy, etc.

I have tried to place before you the fundamental idea of the wave theory of matter in the simplest possible form. I must admit now that in my desire not to tangle the ideas from the very beginning, I have painted the lily. Not as regards the high degree to which all sufficiently, carefully drawn conclusions are confirmed by experience, but with regard to the conceptual ease and simplicity with which the conclusions are reached. I am not speaking here of the mathematical difficulties, which always turn out to be trivial in the end, but of the conceptual difficulties. It is, of course, easy to say that we turn from the concept of a *curved path* to a system of wave surfaces normal to it. The wave surfaces, however, even if we consider only small parts of them (see Fig. 7) include at least a narrow *bundle* of possible curved paths,

Fig. 7.

to all of which they stand in the same relationship. According to the old view, but not according to the new, one of them in each concrete individual case is distinguished from all the others which are « only possible », as that « really travelled ». We are faced here with the full force of the logical opposition between an

either – or   (point mechanics)

and a

both – and   (wave mechanics)

This would not matter much, if the old system were to be dropped entirely and to be *replaced* by the new. Unfortunately, this is not the case. From the point of view of wave mechanics, the infinite array of possible point paths would be merely fictitious, none of them would have the prerogative over the others of being that really travelled in an individual case. I have, however, already mentioned that we have yet really observed such individual particle paths in some cases. The wave theory can represent this, either not at all or only very imperfectly. We find it confoundedly difficult to interpret the traces we *see* as nothing more than narrow bundles of equally possible paths between which the wave surfaces establish cross-connections. Yet, these cross-connections are necessary for an understanding of the diffraction and interference phenomena which can be demonstrated for the same particle with the same plausibility–and that on a large scale, not just as a consequence of the theoretical ideas about the interior of the atom, which we mentioned earlier. Conditions are admittedly such that we can always manage to make do in each concrete individual case without the two different aspects leading to different expectations as to the result of certain experiments. We cannot, however, manage to make do with such old, familiar, and seemingly indispensible terms as «real» or «only possible»; we are never in a position to say what really *is* or what really *happens*, but we can only say what will be *observed* in any concrete individual case. Will we have to be permanently satisfied with this…? On principle, yes. On principle, there is nothing new in the postulate that in the end exact science should aim at nothing more than the description of what can really be observed. The question is only whether from now on we shall have to refrain from tying description to a clear hypothesis about the real nature of the world. There are many who wish to pronounce such abdication even today. But I believe that this means making things a little too easy for oneself.

I would define the present state of our knowledge as follows. The ray or the particle path corresponds to a *longitudinal* relationship of the propagation process (i.e. *in the direction* of propagation), the wave surface on the other hand to a *transversal* relationship (i.e. *normal* to it). *Both* relationships are without doubt real; one is proved by photographed particle paths, the other by interference experiments. To combine both in a uniform system has proved impossible so far. Only in extreme cases does either the transversal, shell-shaped or the radial, longitudinal relationship predominate to such an extent that we *think* we can make do with the wave theory alone or with the particle theory alone.

In this short story by a well-known writer of science fiction, the moon explorers make an unexpected discovery, and react in an all-too-human way.

17   **The Sentinel**

Arthur C. Clarke

Chapter from his book, *Expedition to Earth*, 1953.

The next time you see the full moon high in the south, look carefully at its right-hand edge and let your eye travel upward along the curve of the disk. Round about two o'clock you will notice a small, dark oval: anyone with normal eyesight can find it quite easily. It is the great walled plain, one of the finest on the Moon, known as the Mare Crisium—the Sea of Crises. Three hundred miles in diameter, and almost completely surrounded by a ring of magnificent mountains, it had never been explored until we entered it in the late summer of 1996.

Our expedition was a large one. We had two heavy freighters which had flown our supplies and equipment from the main lunar base in the Mare Serenitatis, five hundred miles away. There were also three small rockets which were intended for short-range transport over regions which our surface vehicles couldn't cross. Luckily, most of the Mare Crisium is very flat. There are none of the great crevasses so common and so dangerous elsewhere, and very few craters or mountains of any size. As far as we could tell, our powerful caterpillar tractors would have no difficulty in taking us wherever we wished to go.

I was geologist—or selenologist, if you want to be pedantic—in charge of the group exploring the southern region of the Mare. We had crossed a hundred miles of it in a week, skirting the foothills of the mountains along the shore of what was once the ancient sea, some thousand million years before. When life was beginning on Earth, it was already dying here. The waters were retreating down the flanks of those stupendous cliffs, retreating into the empty heart of the Moon. Over the land which we were crossing, the tideless ocean had once been half a mile deep, and now the only trace of moisture was the hoarfrost one could sometimes find in caves which the searing sunlight never penetrated.

We had begun our journey early in the slow lunar dawn, and still had almost a week of Earth-time before nightfall. Half a dozen times a day we would leave our vehicle and go outside in the space-suits to hunt for interesting minerals, or to place markers for the guidance of future travelers. It was an uneventful routine. There is nothing hazardous or even particularly exciting about lunar exploration. We could live comfortably for a month in our pressurized tractors, and if we ran into trouble we could always radio for help and sit tight until one of the spaceships came to our rescue.

I said just now that there was nothing exciting about lunar exploration, but of course that isn't true. One could never grow tired of those incredible mountains, so much more rugged than the gentle hills of Earth. We never knew, as we rounded the capes and promontories of that vanished sea, what new splendors would be revealed to us. The whole southern curve of the Mare Crisium is a vast delta, where a score of rivers once found their way into the ocean, fed perhaps by the torrential rains that must have lashed the mountains in the brief volcanic age when the Moon was young. Each of these ancient valleys was an invitation, challenging us to climb into the unknown uplands beyond. But we had a hundred miles still to cover, and could only look longingly at the heights which others must scale.

We kept Earth-time aboard the tractor, and precisely at 22.00 hours the final radio message would be sent out to Base and we would close down for the day. Outside, the rocks would still be burning beneath the almost vertical sun, but to us it was night until we awoke again eight hours later. Then one of us would prepare breakfast, there would be a great buzzing of electric razors, and someone would switch on the short-wave radio from Earth. Indeed, when the smell of frying sausages began to fill the cabin, it was sometimes hard to believe that we were not back on our own world—everything was so normal and homely, apart from the feeling of decreased weight and the unnatural slowness with which objects fell.

It was my turn to prepare breakfast in the corner of the main cabin that served as a galley. I can remember that moment quite vividly after all these years, for the radio had just played one of my favorite melodies, the old Welsh air, "David of the White Rock." Our driver was already outside in his space-suit, inspecting our caterpillar treads. My assistant, Louis Garnett, was up forward in the control position, making some belated entries in yesterday's log.

As I stood by the frying pan waiting, like any terrestrial housewife, for the sausages to brown, I let my gaze wander idly over the mountain walls which covered the whole of the southern horizon, marching out of sight to east and west below the curve of the Moon. They seemed only a mile or two from the tractor, but I knew that the nearest was twenty miles away. On the Moon, of course, there is no loss of detail with distance—none of that almost imperceptible haziness which softens and sometimes transfigures all far-off things on Earth.

Those mountains were ten thousand feet high, and they climbed steeply out of the plain as if ages ago some subterranean eruption had smashed them skyward through the molten crust. The base of even the nearest was hidden from sight by the steeply curving surface of the plain, for the Moon is a very little world, and from where I was standing the horizon was only two miles away.

I lifted my eyes toward the peaks which no man had ever climbed, the peaks which, before the coming of terrestrial life, had watched the retreating oceans sink sullenly into their graves, taking with them the hope and the morning promise of a world. The sunlight was beating against those ramparts with a glare that hurt the eyes, yet only a little way above them the stars were shining steadily in a sky blacker than a winter midnight on Earth.

I was turning away when my eye caught a metallic glitter high on the ridge of a great promontory thrusting out into the sea thirty miles to the west. It was a dimensionless point of light, as if a star had been clawed from the sky by one of those cruel peaks, and I imagined that some smooth rock surface was catching the sunlight and heliographing it straight into my eyes. Such things were not uncommon. When the Moon is in her second quarter, observers on Earth can sometimes see the great ranges in the Oceanus Procellarum burning with a blue-white iridescence as the sunlight flashes from their slopes and leaps again from world to world. But I was curious to know what kind of rock could be shining so brightly up there, and I climbed into the observation turret and swung our four-inch telescope round to the west.

I could see just enough to tantalize me. Clear and sharp in the field of vision, the mountain peaks seemed only half a mile away, but whatever was catching the sunlight was still too small to be resolved. Yet it seemed to have an elusive symmetry, and the summit upon which it rested was curiously flat. I stared for a long time at that glittering enigma, straining my eyes into space, until presently a smell of burning from the galley told me that our breakfast sausages had made their quarter-million mile journey in vain.

All that morning we argued our way across the Mare Crisium while the western mountains reared higher in the sky. Even when we were out prospecting in the space-suits, the discussion would continue over the radio. It was absolutely certain, my companions argued, that there had never been any form of intelligent life on the Moon. The only living things that had ever existed there were a few primitive plants and their slightly less degenerate ancestors. I knew that as well as anyone, but there are times when a scientist must not be afraid to make a fool of himself.

"Listen," I said at last, "I'm going up there, if only for my own peace of mind. That mountain's less than twelve thousand feet high—that's only two thousand under Earth gravity—and I can make the trip in twenty hours at the outside. I've always wanted to go up into those hills, anyway, and this gives me an excellent excuse."

"If you don't break your neck," said Garnett, "you'll be the laughing-stock of the expedition when we get back to Base. That mountain will probably be called Wilson's Folly from now on."

"I won't break my neck," I said firmly. "Who was the first man to climb Pico and Helicon?"

"But weren't you rather younger in those days?" asked Louis gently.

"That," I said with great dignity, "is as good a reason as any for going."

We went to bed early that night, after driving the tractor to within half a mile of the promontory. Garnett was coming with me in the morning; he was a good climber, and had often been with me on such exploits before. Our driver was only too glad to be left in charge of the machine.

At first sight, those cliffs seemed completely unscaleable, but to anyone with a good head for heights, climbing is easy on a world where all weights are only a sixth of their normal value. The real danger in lunar mountaineering lies in overconfidence; a six-hundred-foot drop on the Moon can kill you just as thoroughly as a hundred-foot fall on Earth.

We made our first halt on a wide ledge about four thousand feet above the plain. Climbing had not been very difficult, but my limbs were stiff with the unaccustomed effort, and I was glad of the rest. We could still see the tractor as a tiny metal insect far down at the foot of the cliff, and we reported our progress to the driver before starting on the next ascent.

Inside our suits it was comfortably cool, for the refrigeration units were fighting the fierce sun and carrying away the body-heat of our exertions. We seldom spoke to each other, except to pass climbing instructions and to discuss our best plan of ascent. I do not know what Garnett was thinking, probably that this was the craziest goose-chase he had ever embarked upon. I more than half agreed with him, but the joy of climbing, the knowledge that no man had ever gone this way before and the exhilaration of the steadily widening landscape gave me all the reward I needed.

I don't think I was particularly excited when I saw in front of us the wall of rock I had first inspected through the telescope from thirty miles away. It would level off about fifty feet above our heads, and there on the plateau would be the thing that had lured me over these barren wastes. It was, almost certainly, nothing more than a boulder splintered ages ago by a falling meteor, and with its cleavage planes still fresh and bright in this incorruptible, unchanging silence.

There were no hand-holds on the rock face, and we had to use a grapnel. My tired arms semed to gain new strength as I swung the three-pronged metal anchor round my head and sent it sailing up toward the stars. The first time it broke loose and came falling slowly back when we pulled the rope. On the third attempt, the prongs gripped firmly and our combined weights could not shift it.

Garnett looked at me anxiously. I could tell that he wanted to go first, but I smiled back at him through the glass of my helmet and shook my head. Slowly, taking my time, I began the final ascent.

Even with my space-suit, I weighed only forty pounds here, so I pulled myself up hand over hand without bothering to use my feet. At the rim I paused and waved to my companion, then I scrambled over the edge and stood upright, staring ahead of me.

You must understand that until this very moment I had been almost completely convinced that there could be nothing strange or unusual for me to find here. Almost, but not quite; it was that haunting doubt that had driven me forward. Well, it was a doubt no longer, but the haunting had scarcely begun.

I was standing on a plateau perhaps a hundred feet across. It had once been smooth—too smooth to be natural—but falling meteors had pitted and scored its surface through immeasurable eons. It had been leveled to support a glittering, roughly pyramidal structure, twice as high as a man, that was set in the rock like a gigantic, many-faceted jewel.

Probably no emotion at all filled my mind in those first few seconds. Then I felt a great lifting of my heart, and a strange, inexpressible joy. For I loved the Moon, and now I knew that the creeping moss of Aristarchus and Eratosthenes was not the only life she had brought forth in her youth. The old, discredited dream of the first explorers was true. There had, after all, been a lunar civilization—and I was the first to find it. That I had come perhaps a hundred million years too late did not distress me; it was enough to have come at all.

My mind was beginning to function normally, to analyze and to ask questions. Was this a building, a shrine— or something for which my language had no name? If a building, then why was it erected in so uniquely inaccessible a spot? I wondered if it might be a temple, and I could picture the adepts of some strange priesthood calling on their gods to preserve them as the life of the Moon ebbed with the dying oceans, and calling on their gods in vain.

I took a dozen steps forward to examine the thing more closely, but some sense of caution kept me from going too near. I knew a little of archaeology, and tried to guess the cultural level of the civilization that must have smoothed this mountain and raised the glittering mirror surfaces that still dazzled my eyes.

The Egyptians could have done it, I thought, if their workmen had possessed whatever strange materials these far more ancient architects had used. Because of the thing's smallness, it did not occur to me that I might be looking at the handiwork of a race more advanced than my own. The idea that the Moon had possessed intelligence at all was still almost too tremendous to grasp, and my pride would not let me take the final, humiliating plunge.

And then I noticed something that set the scalp crawling at the back of my neck—something so trivial and so innocent that many would never have noticed it at all. I have said that the plateau was scarred by meteors; it was also coated inches-deep with the cosmic dust that is always filtering down upon the surface of any world where there are no winds to disturb it. Yet the dust and the meteor scratches ended quite abruptly in a wide circle enclosing the little pyramid, as though an invisible wall was protecting it from the ravages of time and the slow but ceaseless bombardment from space.

There was someone shouting in my earphones, and I realized that Garnett had been calling me for some time. I walked unsteadily to the edge of the cliff and signaled him to join me, not trusting myself to speak. Then I went back toward that circle in the dust. I picked up a fragment of splintered rock and tossed it gently toward the shining enigma. If the pebble had vanished at that invisible barrier I should not have been surprised, but it seemed to hit a smooth, hemispherical surface and slide gently to the ground.

I knew then that I was looking at nothing that could be matched in the antiquity of my own race. This was not a building, but a machine, protecting itself with forces that had challenged Eternity. Those forces, whatever they might be, were still operating, and perhaps I had already come too close. I thought of all the radiations man had trapped and tamed in the past century. For all I knew, I might be as irrevocably doomed as if I had stepped into the deadly, silent aura of an unshielded atomic pile.

I remember turning then toward Garnett, who had joined me and was now standing motionless at my side. He seemed quite oblivious to me, so I did not disturb him but walked to the edge of the cliff in an effort to marshal my thoughts. There below me lay the Mare Crisium—Sea of Crises, indeed—strange and weird to most men, but reassuringly familiar to me. I lifted my eyes toward the crescent Earth, lying in her cradle of stars, and I wondered what her clouds had covered when these unknown builders had finished their work. Was it the steaming jungle of the Carboniferous, the bleak shoreline over which the first amphibians must crawl to conquer the land —or, earlier still, the long loneliness before the coming of life?

Do not ask me why I did not guess the truth sooner— the truth that seems so obvious now. In the first excitement of my discovery, I had assumed without question that this crystalline apparition had been built by some race belonging to the Moon's remote past, but suddenly, and with overwhelming force, the belief came to me that it was as alien to the Moon as I myself.

In twenty years we had found no trace of life but a few degenerate plants. No lunar civilization, whatever its doom, could have left but a single token of its existence.

I looked at the shining pyramid again, and the more remote it seemed from anything that had to do with the Moon. And suddenly I felt myself shaking with a foolish, hysterical laughter, brought on by excitement and overexertion: for I had imagined that the little pyramid was speaking to me and was saying: "Sorry, I'm a stranger here myself."

It has taken us twenty years to crack that invisible shield and to reach the machine inside those crystal walls. What we could not understand, we broke at last with the savage might of atomic power and now I have seen the fragments of the lovely, glittering thing I found up there on the mountain.

They are meaningless. The mechanisms—if indeed they are mechanisms—of the pyramid belong to a technology that lies far beyond our horizon, perhaps to the technology of para-physical forces.

The mystery haunts us all the more now that the other planets have been reached and we know that only Earth has ever been the home of intelligent life in our Universe. Nor could any lost civilization of our own world have built that machine, for the thickness of the meteoric dust on the plateau has enabled us to measure its age. It was set there upon its mountain before life had emerged from the seas of Earth.

When our world was half its present age, *something* from the stars swept through the Solar System, left this token of its passage, and went again upon its way. Until we destroyed it, that machine was still fulfilling the purpose of its builders; and as to that purpose, here is my guess.

Nearly a hundred thousand million stars are turning in the circle of the Milky Way, and long ago other races on the worlds of other suns must have scaled and passed the heights that we have reached. Think of such civilizations, far back in time against the fading afterglow of Creation, masters of a universe so young that life as yet had come only to a handful of worlds. Theirs would have been a loneliness we cannot imagine, the loneliness of gods looking out across infinity and finding none to share their thoughts.

They must have searched the star-clusters as we have searched the planets. Everywhere there would be worlds, but they would be empty or peopled with crawling, mindless things. Such was our own Earth, the smoke of the great volcanoes still staining the skies, when that first ship of the peoples of the dawn came sliding in from the abyss beyond Pluto. It passed the frozen outer worlds, knowing that life could play no part in their destinies. It came to rest among the inner planets, warming themselves around the fire of the Sun and waiting for their stories to begin.

Those wanderers must have looked on Earth, circling safely in the narrow zone between fire and ice, and must have guessed that it was the favorite of the Sun's children. Here, in the distant future, would be intelligence; but there were countless stars before them still, and they might never come this way again.

So they left a sentinel, one of millions they have scattered throughout the Universe, watching over all worlds with the promise of life. It was a beacon that down the ages has been patiently signaling the fact that no one had discovered it.

Perhaps you understand now why that crystal pyramid was set upon the Moon instead of on the Earth. Its builders were not concerned with races still struggling up from savagery. They would be interested in our civilization only if we proved our fitness to survive—by crossing space and so escaping from the Earth, our cradle. That is the challenge that all intelligent races must meet, sooner or later. It is a double challenge, for it depends in turn upon the conquest of atomic energy and the last choice between life and death.

Once we had passed that crisis, it was only a matter of time before we found the pyramid and forced it open. Now its signals have ceased, and those whose duty it is will be turning their minds upon Earth. Perhaps they wish to help our infant civilization. But they must be very, very old, and the old are often insanely jealous of the young.

I can never look now at the Milky Way without wondering from which of those banked clouds of stars the emissaries are coming. If you will pardon so commonplace a simile, we have set off the fire-alarm and have nothing to do but to wait.

I do not think we will have to wait for long.

A distinguished mathematical physicist, the nephew of the great Irish playwright John Millington Synge, uses an amusing allegory to discuss the nature of scientific knowledge.

18 The Sea-Captain's Box

John L. Synge

Excerpt from his book, *Science: Sense and Nonsense,*

published in 1951.

Long ago there lived a retired sea-captain who liked to go to auctions where he bought all sorts of queer things, much to the annoyance of his wife. One day he brought home a box with strange hieroglyphics painted all over it and set it down in a place of honour on the table where he kept his trophies.

As far as could be seen, there was no way of opening the box. This aroused the curiosity of the sea-captain and he started carefully to scrape off the rust and grime with which the box was covered. To his great delight he found a small shaft or axle protruding from one side of the box, as shown in Fig. 1

He discovered that he could turn this shaft with a pair of pliers, but nothing seemed to happen when he did so. Certainly the box did not open. 'Perhaps I haven't turned the shaft far enough,' he said to himself, 'or perhaps I'm turning it the wrong way.'

He realized then that he had lost track of the amount by which he had turned the shaft, and rebuked himself severely for not keeping a log. He must be more systematic.

There was a tiny arrow on the end of the shaft, and when the shaft was turned so that this arrow was vertical, it would go no further to the left. That he called 'the zero position'. Then he set to work and fixed a knob on the end of the shaft with a pointer attached and a graduated scale running round the shaft so that he could take readings with the pointer when he turned the shaft (see Fig. 2). He marked off the scale in units, tenths of units and hundredths of units, but he could not draw any finer divisions.

He got out one of the old log books he had brought back from the sea and wrote the words 'Log of my box' at the top of a blank page. He ruled two columns very neatly and wrote at the head of the first column 'Date of observation' and at the head of the second column 'Reading of pointer'.

Then he turned the knob, looked at the calendar and the pointer, and made this entry:

Date of observation	Reading of pointer
3 March 1453, morning, cloudy, wind fresh S.E. by E.	2·00

There was an auction in the neighbourhood that day. The sea-captain came home from it in the evening and made another entry:

3 March 1453, evening, fair, wind slight S.E. by S.	2·00

'We'll never reach port at this rate,' said the sea-captain to himself. 'Man the capstan!' Then he took the knob and turned the pointer to another position, which he noted in his log; but the box did not open. He turned the knob to various positions, noting them all, but still the box did not open.

By this time he was pretty disgusted and half resolved to throw the box away, but he was afraid his wife would laugh at him. He opened his clasp knife and attacked the box in a fury, but succeeded only in knocking off a few flakes of rust and breaking his knife. But he was excited to see that he had

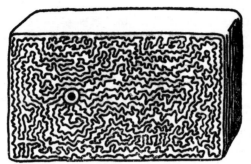

FIG. 1. The Box and the Shaft

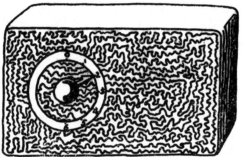

FIG. 2. The Pointer and the Scale

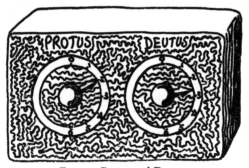

FIG. 3. Protus and Deutus

exposed a second shaft! He quickly went to work and fitted this shaft with a knob, pointer and graduated scale, so that it looked as in Fig. 3.

Then he turned over a fresh page in his log and ruled three columns. The first he headed as before 'Date of observation'. Then he hesitated. He must not get the two pointers mixed up — he must give them names — what would he call them? Castor and Pollux? Scylla and Charybdis? Port and starboard?

The sea-captain was a long time making up his mind. An unlucky name might send a good ship to the bottom on her maiden voyage. He rejected for reasons of domestic peace the idea of naming the pointers after girl friends of his youth or even after Greek goddesses. He must choose names which would apply to his pointers only and to nothing else, and the only thing to do was to make up names. He finally decided on PROTUS for the one he had discovered first and DEUTUS for the one he had discovered second. The grammarians might not think much of these names, but the mixture of Greek and Latin sounds had a pleasant ring and should make them safe from confusion with anything else. So he now prepared three columns in his log like this:

Date of observation	PROTUS	DEUTUS

The sea-captain's wife thought that he bought things at auctions merely to satisfy a childish yearning to possess curious pieces of rubbish, but that was not the real reason. Actually, he was a very avaricious man, and he was convinced that sooner or later he would find a hoard of gold in some trunk or box picked up for next to nothing at an auction. That is the reason for the gleam in his eyes as he now grasps the two knobs on the box and prepares to turn them. Surely the box will open now!

But the box does not open. Instead, the sea-captain jumps back, shaking in every limb and with his hair on end. 'Shiver my timbers!' he cries. 'There's a witch in the fo'c'sle!'

For, as he had tried to turn the knobs, there seemed to be human hands inside the box resisting his efforts.

Then cautiously, as if afraid of getting burned, he stretches out his hand to Protus and turns it gently. No resistance. But he draws back his hand in alarm. When he turned Protus, Deutus turned at the same time!

The sea-captain is no coward. In his time he has fought pirates in the Levant and dived last from the bridge of his ship sinking under him in the Bay of Biscay. But this is a different matter. There is magic in this box, and his conscience is troubled by his secret avarice for gold. Muttering a prayer and an incantation he picked up in an Eastern port, he takes up his pen in a shaky hand and with the other starts to manipulate Protus, writing down the figures as he does so. He is so excited that he forgets to record the date and the weather.

Here are his readings:

PROTUS	DEUTUS
0·00	0·00
1·00	2·00
2·00	2·83
3·00	3·46
4·00	4·00

The box does not open, but he does not care. The lust for gold has been replaced by scientific curiosity. His sporting instinct is roused. 'Good old Protus!' he cries. 'You made a poor start but you're gaining. Two to one on Protus!'

He turns Protus further and gets these readings:

PROTUS	DEUTUS
5·00	4·47
6·00	4·90

'Protus wins!' roars the sea-captain, springing to his feet and nearly knocking the table over. His wife puts her head round the door. 'What's all the noise about?' Then she sneers: 'Still playing with that silly old box! A man of your age!'

As the days pass, the sea-captain plays the game of Protus versus Deutus over and over again. Protus always makes a bad start and Protus always wins. It gets boring and he begins to dream a little. He forgets that Protus and Deutus were names he made up to distinguish one pointer from the other. They take on reality and he begins to think of them as two ships. Protus must be a heavy ship and Deutus a little sloop, very quick at the get-away but not able to hold the pace against the sail-spread of Protus.

But he pulls himself together. The lust for gold is now completely gone and the sea-captain starts to ask himself questions.

What is there really inside the box? He toys again with the idea that there may be a witch inside the box, but reason tells him that witches don't behave like that. No witch would reproduce the same readings over and over again.

Since Deutus moves whenever you move Protus, there must be some connection between them. Ha! Blocks and tackle, that's what it must be! Very small ivory pulley-blocks and silk threads!

So the sea-captain stumps down to the dock and gets one of his friends to put his ship at his disposal. He tries all sorts of ways of connecting two windlasses so that their motions will reproduce the motions of Protus and Deutus, but it will not work. He can easily make one windlass turn faster than the other, but he can never arrange matters so that one windlass makes a bad start and then overtakes the other. He returns home dejected. He is as wise as before about the contents of the mysterious box.

He reads over his log again and notices that he has always set Protus to an integer value. What would happen if he moved Protus through half a unit to 0·50? He is about to set Protus to 0·50 when his pride explodes in an oath. 'Sacred catfish!' he cries. 'What am I? A knob-twiddler and pointer-reader? No. I am a man — a man endowed with the gift of reason. I shall *think* it out for myself!'

Then he ponders: 'When Protus goes from 0·00 to 1·00, Deutus goes from 0·00 to 2·00. That means that Deutus goes twice as fast as Protus, at least at the start of the race. So when Protus goes from 0·00 to 0·50, Deutus will go from 0.00 to 1.00. That's obvious!' And he writes in the log

PROTUS	DEUTUS
0·50	1·00 (theoretical)

By adding that word 'theoretical' the sea-captain shows himself to be a cautious, conscientious man, distinguishing what he has deduced from his 'theory' from what he observes directly. (A noble precedent, often sadly neglected, but much harder to follow than one might suppose at first sight!)

Was the sea-captain right? No. When he actually turned Protus, he had to record the readings as follows:

PROTUS	DEUTUS
0·50	1·41 (observed)

What do you think of the sea-captain's 'theory'? Not bad for 1453, but any modern schoolboy could tell him how to do better. He should have taken a sheet of squared paper and plotted a graph, Protus versus Deutus, marking first the points corresponding to the observations made and then drawing a smooth curve through them. Then he could have read off from the curve the 'theoretical' Deutus-reading corresponding to the Protus-reading 0·50. That might have saved him from making a fool of himself, provided that nature does not make jumps. That is an assumption always made in the absence of evidence to the contrary, and (as we shall see later) it might have been made here.

But a graph is not completely satisfactory. It is hard to *tell* another person in a letter the precise shape of the graph; you have to enclose a copy of the graph, and the making of copies of a graph is a nuisance unless you use photography. A *mathematical formula* is always regarded as a much more convenient and satisfactory way of describing a natural law. The sea-captain had never heard of graphs or photography, but the other idea slowly evolved in his mind. Let us continue the story.

After thinking the matter over for several years, the sea-captain walked down to the pier one evening and stuck up a notice which read as follows:

DEUTUS IS TWICE THE SQUARE ROOT OF PROTUS

The people of the sea-port were of course very proud of the sea-captain, and they crowded cheering round the notice-board. But there was one young man who did not cheer. He had just returned from the University of Paris and took all scientific matters very seriously. This young man now pressed through the crowd until he reached the sea-captain, and, taking him by the lapel of his coat, said earnestly 'This notice, what does it mean?'

The sea-captain had been celebrating his discovery and was a little unsteady on his feet. He stared belligerently at the young man. 'Deutus is twice the square root of Protus,' he said. 'That's what it means. Can't you read?'

'And who is Deutus?' said the young man. 'And who is this creature Protus that has a square root?'

'You don't know Protus and Deutus?' cried the sea-captain.

'Why, everyone knows Protus and Deutus! Come up to my house and meet them over a glass of grog!'

So they went up to the sea-captain's house and he introduced the young man to Protus and Deutus. 'That's Protus on the left,' said he, 'and Deutus on the right.' Then he leaned over and whispered confidentially in the young man's ear: 'Protus carries more sail, but Deutus is quicker on the get-away!'

The young man looked at the sea-captain coldly. 'You mean,' he said, 'that Protus is a word which stands for the number indicated by the left-hand pointer and Deutus is a word which stands for the number indicated by the right-hand pointer. When you say that Protus is twice the square root of Deutus, you mean that one of these numbers is twice the square root of the other. In Paris we do not use words like Protus and Deutus for numbers. We use letters. We would write your result

$$D = 2 \sqrt{P}.$$

But is it really true?'

'Of course it's true,' said the sea-captain, 'and we don't need all your French fancy-talk to prove it. Here, read my ship's log.' He opened the log and showed the young man the readings which you have read on p. 65.

'Let us see,' said the young man. 'These things are not so obvious. Let us do a little calculation. The square root of zero is zero, and twice zero is zero, so the first line is right.'

He was about to put a check mark opposite the first line when the sea-captain roared 'Keep your hands off my log! Time enough to start writing when you find a mistake, which you won't. You can't teach a master mariner how to reckon!'

'To proceed,' went on the young man, 'in the second line P is one; the square root of one is one, and twice one is two.

Quite correct.' He put out his hand to make a check mark, but withdrew it hastily.

'In the next line,' he continued, 'P is two. The square root of two is an irrational number and cannot be represented by a terminating decimal. The third line is wrong, in the sense that the law $D = 2\sqrt{P}$ is not satisfied by these numbers.'

The sea-captain was taken aback. 'What's that?' he said. 'An irrational number? I've sailed the seven seas, but never did I meet up with an irrational number. Take your irrational numbers back where they come from, and don't try to teach me about Protus and Deutus!'

'I can put it another way,' said the young man. 'If you square both sides of your equation, and then interchange the sides of the equation, you get

$$4P = D^2.$$

Now we shall put in the figures from the third line of your log. P is 2·00 and D = 2·83. Four times P is therefore eight. Now we calculate the square of 2·83; it comes out to be 8·0089. So you assert — or do you? — that

$$8 = 8·0089.$$

Surely you cannot mean that?'

The sea-captain scratched his head. 'That's not the way I figured it,' he said. 'Let's see now. Protus is 2·00. What is the square root of 2·00? Why, it's 1·4142. If you double that you get 2·8284, and that is 2·83 to the nearest second decimal place. You can't trip me up, my boy. The law is satisfied all right.'

'Honest sir,' said the young man, smoothing his Parisian hair-cut, 'do you tell me that

$$2·8284 = 2·83?'$$

'Yes,' said the sea-captain stoutly, 'it is. Those numbers are equal to two decimal places.'

The young man jumped to his feet in anger. 'What a waste of my time!' he cried. 'It is a lying notice you have posted on the pier! Go down and add to it those words which will make it true.'

'And what words might those be?' asked the sea-captain suspiciously.

'Write that Deutus is twice the square root of Protus *to two decimal places.*'

'I will not,' replied the sea-captain stubbornly. 'Everybody knows that Protus and Deutus have only two decimal places and they don't need to be told. Keep your irrational numbers and other French fiddle-faddle away from Protus and Deutus. Commonsense is enough for them. But,' he added, 'you're a nice young fellow for a land-lubber, so sit ye down and we'll have a glass of grog together.'

So the young man sat down for a glass of grog and as the evening wore on the two became more and more friendly and open-hearted with one another. Finally, speaking at once, they both broke out with the question: 'What *is* inside the box?'

The sea-captain told the young man how he had first thought that there was gold in the box, how then he had thought that there must be a witch, and now for the life of him he could think of nothing but that there were two ships, Protus with a great sail-spread and Deutus smaller and quicker on the get-away. 'But,' he added, 'it bothers me how you could fit ships in such a little box, with a sea for them to sail on and a wind to sail by. And how is it that they always sail the same, with Protus slow at first and Deutus quick on the get-away?'

Not having followed the sea, the young man paid little attention to the idea of the two ships. Then suddenly he stood up and stared at the box. He had now drunk several glasses of grog, so he stood with difficulty and leaned heavily on the table.

'I see it,' he said. 'Yes, I see it!'

'What do you see?' asked the sea-captain. 'Protus with her tops'ls set?' And he too stared at the box.

'I see no ships,' said the young man, speaking slowly at first and then more and more rapidly. 'I see a world of mathematics. I see two variable numbers, P and D, taking all values rational and irrational from zero to infinity. What fools we were to talk of two decimal places! The law is *exact*! $D = 2 \sqrt{P}$. It is true for all values, rational and irrational. Protus is a number and Deutus is a number, and if you cannot measure them to more than two decimal places, that is your infirmity, not theirs. Go,' he cried to the sea-captain, 'go to the silversmith and make him contrive for you more cunning scales so that they may be read more accurately. I will go to Paris and procure some optic glasses wherewith to read the scales. Then you will see that I am right. The law $D = 2 \sqrt{P}$ is an exact mathematical law and you will verify it with readings that go to four or five or six decimal places.'

The sea-captain yawned. 'The silversmith is now abed,' he said, 'and with the wind now holding you cannot sail for France. It may be that this grog has been too much for your young stomach. Lie down on the couch there and sleep it off.'

But before long the silversmith made the cunning scales and the young man brought the optic glasses from Paris; to the great surprise of the sea-captain, the young man was right — the law was satisfied to two more decimal places. Beyond that they could not go, although the young man married the sea-captain's daughter and worked with his father-in-law on the box for many years. The sea-captain died thinking of Protus and Deutus racing in a stiff breeze and bequeathed the box to the young man, who in course of time grew old and died too. The box was handed down from generation to generation as a family heirloom, and it was a point of honour with each generation to try to add a decimal place to the readings and see whether the law $D = 2 \sqrt{P}$ remained true. Generation after generation found that it did remain true, and finally the idea that there might be any doubt about it faded.

No one has ever succeeded in getting inside the box, and there is a mixed tradition as to what its contents are. Gold and witches were ruled out long ago, but still some members of the family see Protus and Deutus sailing with foaming wakes where others see two variable numbers capable of taking all positive values, rational and irrational.

An allegory must not be pushed too far, and so one hesitates to say what has happened to the sea-captain's box in these days of relativity and quantum mechanics. You might say that if you look very hard at Protus, your mere inspection disturbs him, and when you feel quite certain you have pinned him down to a definite reading Deutus is dancing all over the place. Or perhaps you might say that the two pointers do not move continuously but only in definite small jumps.

However, the whole picture is blurred by the discovery of a vast number of shafts, connected to one another by many complicated laws which the sea-captain would find it impossible to visualize in terms of nautical manœuvres.

But the essential feature of the allegory remains — the unopened and unopenable box, and the question: 'What is really inside it?' Is it the world of mathematics, or can it be explained in terms of ships and shoes and sealing wax?

The answer must surely be a subjective matter; if you ask for an 'explanation', you cannot be satisfied unless the explanation you get rings a bell somewhere inside you. If you are a mathematician, you will respond to a mathematical explanation, but if you are not, then probably you will want an explanation which establishes analogies between the deep laws of nature and simple facts of ordinary life.

Up to the year 1900, roughly, such homely explanations were available. It is true that they never told the whole story (that inevitably involved mathematics), but they provided crusts for the teeth of the mind to bite on. The earth pursues its orbit round the sun on account of the pull of gravity; then think of an apple with a string through it which you whirl round your head. Light travels from the sun to the earth in ether-waves; then think of the ripples on the surface of a pond when you throw a stone into it.

Modern physics tends to decry 'explanations' of this sort — not out of any malevolent desire to hide secrets, but because the simple analogies prove too deceptive and inadequate. In fact there are those who deny that physicists have the responsibility of giving explanations. This modern attitude has been expressed compactly by Professor Dirac: 'The only object of theoretical physics is to calculate results that can be compared with experiment, and it is quite unnecessary that any satisfying description of the whole course of the phenomena should be given.'[1]

A new creed! Something to weigh and consider and contrast with the old creed implicit in science for centuries.

[1] DIRAC, P. A. M., *Quantum Mechanics*, Clarendon Press (Oxford, 1930), p. 7.

This article, based on lectures of Edward M. Purcell,
distinguishes between sound proposals and unworkable
fantasies about space travel.

---

19 Space Travel: Problems of Physics and Engineering

Harvard Project Physics Staff

1960

Traveling through empty space. After centuries of gazing curiously at
stars, moon, and planets from the sanctuary of his own planet with its
blanket of lifegiving atmosphere, man has learned to send instruments
to some of the nearer celestial objects; and he will no doubt soon try
to make such a trip himself.

Starting with Johannes Kepler's Somnium, a flood of fanciful stories
dealt with journeys to the moon, often in balloons equipped with all
the luxuries of a modern ocean liner. These stories, of course, ignored something that had already been known for almost a century, namely, that the earth's atmosphere must be only a thin shell of gas, held
in place by gravity, and that beyond it must lie a nearly perfect
vacuum. In this vacuum of outer space there is no friction to retard
the motion of a space ship, and this is a great advantage. But the
forces of gravity from the sun and other bodies will not always take
a vehicle where we want it to go, and we must be able to produce oc-
casional bursts of thrust to change its course from time to time. Thus,
quite aside from how we may launch such a space vehicle, we must equip
it with an engine that can exert a thrust in empty space.

The only way to obtain a thrust in a completely empty space is to use
recoil forces like those acting on a gun when it fires a projectile.
Indeed, Newton's third law says that to obtain a thrusting force on the
space vehicle an equal and opposite force must be exerted on something
else, and in empty space this "something else" can only be a matter that
comes from the space vehicle itself, a matter that we are willing to
leave behind us. Only by throwing out a part of its own mass can a
vehicle achieve recoil forces to change its own velocity—or at least
the velocity of the part of it that remains intact.

A rocket is a recoil engine of this type. It carries its own oxygen
(or other oxidizer) with which to burn its fuel, and the mass of the
burned fuel and oxygen is ejected from the rear and left behind. The
rocket is much like a continuously firing gun that constantly sprays
out an enormous number of very tiny bullets. The recoil from these
"bullets" is precisely the thrusting force on the body of the rocket.

Obviously there is a limit to the length of time that such a process
can continue, for the mass remaining in the space ship gets smaller all
the time, except when the engine is turned off entirely. In this chapter we will examine this limitation and see what it implies about space
travel. To be definite, we shall usually speak about rocket engines,
but it will be clear that what we have to say applies to any recoil
engine whether it is run by chemical power, nuclear power, or any other
source of power. All such engines, to produce a thrust in empty space,
must eject some of the mass that has been carried along.

The rocket equation. It turns out, as we shall see, that the only property of a rocket engine that seriously limits its performance is the
"exhaust velocity" of the burned fuel gases, i.e. the velocity of the
exhaust material as seen from the rocket. This exhaust velocity, which
we denote by v_{ex}, is determined by the energy released inside the combustion chamber and hence by the fuel (and oxidizer) used by the rocket.
The same "kick" backward is given to the exhaust-gas molecule whether
or not the rocket is already moving. Therefore, to a man standing on
the rocket using a specific combustion process, the gases rushing out
the exhaust will always appear to have the same velocity relative to
the rocket, whatever the motion of the rocket itself with respect to
another body.

Imagine you are watching a rocket coasting along at constant velocity, far away from any other massive bodies. Suppose that the engine is ignited briefly and ejects a small mass Δm of burned gases. The situation is sketched in Fig. 1, where we have denoted the initial mass and velocity of the vehicle by m and v respectively. The velocity v may be measured with respect to any (unaccelerated) coordinate system, for example, another space ship coasting alongside the first, or the sun-centered coordinate system that we commonly use to analyze the motions of the planets. (The actual value of v will cancel out of our final results. Why is this expected?) After the burst of power, the rocket will move away from us at velocity $v + \Delta v$, having a mass $m - \Delta m$; and the "cloud" of exhaust gases, of mass Δm, will be moving away from us at a velocity equal to the exhaust velocity diminished by the forward velocity of the rocket, $v_{ex} - v$.

Since no external forces are acting on the system, we know that momentum must be conserved. In Fig. 1(a), before the burst of power, the momentum is mv; right afterwards, in Fig. 1(b), it is $(m - \Delta m)(v + \Delta v) - (\Delta m)(v_{ex} - v)$. These momenta must be the same:

$$(m - \Delta m)(v + \Delta v) - (\Delta m)(v_{ex} - v) = mv \ .$$

Multiplying out the terms on the left-hand side, we find that all terms containing v cancel out (as they must), and the result can be written in the form,

$$(\Delta m)v_{ex} + (\Delta m)(\Delta v) = m(\Delta v) \ .$$

If we consider a sufficiently small burst of thrust, we can make Δv as small as we wish compared to v_{ex}, and the second term on the left-hand side of this equation can be made completely negligible compared to the first term. Then we can write (for very small bursts of thrust):

$$\frac{\Delta m}{m} = \frac{\Delta v}{v_{ex}} \ . \tag{1}$$

Notice that this relation does not depend in any way on the length of time during which the change Δv occurs. The fuel Δm may be burned very rapidly or very slowly. As long as the exhaust gases emerge with velocity v_{ex} relative to the rocket, the resulting momentum changes will be the same, and will lead to the same relation Eq. (1), whenever the changes are sufficiently small. Notice also that this result depends only on the conservation of momentum; we have used no other law in deriving it.

Now, a moderately large burst of power can be divided conceptually into a great many consecutive small bursts, and Eq. (1) shows that each small increase in velocity requires ejecting a given fraction of the remaining mass of the rocket. The rules of this "inverted compound-interest payment" are examined in the appendix to this chapter. There we find (Eq. A6) that any velocity change v_c, large or small, requires reducing the mass of the rocket as follows:

$$m = m_o \, e^{-(v_c/v_{ex})}$$

or

$$m/m_o = e^{-(v_c/v_{ex})} \ . \tag{2}$$

Here m_o is the mass before the change, and m is the mass after the change. The quantity e is a certain number whose value is

(a) JUST BEFORE FIRING OFF Δm:

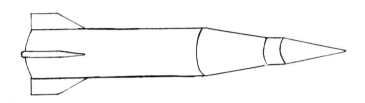

(b) JUST AFTER FIRING OFF Δm:

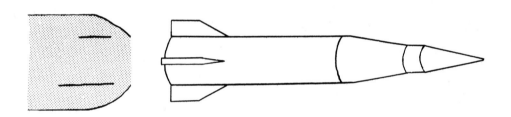

Fig. 1. Analysis of the performance of a rocket. Note that the "backwards" velocity of the spent fuel, namely $v_{ex} - v$, might actually be negative as seen by an external observer. This would happen if v is larger than v_{ex}, in which case the exhaust "cloud" is seen to move off to the right, too, although at a speed less than that of the rocket.

$$e = 2.718\ldots = 10^{0.4343\ldots} . \tag{3}$$

One use of Eq. (2) is in computing the final velocity v_f of a rocket that has initial mass m_0, initial speed v_0, final mass m_f, and exhaust velocity v_{ex}. The result is

$$\frac{m_f}{m_0} = e^{-(v_f/v_{ex})} ,$$

as shown graphically in Fig. 2.

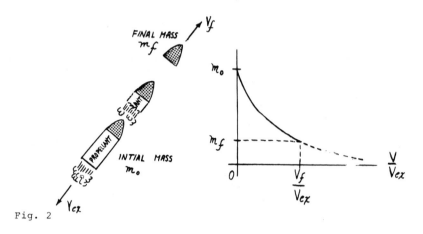

Fig. 2

Eq. (2) is the <u>rocket equation</u>. Unless a table of powers of e happens to be handy, the most convenient way to write this equation is the following:

$$m_0 = (m)\, 10^{(0.4343\, v_c/v_{ex})} \tag{4}$$

or

$$\log_{10}(m_0/m) = 0.4343\, (v_c/v_{ex}). \tag{5}$$

This relation is based only on the conservation of momentum and on the concept of a constant exhaust velocity v_{ex} (constant with respect to the body of the rocket) for the spent part of the fuel. (But the relation is idealized in the sense that we have not taken into account any accelerations due to gravity.)

As an example, suppose that we wish to give a rocket a final velocity equal to twice the exhaust velocity of its engines, starting with the rocket at rest. Then $v_c = 2v_{ex}$, and we have:

$$m_0 = (m)\, 10^{0.8686} = 7.39\, (m).$$

That is, the original takeoff mass m_0 must be over 7 times the final mass. In other words, about 87 percent of the initial mass must be expelled to achieve a velocity of $2v_{ex}$. The useful payload must be somewhat less than the remaining 13 percent of the takeoff mass, because the rocket casing, its fuel tanks, and the like will constitute much of this remaining mass.

Practical rockets. The rocket equation shows that the most important feature of a rocket is v_{ex}, the velocity with which the spent fuel gases are expelled. When chemical fuels are used, there is a limit to how large this exhaust velocity can be. We can see this by applying the law of energy conservation to the interior of the rocket.

Consider what happens when a given mass m of fuel and oxidizer are combined, with the fuel burning in the oxidizer. Let the total energy produced by this chemical reaction be E. Obviously, the ratio E/m, which is the energy per unit mass of fuel and oxidizer, will be a constant that depends only on the chemical nature of the fuel and the oxidizer. After the materials have reacted, the total mass m is ejected from the rocket with velocity v_{ex}, and the kinetic energy of the ejected mass is just $\frac{1}{2}m(v_{ex})^2$. Since this energy comes from burning the fuel, it can be no greater than the chemical energy liberated, namely E:

$$\frac{1}{2}m(v_{ex})^2 \leq E \ .$$

Dividing by $\frac{1}{2}$m and taking square roots, we find:

$$v_{ex} \quad \sqrt{2(E/m)} \ . \tag{6}$$

These relations are not simple equalities because much of the released energy will be wasted, primarily as internal (random motion) heat energy in the still-hot exhaust gases.

Chemists have measured the "heats of reaction" (which determines E/m) for almost all chemical reactions. For example, for typical hydrocarbons such as fuel oil, gasoline, kerosene, and the like, they have found that about 1.1×10^4 kcal are given off for each kilogram of fuel burned. When we add the mass of oxygen required (about 3.4 kg per kg of fuel) and convert to mechanical units, we find that E/m for all of these fuels is very nearly 10^7 j/kg. Therefore, according to Eq. (6),

$$v_{ex} < \sqrt{20} \times 10^3 \text{ m/sec} = 4.5 \text{ km/sec}$$

for hydrocarbon fuels burned in oxygen. This, of course, is the largest value that could possibly be obtained, even if the exhaust gases emerged ice-cold. In actual practice, many current rockets using kerosene and liquid oxygen (called LOX) obtain roughly:

$$v_{ex} = 2.5 \text{ km/sec.} \tag{7}$$

Even liquid hydrogen and liquid fluorine will yield exhaust velocities only about 20 percent greater than this in practice.* Consequently whenever the speed of the rocket has to be substantially more than this value of v_{ex}—and we shall see in the next section that this is indeed so even for orbital flights—the useful payload is in practice only a small fraction of the original mass, by Eq. (2).

In view of this limitation on the fundamental quantity v_{ex} for chemical rockets, a number of proposals and experimental models have been made for nonchemical rockets where v_{ex} may not have these limitations. To date, none of these has offered any real advantage, although they may do so in the future. The difficulty is that today the auxiliary apparatus for ion-beam engines, nuclear reactors, and the like, always contains too much mass relative to the mass allowance needed for any significant payload. Eventually, of course, we might be able to do much better with nonchemical engines.

* Specific impulse is a term often used by rocket engineers who use the symbol I for it. It is essentially impulse per unit weight of fuel and equals the exhaust velocity divided by the acceleration of gravity at the earth's surface: $I = v_{ex}/g$. Typical practical values are therefore about 250 sec.

Artificial satellites. Now let us see what velocities we need to perform the simplest task of space engineering, namely placing an artificial satellite in orbit above the surface of the earth. Since the radius of the earth is about 4000 miles, the force of gravity on a satellite moving perhaps a few hundred miles above the earth's surface will be not very different from that on the surface. Thus, the satellite will experience an acceleration of approximately g toward the center of the earth. As we saw in Chapter 5 if it is travelling in a circular orbit with speed v, its centripetal acceleration must be v^2/R where R is the radius of the orbit. For these two facts to be consistent,

$$v^2/R = g \quad \text{or} \quad v = \sqrt{Rg} \ .$$

Since the satellite is assumed to be fairly close to the earth, the radius of its orbit R will be about the same as the radius of the earth, or about 6400 km. Substituting this value, along with $g = 9.8 \text{ m/sec}^2 = 0.0098 \text{ km/sec}^2$, into our formula, we obtain

$$v = 8 \text{ km/sec} \quad \text{(close orbit)}. \tag{8}$$

This is the approximate speed an object must have if it is to remain in orbit. Eq. (7) displays the rocket-exhaust velocities achieved when chemical engines are used. Are these velocities adequate? From Eqs. (7) and (8), we have

$$v_c/v_{ex} = 8/2.5 = 3.2 \ .$$

Substituting this value into the rocket equation (4) or (5), we find:

$$m_o = (m) \, 10^{1.39} = 24.5 (m) \ .$$

That is, the takeoff mass m_o must be almost 25 times the mass m of the satellite and all other non-fuel structures; thus only about 4 percent of the initial mass can actually go into orbit (even ignoring the problem of lifting it to orbit altitude, which we shall examine shortly).

But the situation is even worse than these numbers may seem to imply at first. The "other nonfuel structures"—the rocket's casing, framework, fuel tanks, fuel pumps, and the like—have much more mass than the payload, the satellite. In fact even with the best of modern structural materials and techniques, there is so far no rocket mechanism with a mass less than about 1/10 of the mass of the fuel it can carry (rather than 1/25). According to our foregoing result, a rocket of this sort could not be put into orbit at all.

The way out of these difficulties is to use the technique of staging, which essentially amounts to putting a small rocket onto a larger rocket (and this combination onto a third, still larger rocket, and so on as necessary). The fundamental rocket equation is not circumvented by this strategem; it remains valid. But heavy casings and fuel tanks can be thrown away as soon as their fuel is used up, and the remaining fuel in the remaining rocket then need only accelerate the remaining mass, which can be much smaller. In this way, the remaining fuel is used more efficiently toward the end of the process, and the ideal limit expressed by the rocket equation can be more nearly approached. It cannot be exceeded, for that would violate the conservation of momentum, upon which the rocket equation is based.

There is one further matter that we should look into. We have neglected to compute the work we must do to lift the payload up into its orbit against the downward force of gravity. (Anyone who has watched pictures of a big rocket taking off has seen how, at the start, thrust must be increased until the rocket's own weight on the launching pad is balanced and the net acceleration upward can begin.) This work, however, is not terribly large, relatively speaking, for a close-in orbit, as we can easily show. In obtaining Eq. (8), we derived the relation $v^2 = Rg$ for the orbital velocity. If we multiply this equation by $\frac{1}{2}m$, we find that the orbital kinetic energy is $\frac{1}{2}mv^2 = \frac{1}{2}mgR$. The potential energy change in lifting the mass m to height h above the surface of the earth is mgh. Since h is only a few hundred miles while R is 4000 miles or more, the work (mgh) required to raise the satellite will be only about 1/10 to 1/5 of the work ($\frac{1}{2}mgR$) required to give it orbiting speed in a close-in orbit. (Naturally, this is not true for a very large orbit with a height of, say, 4000 miles or more above the earth's surface.)

Interplanetary travel. To send instruments to other planets, we must first free them from the gravitational attraction of the earth. This requires that the payload be given a velocity sufficient to prevent it from returning close to the earth of its own accord. The smallest such velocity is called the escape velocity. A vehicle with this velocity will just barely escape, and its final velocity will be nearly zero relative to the earth.

As might be expected, the escape velocity is not enormously greater than orbital velocity, and in the appendix to this chapter, we show that it is about:

$$v \text{ (for escape)} = 11.2 \text{ km/sec}, \qquad (9)$$

as compared to v (for close orbit) = 8 km/sec. (8)

Even this moderately greater (than orbital) velocity for escape requires a rather large increase in the ratio of takeoff mass to payload mass. With v_{ex} equal to 2.5 km/sec as in Eq. (7), we have $v_c/v_{ex} = 11.2/2.5 = 4.48$, and the rocket equation (Eq. 4) yields:

$$m_o = (m) \, 10^{1.95} = 89 \, (m) \, .$$

So, despite the seemingly modest change in velocity (11.2 km/sec instead of 8 km/sec), freeing a payload from the earth with chemically fueled rockets (even in stages) requires about 3½ times as much fuel as required for placing the same payload into a close-in orbit.

Once essentially free of the earth, a body will still be under the direct influence of the sun's gravitational forces. Here it is necessary to recall that the earth already has a rather large orbital velocity around the sun, and that any body launched from the earth will continue to have that orbital velocity if it has been merely freed from the earth with no additional accelerations. This velocity is about 30 km/sec and clearly represents a very substantial bonus for interplanetary travel. Even so, the Mariner 4 probe to Mars, for example, actually required a takeoff mass 400 times as large as the mass of the probe itself. The rocket was an Atlas-Agena with an initial mass of about 200,000 lbs. and a payload of 500 lbs. It was designed to cover the 3×10^8 mile trip in the solar system in about 7 months (this works out at about 16 miles/sec).

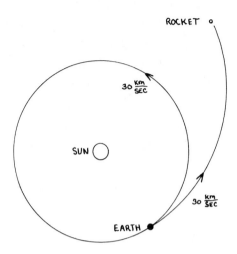

Fig. 3

Travel to a star? When we think of sending a payload to examine a star,
we find once more that the necessary velocity is the crucial factor, but
the origin of the needed velocity is different. The velocity required
to escape from the solar system is about 45 km/sec, but even the nearest
stars are enormously far away, and the payload must travel much faster
than this if it is to complete its journey within a century.

The distances to the nearest stars have been measured by observing
the shift in their apparent positions in, say, summer and winter as
the earth moves from one side of its orbit to the other. Even with this
very large baseline (186 million miles), the apparent shift in direction—
the parallax—is extremely small, and the corresponding distances are
found to be several million million miles, i.e., several trillion miles.
Such large distances are more conveniently expressed in light years, a
light year being the distance that light will travel in one year. A
simple multiplication shows that one light year is about 10^{13} km.

The two nearest stars are in the constellation Centaurus. The nearest
one, Proxima Centauri, is 4.2 light years away but is very dim and emits
only about 10^{-4} times as much light as our sun. The next-to-nearest star,
Alpha Centauri, is 4.3 light years away and is actually a double star,
consisting of two stars similar to our sun and separated by about the
distance between the sun and Jupiter. The brighter of the two emits
energy at about the same rate as our sun, and the other at about 1/5
that rate.

While none of these particular stars seems likely to have habitable
planets comparable to our own, it might be very interesting to send instruments in close to one of them and take pictures of it. To see just
what problems such a project might entail, let us examine this simplest
of all interstellar journeys a little more closely.

The first question to be answered is how long we would be willing to
wait for the results of the journey. Although an unmanned instrument
package need not return to the earth within a man's lifespan, it nevertheless seems that we would be unlikely to plan today for a very expensive
project whose results would be known later than, say, a century from now.

If the payload is to travel 4.2 light years during 100 years, its speed must be 0.042 times the speed of light (3×10^5 km/sec). This speed v_c is 12.6×10^3 km/sec. Let us optimistically assume that we can soon design rockets with exhaust velocities twice as high as the ones we now have, even though it is difficult to see now how this could be done with chemical fuels. Thus, we assume $v_{ex} = 5$ km/sec. Then we have $v_c/v_{ex} = 2.52 \times 10^3$, which we substitute into the rocket equation. (Both speeds are small enough so that we can use this nonrelativistic equation; actually the relativistic one gives slightly more pessimistic results.)

When we make this substitution in Eq. (4), we find a result that can only be described as ridiculous:

$$m_o = (m)\ 10^{1094} \ .$$

To see just how impossibly large this mass ratio is, we might note that the total number of atoms in the entire solar system has been estimated to be less than 10^{58}. There is not enough chemical fuel in the entire solar system to send even one atom on such a journey! In fact, we are short of having enough fuel for even that trivial task by a factor of over 10^{1000}!

These numbers are so large that the mind can not really form an adequate picture of their hugeness. To reduce them, let us throw caution to the winds and allow a much longer time for the journey, for example, 5000 years or 50 centuries—a terribly long wait. Retracing the arithmetic we find that we then obtain

$$m_o = (m)\ 10^{21.9} = 8 \times 10^{21}\ (m) \ .$$

Even this more familiar sort of number is still absurdly large. The mass of the entire earth is only 6×10^{21} tons, less than enough (even if it were all good fuel—and to be so used!) to send a one-ton payload on a journey of 5000 years to the nearest star.

There is only one sensible conclusion: interstellar travel is impossible if chemical fuels are used for propulsion.

Future star travel? Perhaps one of the conceivable nonchemical rockets might someday offer an escape from this pessimistic conclusion. To look at this possibility, let us return to our simplest of interstellar journeys, a trip to the nearest star in 100 years. As we saw, we need a velocity v_c of 12.6×10^3 km/sec for such a journey. (With this velocity, the payload arrives at Alpha Centauri after 100 years; it must contain either a very powerful radio transmitter, or enough fuel to return in another 100 years or so.)

The various "plasma" engines and "magnetohydrodynamic" engines that have been proposed are essentially electric "guns" that shoot out ionized gases. It is difficult to set limiting numbers on the best possible performance from such engines, partly because the exhaust gases are usually accelerated by some separate source of power. Certainly, they can be no better than nuclear engines, which we shall examine later. It is probably fair to say that exhaust velocities much larger than 1/300 the velocity of light could not be expected when very large masses of ionized gas must be expelled.

If we adopt this estimate, then a value of v_{ex} of 1000 km/sec is about the best that could ever be expected from such non-nuclear engines. With this value we obtain the ratio $v_c/v_{ex} = 12.6$, and by inserting this into the rocket equation, Eq. (4), we get the result,

$$m_o = (m) \ 10^{5.47} = 3 \times 10^5 \ (m).$$

Thus, a 3-ton payload would require at least a million tons of "fuel" (material to be expelled as ionized gas). If the payload is to contain a sufficiently powerful radio transmitter, it is likely to weigh at least 3 tons. To form some picture of what a million tons of material might look like, we may note that a million tons of water would cover a football field to a depth of 200 yards.

Abandoning the radio transmitter and waiting another 100 years for the payload to return would be no way to avoid this large mass of "fuel," because the effective payload on the outward journey would then have to include all the "fuel" for reversing the velocity for the return trip. This essentially squares the mass ratio, making m_o/m equal to 10^{11}, which is far worse: even only one pound of true payload then requires 50 million tons of takeoff mass.

These results are not quite so ridiculous as the ones we obtained when we tried to use chemical fuels, but they clearly show that ion-beam engines will not be very practical for interstellar travel unless they can consistently give an exhaust velocity significantly greater than 1/300 the velocity of light.

Nuclear fission yields about 8.2×10^{13} joules per kilogram of fission-able material. According to Eq. (6), this will result in a maximum exhaust velocity of the products of fission of 12.8×10^6 m/sec, or 12.8×10^3 km/sec, about 1/23 the velocity of light.*

These exhaust velocities at last begin to approach what we need for the simplest of interstellar journeys. For the 100-year, one-way trip to Alpha Centauri, the necessary v_c is just about exactly equal to the v_{ex} that we might hope to obtain for nuclear fission products, and the rocket equation then gives $m_o/m = 2.7$ to 3. This, in itself, is so clearly practical that we might begin to consider making the elapsed time some-what shorter or journeying further to a few of the slightly more distant stars. Note, however, that a 20-year, one-way trip to Alpha Centauri would still require $m_o/m = 200$ approximately.

But present day engineering is a long way from being able to put a small nuclear reactor on a rocket to provide these exhaust velocities for fission products. Today's nuclear reactors involve so much additional mass besides their fuel that they would be even less useful than engines working with chemical fuels—and the latter are hopeless for interstellar journeys, as we have seen. It was only by ignoring these auxiliary dif-ficulties that we have made nuclear power appear to be the answer for interstellar travel. What is likely, however, is the development of nuclear reactors that do not emit the relatively heavy fission products, but that provide heat to a supply of hydrogen that is pumped over the reactor, heated by it, and ejected at correspondingly higher speed (see Eq. (6); v_{ex} is proportional to $\sqrt{1/m}$.

* The best possible nuclear fusion reaction, converting 4 hydrogen nuclei into a helium nucleus, gives about 1/8 the velocity of light. But non-explosive "slow" fusion reactors are far from being available on the earth, not to speak of the availability of a portable model for use in rockets!

If we are ever going to send instruments, let alone men, to even the nearest stars, we must first develop an almost ideal nuclear rocket (or an ion-beam rocket virtually equivalent to it). Even then, the simplest such trip will require many decades.

The perfect rocket. If we agree to ignore questions of engineering know-how, is there any absolute limit to how effective any rocket could possibly be? There is indeed such a limit and it is imposed by the facts of physics; physical energy cannot leave the rocket at an exhaust velocity greater than c, the velocity of light. And when any energy (say of amount E) is lost by the rocket, it also loses a (rest) mass of $m = E/c^2$. This is true whether the energy E is carried off in the exhaust of some gas or in the form of a beam of light that escapes from the back of the rocket. This last possibility is suggested by certain reactions between elementary particles, reactions known as annihilations. When an electron (e^-) and a positron (e^+) react sufficiently strongly, both particles disappear and in their place appear two gamma rays; the latter are photons, like light or x-ray photons, that travel at the speed of light and together carry all of the energy represented by the masses of the vanished electron and positron. The reaction suggests that one may call the electron a particle of matter and the positron a particle of anti-matter.

This annihilation of positrons with electrons was the first reaction of this kind that was observed; but in the late 1950's, anti-protons and anti-neutrons were also discovered, and each was observed to annihilate with its ordinary counterpart, the usual proton or neutron respectively, producing two energetic gamma rays in each case. Thus, it became clear that a whole system of anti-matter—anti-hydrogen, anti-helium, and so on—could be constructed from the elementary anti-particles. We do not yet know how to do this to any significant extent, but we know of no physical law that would forbit it.

Since we have already agreed to ignore practical manufacturing problems in this discussion, let us assume that large amounts of anti-matter might be made available. What could we do with such a material if we had it? It would not be an inexpensive supply, because to manufacture it would require at least as much energy as it would later give back. But it would represent a very efficient way of storing energy. Indeed, anti-matter, plus ordinary matter to "burn" it with, would have the smallest ratio of stored energy to total mass that is physically possible, namely $E/m = c^2$. Moreover, because the released (photon) energy will depart at the speed of light, such a "fuel" would constitute the best possible rocket fuel (provided we could find a way of making the photons travel backwards from the rocket).

Naturally, we must use relativistic mechanics to derive the equations for such an exotic rocket. We shall not do so here, but will merely quote the result: if the exhaust velocity equals the velocity of light, then

$$\frac{m_o}{m} = \sqrt{\frac{c + v_c}{c - v_c}} \tag{10}$$

where all the symbols have the same meanings as before. This is the mass equation for a perfect rocket.

[Note, by the way, that a man on the rocket sees the exhaust energy leaving the rocket at the velocity of light; at the same time a man on the earth, say, will see the rocket traveling at the velocity of light relative to the earth. This is one of those paradoxes (seeming contradictions) of relativity that cannot be reconciled with our ordinary experience.]

Would such a "perfect" rocket make it easier for us to travel to the stars? One answer is: "A little, perhaps, but not much." Even this small degree of optimism is justifiable only if we may ignore a number of serious practical difficulties in addition to that of creating the necessary anti-matter for fuel.

Let us analyze a "typical" journey, preferably a rather simple one. As stated before, the nearest stars are about 4 light years away, but an ideal nuclear rocket would suffice for such a trip, so let us consider a slightly longer journey. Within a distance of 12 to 13 light years from the earth there are about 20 stars. (Of these, only Alpha Centauri is closely similar to our sun; two others emit about 1/3 as much energy as does the sun and one other emits about 5 times as much. The remaining ones are either very much brighter or very much dimmer than the sun.)

Accordingly, let us consider a round trip from the earth to a star 12 light years away and back. Since we would have to wait 24 years for light rays to make the round trip, the top speed of the rocket must be close to the speed of light if the rocket is to return to the base on earth during our lifetime. But we would not want the rocket to fly past its distant goal at nearly the speed of light, and it will take about as long to slow the rocket down as it did to speed it up in the first place. Thus the velocity of the rocket would have to vary approximately as shown in Fig. 4.

To avoid imposing unduly large forces on the men inside the rocket, we must keep the accelerations and decelerations small; at an average acceleration of 1 g, one can calculate that about a year will be required to reach full speed, and another year to stop. To keep the total time for the journey reasonably small, we shall choose a top speed of 0.8c, that is, only 20% less than the speed of light.

Journeys of this type involve, therefore, four separate steps: acceleration, deceleration, reacceleration, and a final deceleration. The mass equation applies to each one, but we must remember that, during each step, we must accelerate (or decelerate) all of the fuel mass that will be needed for all the succeeding steps. For one step of the journey in Fig. 4, the mass equation Eq. (1) yields

$$\frac{m_o}{m} = \sqrt{\frac{c + 0.8c}{c - 0.8c}} = \sqrt{\frac{1 + 0.8}{1 - 0.8}} = 3 \ .$$

But if m represents the true payload, this result applies only to the final deceleration. For example, the mass at the beginning of this final step must be $m_o = 3$, and this must be the "payload" for the next-to-last step, the acceleration for the return trip. Thus, the return trip must begin with a total mass of $3m_o = (3^2 m)$. It is easy to show in the same way that the two steps of the outward leg of the journey will introduce two more factors of 3. Thus, if m_{oo} denotes the take-off mass when the rocket leaves the earth (and m denotes the true payload, as before), we find:

$$\frac{m_{oo}}{m} = 3^4 = 81 \ .$$

That is, each ton of payload requires 81 tons of combined take-off mass. A 10-ton payload would require almost a thousand tons of fuel for the journey we have considered—and half of this fuel must be anti-matter. Obviously, we would have to learn how to manufacture anti-matter in very large amounts indeed.

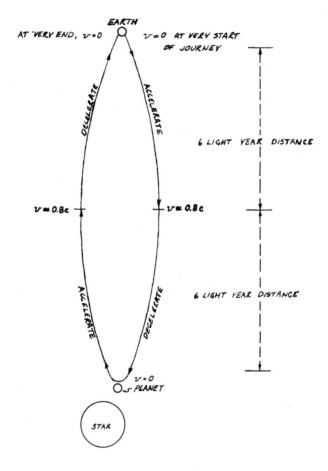

Fig. 4   A modest interstellar journey

With these assumptions about the trip, it is possible to show that the journey we have discussed would take 32 years as measured on the earth. But because of relativistic time-dilation for the inhabitants of the moving systems, it turns out that the crew of the rocket would age by only 20 years. That is, as measured by the crew, the journey would require only 20 years.

The perfect rocket has further difficulties that we have not yet mentioned. First, the energy flux of gamma rays from such a rocket, with a 10-ton payload, can be shown to be 2.4×10^{15} watts, a power that is equivalent to a 1-kilo bomb once every 1.7 seconds! And all of this energy flux is in the form of very penetrating, deadly gamma rays. The payload would have to be shielded very well indeed from even the slightest leakage of all this energy—to say nothing of the difficulties of shielding the earth and its inhabitants as the rocket takes off. Figure 5 indicates how the rocket might look in principle.

Secondly, a glance at Fig. 5 reveals another very serious difficulty. Anti-matter would act as a "universal solvent," reacting readily with any ordinary matter that it contacts. Then, in what can we store it? Within our present knowledge, this problem has no solution.

Thus, we have found that a perfect rocket probably cannot be built, and that, even if it could be built, it would not extend the range of possible space travel very much beyond the meager capabilities of an ideal nuclear rocket. Even the nuclear rocket is presently a long way from being practical. For the time being, of course, there are many exciting possibilities for exploring our own solar system with the chemically fueled rockets we already know how to build. The dreams of space travel are coming true, but only on a "local" basis.

Communicating through space. This final section is closely based on, and copiously cites from, E. M. Purcell's article "Radioastronomy and Communication through Space." Brookhaven National Lecture series #BNL 658 -(T-214); we wish to thank Dr. Purcell and the BNL for permission to use this material.

Now we shall discuss a very different aspect of space engineering, namely, sending signals, rather than physical hardware, across the huge distances of space. The signals that we know how to send most efficiently are coded radio waves, but our discussion will also apply to the light beam from a laser or to any other type of electromagnetic radiation if the necessary engineering "know-how" can be developed. Radio signals suitable for communicating over a distance of a few hundred miles require relatively little energy, but a large amount of energy is needed in communicating across the vast reaches of space.

The simplest possible radio signal is just the presence or absence of a radio wave—or equally well, the presence or absence of a small shift in its frequency (so-called "frequency-shift keying"). Correspondingly, the simplest possible sign that can be written on a piece of paper is the presence or absence of a black dot in some agreed-upon location. Newspaper photographs are arrays of such dots. Television pictures are built up in much the same way.

The simplest possible signal, then, expresses a two-fold ("binary") choice, a simple "yes or no," a "something or nothing" signal. More complicated codes can always be broken down into such signals. For example, a Morse code dot might be called a "yes" and the space between

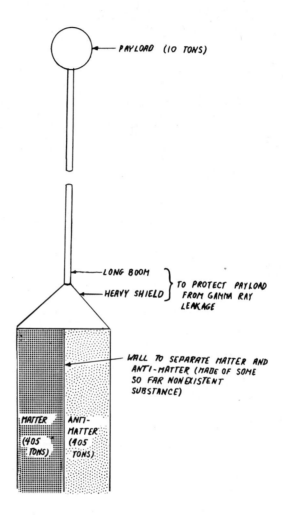

PAYLOAD (IO TONS)

LONG BOOM
HEAVY SHIELD } TO PROTECT PAYLOAD FROM GAMMA RAY LEAKAGE

WALL TO SEPARATE MATTER AND ANTI-MATTER (MADE OF SOME SO FAR NONEXISTENT SUBSTANCE)

MATTER (405 TONS)

ANTI-MATTER (405 TONS)

Fig. 5 A perfect rocket?

two dots a "no"; then the dash becomes two successive "yesses," and the longer space between two letters is represented by two successive "noes," and so on.

This way of analyzing signals was first suggested by the American radio engineer R. V. L. Hartley in 1928, and it was further developed by C. E. Shannon at Bell Telephone Laboratories in 1948. Shannon called the simplest yes-no signal a bit (for "binary digit"), and he first developed much of the analysis that we shall be using in this section. This analysis is a part of "information theory."

For space communication, the important fact is that each bit (each yes-no signal) requires a very small amount of energy. Just as space is filled with very faint light rays from the stars, it is filled also with a background of weak radio waves of all types. If we are to detect a signal from outer space against this "noise," we must receive enough energy to be sure that the supposed signal is not just one of the random mutterings of space itself. Near our solar system, a received signal energy of at least 10^{-21} joule per bit is required. This requirement is essentially independent of the radio frequency or the manner in which the signal is coded in the radio wave, and presumably it remains about the same in many parts of empty space.

As an example, let us consider the task of the Mariner IV space probe, namely to send good television pictures of Mars back to the earth. Since such a picture contains an array of about 1000-by-1000 dots, one picture can be transmitted by a signal consisting of about 10^6 bits. The signal can be detected if, on reaching the earth, it delivers (to our receiving antenna) $10^6 \times 10^{-21}$ joule $= 10^{-15}$ joule for each picture that is to be transmitted.

But what the transmitter emits must be much more energy than what we intercept and receive at a distance. A simple radio antenna sends the energy outward more or less equally in all directions. A properly designed complex antenna can concentrate most of the energy into a narrow beam, but such an antenna must be large (compared to the wavelength of the radio waves), and it must be very accurately shaped. Not only is this difficult to do, but once it is done, the antenna must be pointed toward the receiver, accurately enough to be sure that the receiver lies inside the radio beam, and this pointing operation in turn requires additional machinery and sensors that must be equally accurate. Thus, a space probe such as Mariner must contain either a rather large radio transmitter or else a smaller transmitter and a lot of complex, rather heavy machinery.

The best compromise amongst all the possibilities will depend on the purpose of the space probe and on the status of various engineering arts at the time the probe is designed. But we can obtain a rough idea of the weight of the necessary equipment by analyzing the situation when a simple antenna is used.

Fig. 6 summarizes the situation. Notice that the receiving antenna on the earth can be quite large, and we shall assume that it has a diameter of 100 m (about 100 yards). Only the radio energy that happens to strike the receiving antenna will be useful. Thus, the fraction of the energy that is useful will be given by the ratio of the area of the receiving antenna to the area of a sphere whose radius is equal to the distance from Mars to the earth, about 10^8 km $= 10^{11}$ m (see Fig. 6). The ratio of these areas is

$$\frac{\pi (50)^2}{4\pi (10^{11})^2} = 6 \times 10^{-20} .$$

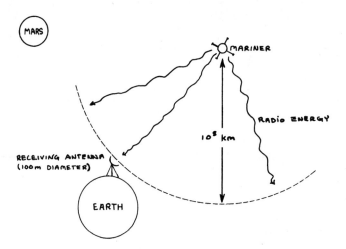

Fig. 6 Sending television pictures from Mars to the
earth. (The diagram is not to scale!)

We have seen that the received energy must be at least 10^{-15} joule per
picture. The energy that must be transmitted for each picture, however,
must be

$$\frac{10^{-15} \text{ j}}{6 \times 10^{-20}} = 16 \times 10^3 \text{ joules per picture .}$$

Although this amounts to only about 0.005 kw-hr, a rather small amount
of energy by our normal standards, it does represent something of a burden to a space probe. To compare it with something familiar, we might
note that the average automobile battery could store only enough energy
for sending about 100 such pictures. Actually, this is a very optimistic
estimate because we have computed it by using the minimum possible energy
per bit of "information," namely 10^{-21} joules per bit. If we are going to
go to all the trouble of sending a probe to Mars, we would want the signal
that it sends back to be quite strong, not just barely detectable, lest we
miss it entirely. Thus, it would be more realistic to say that an automobile battery can store enough energy to send about 10 television pictures from Mars to the earth.

Since such a battery would weigh about 35 lb, and since the ratio of
take-off mass to payload mass was about 400 for Mariner IV, the energy
storage for 10 television pictures of Mars would add about 7 tons to the
take-off mass of such a probe, if a nondirection antenna were used to
send the pictures back to the earth. Actually, Mariner IV used a rather
highly directional "dish" antenna, but note that the antenna and its
pointing equipment must have weighed less than 35 lb if it was to econo-
mize on take-off weight.

Although these energies and masses are perhaps surprisingly large when we consider that they all arose from the very small number of joules per bit (10^{-21}, see p. 16), they are nevertheless small compared to the masses and energies that would be necessary to send physical hardware back from Mars. For example, even a small canister of exposed photographic film might weigh 1 lb, but we would have to send along with it enough fuel to start it on its return journey, namely about 400 lb of fuel. This would add 400 × 400 lb or no less than 80 <u>tons</u> to the original take-off mass when the probe leaves the earth—and we have completely ignored the extra equipment that would be needed to ensure both a proper return orbit and a safe re-entry through the earth's atmosphere.

When we consider the very much greater distances to the nearer stars, the economy of sending signals rather than hardware becomes even more marked. We have seen that nothing short of an ideal nuclear rocket can send a physical payload to the nearest star, and that even then the trip would require several tens of years. On the other hand, if we consider distances as great as 12 light years (containing 20 to 30 stars), it is possible to show that, with 300-ft antennas at the transmitter and receiver, a ten-word telegram can be sent with about a kilowatt-hour of radiated energy (Fig. 7). This is less than one dollar's worth of energy at current prices.

Of course, the trouble is that there is no body at the other end to communicate to. Or is there? In the remainder of this section, we shall discuss the question of communicating with other people out there—if there are any.

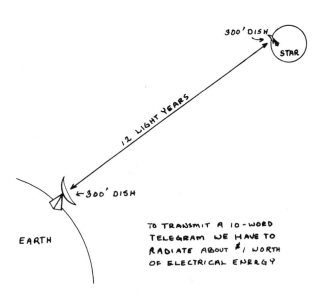

Fig. 7   from E. M. Purcell, "Radioastronomy and Communication through Space" [BNL lecture series #BNL 658 (T-214)] 1960 , p.9.

Let us look at just our own galaxy. There are some 10^{11} stars in the galaxy. Double stars are by no means uncommon, and in fact, there appear to be almost as many double stars as single stars. Astronomers take this as a hint that planetary systems around stars may not be very uncommon either. Moreover, a large number of stars are not rapidly spinning. One good way for a star to lose most of its spin is by interacting with its planets; that is what probably happened in our own solar system. So the chances that there are hundreds of millions of planetary systems among the hundred billion stars in our galaxy seem good. One can elaborate on this, but we shall not try to estimate the probability that a planet occurs at a suitable distance from a star, that it has an atmosphere in which life is possible, that life developed, and so on. Very soon in such speculation, the word "probability" loses any practical meaning. On the other hand, one can scarcely escape the impression that it would be rather remarkable if only one planet in a billion (to speak only of our own galaxy) had become the home of intelligent life.

Since we can communicate so easily over such vast distances, it ought to be easy to establish communication with a society (if we may use that word) in a remote spot. It would be even easier for them to initiate communication with us if they were technologically ahead of us. Should we try to listen for such communications, or should we broadcast a message and hope that someone will hear it? If you think about this a little, you will probably agree that we want to listen before we transmit. The historic time scale of our galaxy is very long, whereas wireless telegraphy on Earth is only 50 years old, and really sensitive receivers are much more recent. If we bank on people who are able to receive our signals but have not surpassed us technologically, that is, people who are not more than 20 years behind us but still not ahead, we are exploring a very thin slice of history. On the other hand, if we listen instead of transmitting, we might hear messages from people anywhere who are ahead of us and happen to have the urge to send out signals. Also, being technologically more advanced than we are, they can presumably transmit much better than we can. So it would not be sensible for us to transmit until we have listened for a long time.

If you want to transmit to someone—and you and he cannot agree on what radio frequency to use—the task is nearly hopeless. To search the entire radio spectrum for a feeble signal entails a vast waste of time. It is like trying to meet someone in New York when you have been unable to communicate and agree on a meeting place. Still, you know you want to meet him and he wants to meet you. Where do you end up? There are only a few likely places: at the clock of Grand Central Station, in the lobby of the Metropolitan Museum, and so on. Here, there is only one Grand Central Station, namely the 1420-megacycle/sec frequency emitted by hydrogen, which is the most prominent radio frequency in the whole galaxy (by a factor of at least 1000). There is no question as to which frequency to use if you want the other fellow to hear: you pick out the frequency that he knows. Conversely, he will pick out the frequency that he knows we know, and that must surely be 1420-megacycle/sec frequency.

Let us assume that his transmitter can radiate a megawatt of power within a 1-cycle/sec bandwidth. This is something that we could do ourselves if we wished to; it is just a modest stretch of the present state of the art. If we receive with a 300-ft dish-antenna and he transmits with a similar one, we should be able to recognize his signal even if it comes from several hundred light years away. With the new maser receivers, which are now being used in radioastronomy, 500 light years ought to be easy. But even a sphere only 100 light years in radius contains about 400 stars of roughly the same brightness as the sun. And the volume accessible to communication increases as the cube of the range. We have previously argued that it is hopelessly difficult to travel even a few light years, and we now see that it is in principle quite easy to communicate over a few hundreds of light years. The ratio of the volumes is about one million. (Fig. 8)

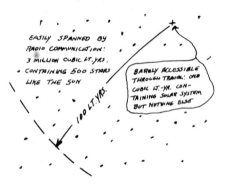

Fig. 8   (From Purcell, op. cit.)

There are other interesting questions. When we get a signal, how do we know it is real and not just some accident of cosmic static? This might be called the problem of the axe head: an archeologist finds a lump of stone that looks vaguely like an axe head; how does he know it is an axe head and not an oddly shaped lump of stone? Actually, the archeologist is usually very sure. An arrowhead can look rather like an elliptical pebble, and still there is no doubt that it is an arrowhead. Our axe head problem can be solved in many ways. Perhaps the neatest suggestion for devising a message having the unmistakable hallmark of intelligent beings is the suggestion made by G. Cocconi and P. Morrison. They would have the sender transmit a few prime numbers, i.e., 1, 3, 5, 7, 11, 13, 17 . . . .   There are no magnetic storms that send messages like this.

What can we talk about with our remote friends? We have a lot in common. To start with, we have mathematics in common, and physics, chemistry, and astronomy. We have the galaxy in which we are near neighbors. So we can open our discourse on common ground before we move into the more exciting exploration of what is not common experience. Of course, the conversation has the peculiar feature of a very long built-in delay. The answer comes back decades later. But it gives one's children something to look forward to.

Appendix A

Appendix A. The rocket equation

In Eq. (1), we showed that, during very small changes of velocity Δv, the following relation is required by the conservation of momentum:

$$\frac{\Delta m}{m} = \frac{\Delta v}{v_{ex}} \ . \tag{A1}$$

Now we want to extend this relation to arbitrarily large changes of velocity.

A large change of velocity can be conceptually divided into a great many steps with a small change in each. Let us choose these in such a manner that all of them involve the same _fractional_ change in the mass of the rocket. For example, we may choose

$$\frac{\Delta m}{m} = \frac{1}{n} \tag{A2}$$

where n is a large number that we will leave unspecified for the moment, but it is to be the same for each small step.

Then if m_o is the original mass of the rocket and m_1 is its mass after the first small step of velocity change, we will have:

$$m_1 = (1 - \frac{1}{n}) \ m_o \ .$$

After the second step, the mass will become:

$$m_2 = (1 - \frac{1}{n}) \ m_1 = (1 - \frac{1}{n})^2 \ m_o \ .$$

After the third step, it will be:

$$m_3 = (1 - \frac{1}{n})^3 \ m_o \ .$$

and it is easy to see that after k of our very small changes in velocity, the mass of the rocket will be

$$m_k = (1 - \frac{1}{n})^k \ m_o \ . \tag{A3}$$

Now, what will be the change in the rocket's velocity during these k steps of acceleration? By substituting Eq. (A2) into Eq. (A1), we find that during each step the velocity change will be:

$$\Delta v = \frac{1}{n} \ v_{ex} \ .$$

Since these are all the same, the total change in velocity during k steps will be just $k(\Delta v)$. If we denote this total change in the rocket's velocity by v_c, we have:

$$v_c = \frac{k}{n} \ v_{ex} \ .$$

Now solve this relation for k:

$$k = n \, (v_c/v_{ex}) \; .$$

And substitute into Eq. (A3):

$$m_k = m_o \, (1 - \frac{1}{n})^{n \, (v_c/v_{ex})} \; .$$

If we write m in place of m_k with the understanding that m now represents the rocket's mass after its velocity has changed by v_c, and if we use the multiplication rule for exponents, we can write our result in the following form:

$$m = m_o \left[(1 - \frac{1}{n})^n\right]^{(v_c/v_{ex})} \; . \tag{A4}$$

We have eliminated k from our relations, by expressing it in terms of the velocity change v_c. Can we eliminate n? In a sense, we cannot, but we can replace it by a less arbitrary quantity.

As we noted earlier, the simple relation Eq. (A1) is valid only for very small bursts of thrust. The smaller the burst, the more accurate Eq. (A1) becomes. In view of Eq. (A2), then our relations will all become more and more accurate as we choose n larger and larger. Obviously, the best thing to do is to choose n so very large that the quantity in square brackets in Eq. (A4) approaches a steady value and no longer changes significantly. Better still, we should take the limit of the square brackets as n "approaches infinity."

Perhaps it is not obvious that this limit exists in the sense that it is a well-defined number, but this fact can be shown by methods that we cannot pursue in this book. To agree with standard mathematical notation, we shall define a number e by the relation:

$$\frac{1}{e} = \text{limit (as } n \to \infty) \left[1 - \frac{1}{n}\right]^n \; . \tag{A5}$$

The number e has been evaluated to very many decimal places, but in physics we seldom need more than a few places: e = 2.718 is usually quite sufficient. Another way of stating the value is often more convenient:

$$e = 10^{0.4343} \; .$$

Now, if we let n approach infinity in Eq. (A4) and substitute the definition (A5), we obtain the result:

$$m = m_o \, (1/e)^{(v_c/v_{ex})}$$

or

$$m = m_o \, e^{-(v_c/v_{ex})} \; . \tag{A6}$$

This final relation can be rewritten in many ways. Eq. (2) of this chapter is the same as Eq. (A6); and Eqs. (4) and (5) are other forms obtained by solving Eq. (A6) for m_o and substituting a numerical value for e.

Appendix B

Appendix B. Escape velocity

If a body is projected away from the earth with sufficient velocity, it will never return. The smallest such velocity is called the escape velocity, and we shall derive it in this section from the law of conservation of energy.

The initial kinetic energy of a body of mass m that has been projected out from the earth with velocity v is equal to $\frac{1}{2}mv^2$. If this is just equal to the work that must be done against the earth's gravitational force on the body as it travels away, then the body will slow down greatly when it gets very far away, but it will never entirely stop, as it would if its initial kinetic energy were less than the work that must be done against the gravitational attraction.

Thus, our main task is to evaluate the work that is done against the earth's gravitational force by a body that moves from the earth's surface to a very large distance away. But to simplify the language of our arguments, we shall evaluate the work done <u>on</u> the body <u>by</u> the earth's gravitational field.

Newton's law of gravitation states that the force on a body of mass m due to the earth (mass M) is

$$F = G \frac{m\,M}{R^2} \qquad \cdot \tag{B1}$$

where G is Newton's gravitational constant and R is the distance from the body to the center of the earth. When the body moves a small distance ΔR further away from the earth, the work done on it by the gravitational force will be

$$\Delta W = -F(\Delta R) = (GmM)\,\frac{-\Delta R}{R^2} \tag{B2}$$

where the minus sign arises because the force opposes the increase in R.

Now we must add up all the ΔW's for all the ΔR's as the body moves from the earth's surface to a very great distance. In Eq. (B2), the quantity (GmM) is a simple constant, but $1/R^2$ changes continually as the body moves away, and we must find some way to express the ratio $-(\Delta R)/R^2$ as a change in some other quantity. One way to find this desired quantity is to guess at it and then try to prove that the guess is correct. From the fact that $-(\Delta R)/R^2$ has the units of a reciprocal length, we might guess that it could equal $\Delta(1/R)$. The change in $1/R$, as R itself changes by ΔR, will be:

$$\Delta\left(\frac{1}{R}\right) = \frac{1}{R+\Delta R} - \frac{1}{R} = \frac{-\Delta R}{R(R+\Delta R)} \qquad \cdot$$

This is almost the result we were seeking, and now we note that we are free to make the individual steps ΔR as small as we like. Thus, we can make $-(\Delta R)/R^2$ equal to $\Delta(1/R)$ to any accuracy that we may wish to choose. In the limit as the steps are made smaller and smaller, the relation becomes exact, although we cannot go into the proof of this here.

Accordingly, we can rewrite Eq. (B2) as follows:

$$\Delta W = (GmM) \; \Delta \left(\frac{1}{R}\right) \; .$$

This equation states that the steps ΔW in the total work done are just equal to the constant (GmM) times the corresponding changes in the quantity $1/R$. The sum of all the ΔW's, therefore, will be equal to the total change in the quantity GmM/R. If the body moves far enough from the earth, we may take the final value of this quantity as zero (because R "approaches infinity"), and the initial value was GmM/R_e, where R_e is the radius of the earth. The total net change is the final value minus the initial one:

$$W = - \frac{GmM}{R_e} \; . \tag{B3}$$

We can simplify this result and eliminate the factor GM by observing that, when $R = R_e$, Eq. (B1) will give the gravitational force on the body when it is at the earth's surface and that this force must be simply mg.

$$\frac{GM}{R_e^2} \; m = F \; (\text{at surface}) = mg.$$

Thus, $GM = gR_e^2$, and when this is substituted into Eq. (B3), we obtain:

$$W = - m \; g \; R_e. \tag{B4}$$

The work done by the body against the gravitational attraction of the earth will be just the negative of this quantity, and we have already observed that, if v is equal to the escape velocity, this work must equal the initial kinetic energy of the body:

$$m \; g \; R_e = \tfrac{1}{2} \; mv^2 \; .$$

Multiplying through by 2/m and taking the square root of both sides of this equation, we obtain the final formula for the escape velocity:

$$v \; (\text{escape}) = \sqrt{2 \; g \; R_e} \; . \tag{B5}$$

Notice that this is independent of the mass of the body. Inserting the numerical values $R_e = 6400$ km, $g = 0.0098$ km/sec^2, we arrive at the value we have been seeking:

$$v \; (\text{escape}) = 11.2 \; \text{km/sec.}$$

One of the foremost theoretical physicists discusses informally
in this talk the process of discovering physical theories.

20 **Looking for a New Law**

Richard P. Feynman

Excerpt from his book, *The Character of Physical Law,* published

in 1965.

In general we look for a new law by the following process.
First we guess it. Then we compute the consequences of the
guess to see what would be implied if this law that we guessed
is right. Then we compare the result of the computation to
nature, with experiment or experience, compare it directly
with observation, to see if it works. If it disagrees with experiment it is wrong. In that simple statement is the key to
science. It does not make any difference how beautiful your
guess is. It does not make any difference how smart you are,
who made the guess, or what his name is – if it disagrees
with experiment it is wrong. That is all there is to it. It is
true that one has to check a little to make sure that it is
wrong, because whoever did the experiment may have reported incorrectly, or there may have been some feature in
the experiment that was not noticed, some dirt or something;
or the man who computed the consequences, even though it
may have been the one who made the guesses, could have
made some mistake in the analysis. These are obvious remarks, so when I say if it disagrees with experiment it is
wrong, I mean after the experiment has been checked, the

calculations have been checked, and the thing has been rubbed back and forth a few times to make sure that the consequences are logical consequences from the guess, and that in fact it disagrees with a very carefully checked experiment.

This will give you a somewhat wrong impression of science. It suggests that we keep on guessing possibilities and comparing them with experiment, and this is to put experiment into a rather weak position. In fact experimenters have a certain individual character. They like to do experiments even if nobody has guessed yet, and they very often do their experiments in a region in which people know the theorist has not made any guesses. For instance, we may know a great many laws, but do not know whether they really work at high energy, because it is just a good guess that they work at high energy. Experimenters have tried experiments at higher energy, and in fact every once in a while experiment produces trouble; that is, it produces a discovery that one of the things we thought right is wrong. In this way experiment can produce unexpected results, and that starts us guessing again. One instance of an unexpected result is the mu meson and its neutrino, which was not guessed by anybody at all before it was discovered, and even today nobody yet has any method of guessing by which this would be a natural result.

You can see, of course, that with this method we can attempt to disprove any definite theory. If we have a definite theory, a real guess, from which we can conveniently compute consequences which can be compared with experiment, then in principle we can get rid of any theory. There is always the possibility of proving any definite theory wrong; but notice that we can never prove it right. Suppose that you invent a good guess, calculate the consequences, and discover every time that the consequences you have calculated agree with experiment. The theory is then right? No, it is simply not proved wrong. In the future you could compute a wider range of consequences, there could be a wider range of experiments, and you might then discover that the thing is wrong. That is why laws like Newton's laws for the motion of planets last such a long time. He guessed the law of gravitation, calculated all kinds of consequences for the system and so on, compared them with experiment – and it took several hundred years before the slight error of the motion of Mercury was observed. During all that time the theory had not been proved wrong, and could be taken temporarily to be right. But it could never be proved right, because tomorrow's experiment might succeed in proving wrong what you thought was right. We never are definitely right, we can only be sure we are wrong. However, it is rather remarkable how we can have some ideas which will last so long.

One of the ways of stopping science would be only to do experiments in the region where you know the law. But experimenters search most diligently, and with the greatest effort, in exactly those places where it seems most likely that we can prove our theories wrong. In other words we are trying to prove ourselves wrong as quickly as possible, because only in that way can we find progress. For example, today among ordinary low energy phenomena we do not know where to look for trouble, we think everything is all right, and so there is no particular big programme looking for trouble in nuclear reactions, or in super-conductivity. In these lectures I am concentrating on discovering fundamental laws. The whole range of physics, which is interesting, includes also an understanding at another level of these phenomena like super-conductivity and nuclear reactions, in terms of the fundamental laws. But I am talking now about discovering trouble, something wrong with the fundamental laws, and since among low energy phenomena nobody knows where to look, all the experiments today in this field of finding out a new law, are of high energy.

Another thing I must point out is that you cannot prove a vague theory wrong. If the guess that you make is poorly expressed and rather vague, and the method that you use for figuring out the consequences is a little vague – you are not sure, and you say, 'I think everything's right because it's all due to so and so, and such and such do this and that more or less, and I can sort of explain how this works . . .', then you see that this theory is good, because it cannot be proved wrong! Also if the process of computing the consequences is indefinite, then with a little skill any experimental results can be made to look like the expected consequences. You are probably familiar with that in other fields. 'A' hates his mother. The reason is, of course, because she did not caress him or love him enough when he was a child. But if you investigate you find out that as a matter of fact she did love him very much, and everything was all right. Well then, it was because she was over-indulgent when he was a child! By having a vague theory it is possible to get either result. The cure for this one is the following. If it were possible to state exactly, ahead of time, how much love is not enough, and how much love is over-indulgent, then there would be a perfectly legitimate theory against which you could make tests. It is usually said when this is pointed out, 'When you are dealing with psychological matters things can't be defined so precisely'. Yes, but then you cannot claim to know anything about it.

You will be horrified to hear that we have examples in physics of exactly the same kind. We have these approximate symmetries, which work something like this. You have an approximate symmetry, so you calculate a set of consequences supposing it to be perfect. When compared with experiment, it does not agree. Of course – the symmetry you are supposed to expect is approximate, so if the agreement is pretty good you say, 'Nice!', while if the agreement is very poor you say, 'Well, this particular thing must be especially sensitive to the failure of the symmetry'. Now you may laugh, but we have to make progress in that way. When a subject is first new, and these particles are new to us, this jockeying around, this 'feeling' way of guessing at the results, is the beginning of any science. The same thing is true of the symmetry proposition in physics as is true of psychology, so do not laugh too hard. It is necessary in the beginning to be very careful. It is easy to fall into the deep end by this kind of vague theory. It is hard to prove it wrong, and it takes a certain skill and experience not to walk off the plank in the game.

In this process of guessing, computing consequences, and comparing with experiment, we can get stuck at various stages. We may get stuck in the guessing stage, when we have no ideas. Or we may get stuck in the computing stage. For example, Yukawa* guessed an idea for the nuclear forces in 1934, but nobody could compute the consequences because the mathematics was too difficult, and so they could not compare his idea with experiment. The theories remained for a long time, until we discovered all these extra particles which were not contemplated by Yukawa, and therefore it is undoubtedly not as simple as the way Yukawa did it. Another place where you can get stuck is at the experimental end. For example, the quantum theory of gravitation is going very slowly, if at all, because all the experiments that you can do never involve quantum mechanics and gravitation at the same time. The gravity force is too weak compared with the electrical force.

Because I am a theoretical physicist, and more delighted with this end of the problem, I want now to concentrate on how you make the guesses.

As I said before, it is not of any importance where the guess comes from; it is only important that it should agree with experiment, and that it should be as definite as possible. 'Then', you say, 'that is very simple. You set up a machine, a great computing machine, which has a random wheel in it that makes a succession of guesses, and each time it guesses a hypothesis about how nature should work it computes immediately the consequences, and makes a comparison with a list of experimental results it has at the other end'. In other words, guessing is a dumb man's job. Actually it is quite the opposite, and I will try to explain why.

The first problem is how to start. You say, 'Well I'd start off with all the known principles'. But all the principles

*Hideki Yukawa, Japanese physicist. Director of Research Institute for Fundamental Physics at Kyoto. Nobel Prize 1949.

that are known are inconsistent with each other, so something has to be removed. We get a lot of letters from people insisting that we ought to makes holes in our guesses. You see, you make a hole, to make room for a new guess. Somebody says, 'You know, you people always say that space is continuous. How do you know when you get to a small enough dimension that there really are enough points in between, that it isn't just a lot of dots separated by little distances?' Or they say, 'You know those quantum mechanical amplitudes you told me about, they're so complicated and absurd, what makes you think those are right? Maybe they aren't right'. Such remarks are obvious and are perfectly clear to anybody who is working on this problem. It does not do any good to point this out. The problem is not only what might be wrong but what, precisely, might be substituted in place of it. In the case of the continuous space, suppose the precise proposition is that space really consists of a series of dots, and that the space between them does not mean anything, and that the dots are in a cubic array. Then we can prove immediately that this is wrong. It does not work. The problem is not just to say something might be wrong, but to replace it by something – and that is not so easy. As soon as any really definite idea is substituted it becomes almost immediately apparent that it does not work.

The second difficulty is that there is an infinite number of possibilities of these simple types. It is something like this. You are sitting working very hard, you have worked for a long time trying to open a safe. Then some Joe comes along who knows nothing about what you are doing, except that you are trying to open the safe. He says 'Why don't you try the combination 10:20:30?' Because you are busy, you have tried a lot of things, maybe you have already tried 10:20:30. Maybe you know already that the middle number is 32 not 20. Maybe you know as a matter of fact that it is a five digit combination. . . . So please do not send me any letters trying to tell me how the thing is going to work. I read them – I always read them to make sure that I have not already thought of what is suggested – but it takes too long to answer them, because they are usually in the class 'try 10:20:30'. As usual, nature's imagination far surpasses our own, as we have seen from the other theories which are subtle and deep. To get such a subtle and deep guess is not so easy. One must be really clever to guess, and it is not possible to do it blindly by machine.

I want to discuss now the art of guessing nature's laws. It is an art. How is it done? One way you might suggest is to look at history to see how the other guys did it. So we look at history.

We must start with Newton. He had a situation where he had incomplete knowledge, and he was able to guess the laws by putting together ideas which were all relatively close to experiment; there was not a great distance between the observations and the tests. That was the first way, but today it does not work so well.

The next guy who did something great was Maxwell, who obtained the laws of electricity and magnetism. What he did was this. He put together all the laws of electricity, due to Faraday and other people who came before him, and he looked at them and realized that they were mathematically inconsistent. In order to straighten it out he had to add one term to an equation. He did this by inventing for himself a model of idler wheels and gears and so on in space. He found what the new law was – but nobody paid much attention because they did not believe in the idler wheels. We do not believe in the idler wheels today, but the equations that he obtained were correct. So the logic may be wrong but the answer right.

In the case of relativity the discovery was completely different. There was an accumulation of paradoxes; the known laws gave inconsistent results. This was a new kind of thinking, a thinking in terms of discussing the possible symmetries of laws. It was especially difficult, because for the first time it was realized how long something like Newton's laws could seem right, and still ultimately be wrong. Also it was difficult to accept that ordinary ideas of time and space, which seemed so instinctive, could be wrong.

Quantum mechanics was discovered in two independent ways – which is a lesson. There again, and even more so, an enormous number of paradoxes were discovered experimentally, things that absolutely could not be explained in any way by what was known. It was not that the knowledge was incomplete, but that the knowledge was too complete. Your prediction was that this should happen – it did not. The two different routes were one by Schrödinger,* who guessed the equation, the other by Heisenberg, who argued that you must analyse what is measurable. These two different philosophical methods led to the same discovery in the end.

More recently, the discovery of the laws of the weak decay I spoke of, when a neutron disintegrates into a proton, an electron and an anti-neutrino – which are still only partly known – add up to a somewhat different situation. This time it was a case of incomplete knowledge, and only the equation was guessed. The special difficulty this time was that the experiments were all wrong. How can you guess the right answer if, when you calculate the result, it disagrees with experiment? You need courage to say the experiments must be wrong. I will explain where that courage comes from later.

Today we have no paradoxes – maybe. We have this infinity that comes in when we put all the laws together, but the people sweeping the dirt under the rug are so clever that one sometimes thinks this is not a serious paradox. Again, the fact that we have found all these particles does not tell us anything except that our knowledge is incomplete. I am sure that history does not repeat itself in physics, as you can tell from looking at the examples I have given. The reason is this. Any schemes – such as 'think of symmetry laws', or 'put the information in mathematical form', or 'guess equations' – are known to everybody now, and they are all tried all the time. When you are stuck, the answer cannot be one of these, because you will have tried these right away.

*Erwin Schrödinger, Austrian theoretical physicist. Won Nobel Prize for Physics 1933 with Paul Dirac.

There must be another way next time. Each time we get into this log-jam of too much trouble, too many problems, it is because the methods that we are using are just like the ones we have used before. The next scheme, the new discovery, is going to be made in a completely different way. So history does not help us much.

I should like to say a little about Heisenberg's idea that you should not talk about what you cannot measure, because many people talk about this idea without really understanding it. You can interpret this in the sense that the constructs or inventions that you make must be of such a kind that the consequences that you compute are comparable with experiment – that is, that you do not compute a consequence like 'a moo must be three goos', when nobody knows what a moo or a goo is. Obviously that is no good. But if the consequences can be compared to experiment, then that is all that is necessary. It does not matter that moos and goos cannot appear in the guess. You can have as much junk in the guess as you like, provided that the consequences can be compared with experiment. This is not always fully appreciated. People often complain of the unwarranted extension of the ideas of particles and paths, etc., into the atomic realm. Not so at all; there is nothing unwarranted about the extension. We must, and we should, and we always do, extend as far as we can beyond what we already know, beyond those ideas that we have already obtained. Dangerous? Yes. Uncertain? Yes. But it is the only way to make progress. Although it is uncertain, it is necessary to make science useful. Science is only useful if it tells you about some experiment that has not been done; it is no good if it only tells you what just went on. It is necessary to extend the ideas beyond where they have been tested. For example, in the law of gravitation, which was developed to understand the motion of planets, it would have been no use if Newton had simply said, 'I now understand the planets', and had not felt able to try to compare it with the earth's pull on the moon, and for later men to say 'Maybe what holds the galaxies together is gravitation'. We must try that. You could say, 'When you get to the size of the galaxies, since you know nothing about it, anything can happen'. I know, but there is no science in accepting this type of limitation. There is no ultimate understanding of the galaxies. On the other hand, if you assume that the entire behaviour is due only to known laws, this assumption is very limited and definite and easily broken by experiment. What we are looking for is just such hypotheses, very definite and easy to compare with experiment. The fact is that the way the galaxies behave so far does not seem to be against the proposition.

I can give you another example, even more interesting and important. Probably the most powerful single assumption that contributes most to the progress of biology is the assumption that everything animals do the atoms can do, that the things that are seen in the biological world are the results of the behaviour of physical and chemical phenomena, with no 'extra something'. You could always say, 'When you come to living things, anything can happen'. If you accept that you will never understand living things. It is very hard to believe that the wiggling of the tentacle of the octopus is nothing but some fooling around of atoms according to the known physical laws. But when it is investigated with this hypothesis one is able to make guesses quite accurately about how it works. In this way one makes great progress in understanding. So far the tentacle has not been cut off – it has not been found that this idea is wrong.

It is not unscientific to make a guess, although many people who are not in science think it is. Some years ago I had a conversation with a layman about flying saucers – because I am scientific I know all about flying saucers! I said 'I don't think there are flying saucers'. So my antagonist said, 'Is it impossible that there are flying saucers? Can you prove that it's impossible?' 'No', I said, 'I can't prove it's impossible. It's just very unlikely'. At that he said, 'You are very unscientific. If you can't prove it impossible then how can you say that it's unlikely?' But that is the way that *is* scientific. It is scientific only to say what is more likely and what less likely, and not to be proving all the time the possible and impossible. To define what I mean, I might have said to him, 'Listen, I mean that from my knowledge of the world that I see around me, I think that it is much more likely that the reports of flying saucers are the results of the known irrational characteristics of terrestrial intelligence than of the unknown rational efforts of extra-terrestrial intelligence'. It is just more likely, that is all. It is a good guess. And we always try to guess the most likely explanation, keeping in the back of the mind the fact that if it does not work we must discuss the other possibilities.

How can we guess what to keep and what to throw away? We have all these nice principles and known facts, but we are in some kind of trouble: either we get the infinities, or we do not get enough of a description – we are missing some parts. Sometimes that means that we have to throw away some idea; at least in the past it has always turned out that some deeply held idea had to be thrown away. The question is, what to throw away and what to keep. If you throw it all away that is going a little far, and then you have not much to work with. After all, the conservation of energy looks good, and it is nice, and I do not want to throw it away. To guess what to keep and what to throw away takes considerable skill. Actually it is probably merely a matter of luck, but it looks as if it takes considerable skill.

Probability amplitudes are very strange, and the first thing you think is that the strange new ideas are clearly cock-eyed. Yet everything that can be deduced from the ideas of the existence of quantum mechanical probability amplitudes, strange though they are, do work, throughout the long list of strange particles, one hundred per cent. Therefore I do not believe that when we find out the inner guts of the composition of the world we shall find these ideas are wrong. I think this part is right, but I am only guessing: I am telling you how I guess.

On the other hand, I believe that the theory that space is continuous is wrong, because we get these infinities and other difficulties, and we are left with questions on what determines the size of all the particles. I rather suspect that the simple ideas of geometry, extended down into infinitely small space, are wrong. Here, of course, I am only making a hole, and not telling you what to substitute. If I did, I should finish this lecture with a new law.

Some people have used the inconsistency of all the principles to say that there is only one possible consistent world, that if we put all the principles together, and calculate very exactly, we shall not only be able to deduce the principles, but we shall also discover that these are the only principles that could possibly exist if the thing is still to remain consistent. That seems to me a big order. I believe that sounds like wagging the dog by the tail. I believe that it has to be given that certain things exist – not all the 50-odd particles, but a few little things like electrons, etc. – and then with all the principles the great complexities that come out are probably a definite consequence. I do not think that you can get the whole thing from arguments about consistencies.

Another problem we have is the meaning of the partial symmetries. These symmetries, like the statement that neutrons and protons are nearly the same but are not the same for electricity, or the fact that the law of reflection symmetry is perfect except for one kind of reaction, are very annoying. The thing is almost symmetrical but not completely. Now two schools of thought exist. One will say that it is really simple, that they are really symmetrical but that there is a little complication which knocks it a bit cock-eyed. Then there is another school of thought, which has only one representative, myself, which says no, the thing may be complicated and become simple only through the complications. The Greeks believed that the orbits of the planets were circles. Actually they are ellipses. They are not quite symmetrical, but they are very close to circles. The question is, why are they very close to circles? Why are they nearly symmetrical? Because of a long complicated effect of tidal friction – a very complicated idea. It is possible that nature in her heart is completely unsymmetrical in these things, but in the complexities of reality it gets to look approximately as if it is symmetrical, and the ellipses look almost like circles. That is another possibility; but nobody knows, it is just guesswork.

Suppose you have two theories, A and B, which look completely different psychologically, with different ideas in them and so on, but that all the consequences that are computed from each are exactly the same, and both agree with experiment. The two theories, although they sound different at the beginning, have all consequences the same, which is usually easy to prove mathematically by showing that the logic from A and B will always give corresponding consequences. Suppose we have two such theories, how are we going to decide which one is right? There is no way by science, because they both agree with experiment to the same extent. So two theories, although they may have deeply different ideas behind them, may be mathematically identical, and then there is no scientific way to distinguish them.

However, for psychological reasons, in order to guess new theories, these two things may be very far from equivalent, because one gives a man different ideas from the other. By putting the theory in a certain kind of framework you get an idea of what to change. There will be something, for instance, in theory A that talks about something, and you will say, 'I'll change that idea in here'. But to find out what the corresponding thing is that you are going to change in B may be very complicated – it may not be a simple idea at all. In other words, although they are identical before they are changed, there are certain ways of changing one which looks natural which will not look natural in the other. Therefore psychologically we must keep all the theories in our heads, and every theoretical physicist who is any good knows six or seven different theoretical representations for exactly the same physics. He knows that they are all equivalent, and that nobody is ever going to be able to decide which one is right at that level, but he keeps them in his head, hoping that they will give him different ideas for guessing.

That reminds me of another point, that the philosophy or

ideas around a theory may change enormously when there are very tiny changes in the theory. For instance, Newton's ideas about space and time agreed with experiment very well, but in order to get the correct motion of the orbit of Mercury, which was a tiny, tiny difference, the difference in the character of the theory needed was enormous. The reason is that Newton's laws were so simple and so perfect, and they produced definite results. In order to get something that would produce a slightly different result it had to be completely different. In stating a new law you cannot make imperfections on a perfect thing; you have to have another perfect thing. So the differences in philosophical ideas between Newton's and Einstein's theories of gravitation are enormous.

What are these philosophies? They are really tricky ways to compute consequences quickly. A philosophy, which is sometimes called an understanding of the law, is simply a way that a person holds the laws in his mind in order to guess quickly at consequences. Some people have said, and it is true in cases like Maxwell's equations, 'Never mind the philosophy, never mind anything of this kind, just guess the equations. The problem is only to compute the answers so that they agree with experiment, and it is not necessary to have a philosophy, or argument, or words, about the equation'. That is good in the sense that if you only guess the equation you are not prejudicing yourself, and you will guess better. On the other hand, maybe the philosophy helps you to guess. It is very hard to say.

For those people who insist that the only thing that is important is that the theory agrees with experiment, I would like to imagine a discussion between a Mayan astronomer and his student. The Mayans were able to calculate with great precision predictions, for example, for eclipses and for the position of the moon in the sky, the position of Venus, etc. It was all done by arithmetic. They counted a certain number and subtracted some numbers, and so on. There was no discussion of what the moon was. There was no discussion even of the idea that it went around. They just calculated the time when there would be an eclipse, or when the moon would rise at the full, and so on. Suppose that a young man went to the astronomer and said, 'I have an idea. Maybe those things are going around, and there are balls of something like rocks out there, and we could calculate how they move in a completely different way from just calculating what time they appear in the sky'. 'Yes', says the astronomer, 'and how accurately can you predict eclipses?' He says, 'I haven't developed the thing very far yet'. Then says the astronomer, 'Well, we can calculate eclipses more accurately than you can with your model, so you must not pay any attention to your idea because obviously the mathematical scheme is better'. There is a very strong tendency, when someone comes up with an idea and says, 'Let's suppose that the world is this way', for people to say to him, 'What would you get for the answer to such and such a problem?' And he says, 'I haven't developed it far enough'. And they say, 'Well, we have already developed it much further, and we can get the answers very accurately'. So it is a problem whether or not to worry about philosophies behind ideas.

Another way of working, of course, is to guess new principles. In Einstein's theory of gravitation he guessed, on top of all the other principles, the principle that corresponded to the idea that the forces are always proportional to the masses. He guessed the principle that if you are in an accelerating car you cannot distinguish that from being in a gravitational field, and by adding that principle to all the other principles, he was able to deduce the correct laws of gravitation.

That outlines a number of possible ways of guessing. I would now like to come to some other points about the final result. First of all, when we are all finished, and we have a mathematical theory by which we can compute consequences, what can we do? It really is an amazing thing. In order to figure out what an atom is going to do in a given situation we make up rules with marks on paper, carry them into a machine which has switches that open and close in some complicated way, and the result will tell us what the atom is going to do! If the way that these switches open and close were some kind of model of the atom, if we thought that the atom had switches in it, then I would say that I understood more or less what is going on. I find it quite amazing that it is possible to predict what will happen by mathematics, which is simply following rules which really have nothing to do with what is going on in the original thing. The closing and opening of switches in a computer is quite different from what is happening in nature.

One of the most important things in this 'guess – compute consequences – compare with experiment' business is to know when you are right. It is possible to know when you are right way ahead of checking all the consequences. You can recognize truth by its beauty and simplicity. It is always easy when you have made a guess, and done two or three little calculations to make sure that it is not obviously wrong, to know that it is right. When you get it right, it is obvious that it is right – at least if you have any experience – because usually what happens is that more comes out than goes in. Your guess is, in fact, that something is very simple. If you cannot see immediately that it is wrong, and it is simpler than it was before, then it is right. The in-experienced, and crackpots, and people like that, make guesses that are simple, but you can immediately see that they are wrong, so that does not count. Others, the inex-perienced students, make guesses that are very complicated, and it sort of looks as if it is all right, but I know it is not true because the truth always turns out to be simpler than you thought. What we need is imagination, but imagination in a terrible strait-jacket. We have to find a new view of the world that has to agree with everything that is known, but disagree in its predictions somewhere, otherwise it is not interesting. And in that disagreement it must agree with nature. If you can find any other view of the world which agrees over the entire range where things have already been observed, but disagrees somewhere else, you have made a great discovery. It is very nearly impossible, but not quite, to find any theory which agrees with experiments over the entire range in which all theories have been checked, and yet gives different consequences in some other range, even a theory whose different consequences do not turn out to agree with nature. A new idea is extremely difficult to think of. It takes a fantastic imagination.

What of the future of this adventure? What will happen ultimately? We are going along guessing the laws; how many laws are we going to have to guess? I do not know. Some of my colleagues say that this fundamental aspect of our science will go on; but I think there will certainly not be perpetual novelty, say for a thousand years. This thing cannot keep on going so that we are always going to discover more and more new laws. If we do, it will become boring that there are so many levels one underneath the other. It seems to me that what can happen in the future is either that all the laws become known – that is, if you had enough laws you could compute consequences and they would always agree with experiment, which would be the end of the line – or it may happen that the experiments get harder and harder to make, more and more expensive, so you get 99·9 per cent of the phenomena, but there is always some phenomenon which has just been discovered, which is very hard to measure, and which disagrees; and as soon as you have the explanation of that one there is always another one, and it gets slower and slower and more and more uninteresting. That is another way it may end. But I think it has to end in one way or another.

We are very lucky to live in an age in which we are still making discoveries. It is like the discovery of America – you only discover it once. The age in which we live is the age in which we are discovering the fundamental laws of nature, and that day will never come again. It is very exciting, it is marvellous, but this excitement will have to go. Of course in the future there will be other interests. There will be the interest of the connection of one level of phenomena to another – phenomena in biology and so on, or, if you are talking about exploration, exploring other planets, but there will not still be the same things that we are doing now.

Another thing that will happen is that ultimately, if it turns out that all is known, or it gets very dull, the vigorous philosophy and the careful attention to all these things that I have been talking about will gradually disappear. The philosophers who are always on the outside making stupid remarks will be able to close in, because we cannot push them away by saying, 'If you were right we would be able to guess all the rest of the laws', because when the laws are all there they will have an explanation for them. For instance, there are always explanations about why the world is three-dimensional. Well, there is only one world, and it is hard to tell if that explanation is right or not, so that if everything were known there would be some explanation about why those were the right laws. But that explanation would be in a frame that we cannot criticize by arguing that that type of reasoning will not permit us to go further. There will be a degeneration of ideas, just like the degeneration that great explorers feel is occurring when tourists begin moving in on a territory.

In this age people are experiencing a delight, the tremendous delight that you get when you guess how nature will work in a new situation never seen before. From experiments and information in a certain range you can guess what is going to happen in a region where no one has ever explored before. It is a little different from regular exploration in that there are enough clues on the land discovered to guess what the land that has not been discovered is going to look like. These guesses, incidentally, are often very different from what you have already seen – they take a lot of thought.

What is it about nature that lets this happen, that it is possible to guess from one part what the rest is going to do? That is an unscientific question: I do not know how to answer it, and therefore I am going to give an unscientific answer. I think it is because nature has a simplicity and therefore a great beauty.

A Portfolio of Computer-made Drawings

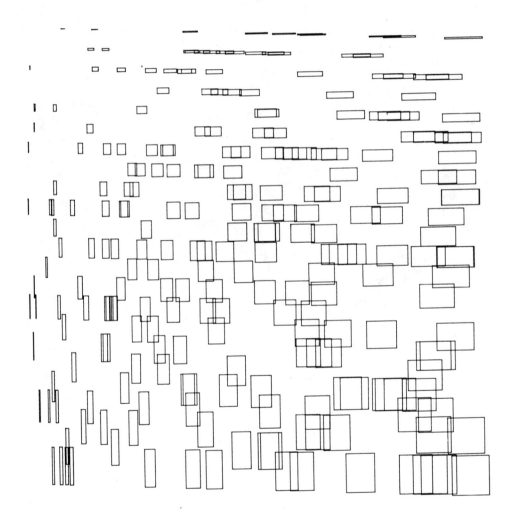

A Computer Drawing, Darel Eschbach, Jr.

A Computer Drawing, Calcomp Test Pattern

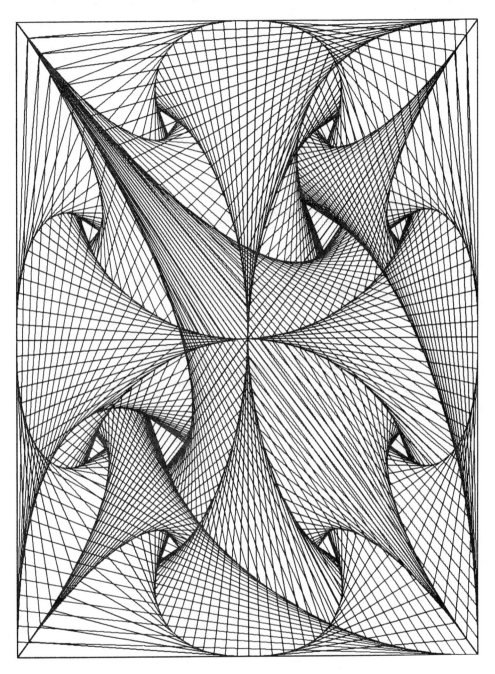

Spires of Contribution, Lloyd Sumner

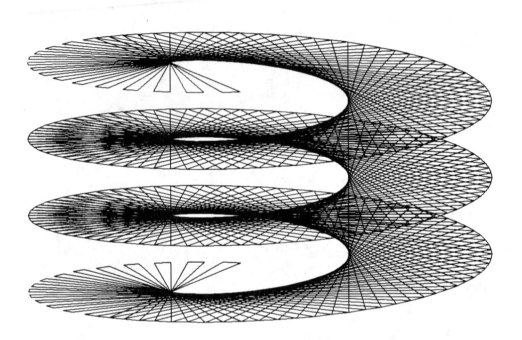

Devil's Staircase, A Computer Drawing Lloyd Sumner

Yesterday & Forever, A Computer Drawing   Lloyd Sumner

Krystollos, by CalComp

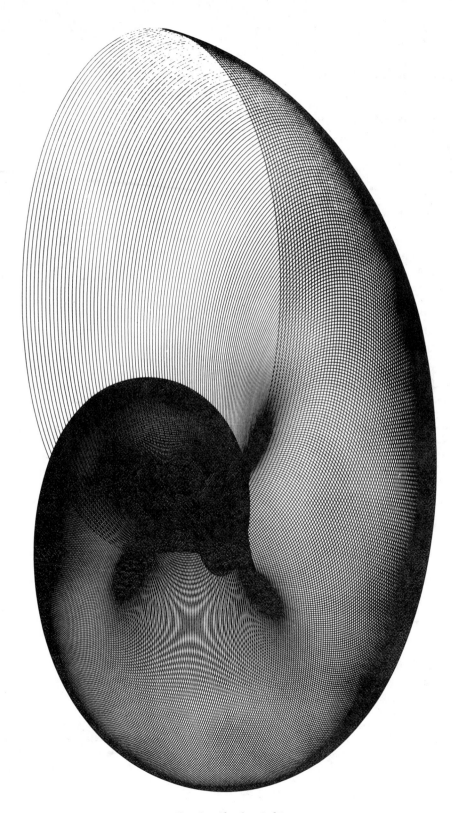

The Snail, by CalComp

JEREMY BERNSTEIN

Jeremy Bernstein, born in Rochester, New York in 1929, is Professor of Physics at Stevens Institute of Technology in New Jersey. He was educated at Columbia Grammar School in New York City and received a bachelor's and master's degree in mathematics, and a doctorate in physics from Harvard University. He has done research at the Harvard Cyclotron Laboratory, the Institute for Advanced Study at Princeton, Los Alamos, at the Brookhaven National Laboratories, and is frequently a visiting physicist at CERN (Conseil Européan pour la Recherche Nucléaire) in Geneva. Bernstein is the author of The Analytical Engine: Computers, Past, Present and Future, Ascent, an account of mountaineering in the Alps, and has written book reviews and profile articles for the magazine, The New Yorker.

ARTHUR C. CLARKE

Arthur C. Clark, British scientist and writer, is a Fellow of the Royal Astronomical Society. During World War II he served as technical officer in charge of the first aircraft ground-controlled approach project. He has won the Kalinga Prize, given by UNESCO for the popularization of science. The feasibility of many of the current space developments was perceived and outlined by Clarke in the 1930's. His science fiction novels include Childhoods End and The City and the Stars.

SIR CHARLES GALTON DARWIN

Charles Galton Darwin, British physicist, and grandson of the founder of the theory of evolution, was born in Cambridge, England in 1887, and died in 1962. He was educated at Trinity College, Cambridge University, and held positions at Manchester University, Cambridge University, and Edinburgh University. In 1938 he became director of the National Physical Laboratory. Charles Galton Darwin was the author of The New Conceptions of Matter (1931), The Next Million Years (1952), and he wrote many papers on theoretical physics.

PAUL ADRIEN MAURICE DIRAC

Paul Adrien Maurice Dirac is one of the major figures in modern mathematics and theoretical physics. He received the Nobel Prize in 1933 for his contribution to quantum mechanics. Dirac was born in 1902 in Bristol and received his bachelor's degree in engineering from Bristol University. Later he became a research student in mathematics at St. John's College, Cambridge, and received his Ph.D. in 1926. He is now Lucasian Professor of Mathematics at Cambridge, England.

ALBERT EINSTEIN

Albert Einstein, considered to be the most creative physical scientist since Newton, was nevertheless a humble and sometimes rather shy man. He was born in Ulm, Germany, in 1879. He seemed to learn so slowly that his parents feared that he might be retarded. After graduating from the Polytechnic Institute in Zurich, he became a junior official at the Patent Office at Berne. At the age of twenty-six, and quite unknown, he published three revolutionary papers in theoretical physics in 1905. The first paper extended Max Planck's ideas of quantization of energy, and established the quantum theory of radiation. For this work he received the Nobel Prize for 1921. The second paper gave a mathematical theory of Brownian motion, yielding a calculation of the size of a molecule. His third paper founded the special theory of relativity. Einstein's later work centered on the general theory of relativity. His work had a profound influence not only on physics, but also on philosophy. An eloquent and widely beloved man, Einstein took an active part in liberal and anti-war movements. Fleeing from Nazi Germany, he settled in the United States in 1933 at the Institute for Advanced Study in Princeton. He died in 1955.

GEORGE GAMOW

George Gamow, a theoretical physicist from Russia, received his Ph.D. in physics at the University of Leningrad. At Leningrad he became professor after being a Carlsberg fellow and a university fellow at the University of Copenhagen and a Rockefeller fellow at Cambridge University. He came to the United States in 1933 to teach at the George Washington University and later at the University of Colorado. His popularizations of physics are much admired.

VICTOR GUILLEMIN, Jr.

Victor Guillemin, Jr., an American physicist, was born in Milwaukee in 1896. He was educated at the University of Wisconsin, Harvard, and the University of Munich. He taught at Harvard from 1930 to

1935, was research associate at the Fatigue Laboratories from 1935–41, senior physicist at the United States Army Air Force in Dayton, Ohio, from 1941 to 1948, and professor of biophysics at the University of Illinois from 1948 to 1959. He is author of The Story of Quantum Mechanics (1968). His research interests are in atomic and molecular structure, and biological and aero-medical sciences.

BANESH HOFFMAN

Banesh Hoffman, born in Richmond, England in 1906, attended Oxford and Princeton. He has been a member of the Institute of Advanced Study, electrical engineer at the Federal Telephone and Radio Laboratories, researcher at King's College, London, and a consultant for Westinghouse Electric Corporation's science talent search tests. He has won the distinguished teacher award at Queen's College, where he is Professor of Mathematics. During the 1966–67 year he was on the staff of Harvard Project Physics.

LEOPOLD INFELD

Leopold Infeld, a co-worker with Albert Einstein in general relativity theory, was born in 1898 in Poland. After studying at the Cracow and Berlin Universities, he bacame a Rockefeller Fellow at Cambridge where he worked with Max Born in electromagnetic theory, and then a member of the Institute for Advanced Study at Princeton. For eleven years he was Professor of Applied Mathematics at the University of Toronto. He then returned to Poland and became Professor of Physics at the University of Warsaw and until his death on 16 January 1968 he was director of the Theoretical Physics Institute at the university. A member of the presidium of the Polish Academy of Science, Infeld conducted research in theoretical physics, especially relativity and quantum theories. Infeld was the author of The New Field Theory, The World in Modern Science, Quest, Albert Einstein, and with Einstein The Evolution of Physics.

MARTIN J. KLEIN

Martin J. Klein was born in New York City and attended Columbia University and Massachusetts Institute of Technology. He has been a National Research Fellow at the Dublin Institute for Advanced Studies and a Guggenheim Fellow at the University of Leyden, Holland. He has taught at MIT and Case Institute and is now Professor at Yale University. His main interest is in the history of relativity and quantum mechanics.

EDWARD MILLS PURCELL

E. M. Purcell, Professor of Physics at Harvard University, was born in 1912 in Taylorville, Illinois. He was educated at Purdue University and at Harvard. During World War II he worked as a researcher at the Radiation Laboratory, and he has been a member of the Science Advisory Board for the United States Air Force and of the President's Science Advisory Committee. For his work in nuclear magnetism, E. M. Purcell was awarded the 1952 Nobel Prize in Physics. He has worked on microwave phenomena and radio-frequency spectroscopy, and has also written physics textbooks.

ERIC M. ROGERS

Eric M. Rogers, Professor of Physics at Princeton University, was born in Bickley, England in 1902. He received his education at Cambridge and later was a demonstrator at the Cavendish Laboratory. Since 1963 he has been the organizer in physics for the Nuffield Foundation Science Teaching Project. He is the author of the textbook, Physics for the Inquiring Mind.

ERWIN SCHRÖDINGER

Erwin Schrödinger (1887–1961) was born in Vienna and became successor of Max Planck as professor of physics at the University of Berlin. His work provided some of the basic equations of the quantum theory. Jointly with Paul A. M. Dirac he was awarded the Nobel Prize in physics in 1933 for the discovery of new productive forms of atomic theory. Originally he had planned to be a philosopher, and he wrote widely-read books concerning the relation between science and the humanities, as well as some poetry.

CYRIL STANLEY SMITH

Cyril Stanley Smith, Professor of Physics at Massachusetts Institute of Technology, was born in Birmingham, England, in 1903. In 1926 he received his doctor of science from MIT. He has done research in physical metallurgy at MIT, the American Brass Company, and during World War II, the Los Alamos Laboratory. For his work there he received the United States Medal of Merit in 1946. Professor Smith has served on the General Advisory Committee to the Atomic Energy Commission and on the President's Scientific Advisory Committee. His interest reaches deeply into history of science and technology; he is also an art collector.

CHARLES PERCY SNOW

Charles Percy Snow, Baron of Leicester, was born in 1905 and educated at University College, Leicester, and at Christ's College, Cambridge. Although well known as a novelist, especially dealing with the lives and problems of professional men, he has held such diverse positions as chief of scientific personnel for the Ministry of Labour, Civil Service Commissioner, and a Director of the English Electric Co., Ltd. His writings have been widely acclaimed; among his novels are The Search, The New Men, and Corridors of Power. His nonfiction books on science and its consequences include The Two Cultures and The Scientific Revolution, and Science and Government.

JOHN LIGHTON SYNGE

J. L. Synge was born in Ireland in 1897. He has taught at universities in Ireland, Canada, and the United States, and is currently Professor of Mathematics at the Institute for Advanced Studies in Dublin. He is the President of the Royal Irish Academy. Synge has written papers on Riemannian geometry, relativity, hydrodynamics, and elasticity, has been author or co-author of Geometrical Optics and Principles of Mechanics, and has coedited the Mathematical Papers of Sir W. R. Hamilton.

SIR JOSEPH JOHN THOMSON

Sir Joseph John Thomson (1856–1940) was born near Manchester, England. At fourteen he entered a college in Manchester, at twenty he entered Cambridge on a scholarship, and at twenty-seven became professor of physics at Cambridge. It was Thomson whose work ushered in the period of subatomic research when he showed conclusively that "cathode rays" consisted of electrons. With this as a building block he constructed the "Thomson" model of the atom—a sphere of positive electricity in which were embedded negatively charged electrons. In 1906 J. J. Thomson was awarded the Nobel Prize, and in 1908 he was knighted. During Thomson's period as Director of the Cavendish Laboratory at Cambridge, eight Nobel Prizes were won by his colleagues. With this start England remained the leader in subatomic experimental physics for almost forty years.